ATLANTIS COMPUTATIONAL INTELLIGENCE SYSTEMS

VOLUME 5

SERIES EDITORS: JIE LU, JAVIER MONTERO

Atlantis Computational Intelligence Systems

Series Editors:

Jie Lu

Faculty of Engineering and Information Technology, University of Technology
Sydney, Australia

Javier Montero

Department of Statistics and Operational Research, Faculty of Mathematics
Complutense University of Madrid, Spain

(ISSN: 1875-7650)

Aims and scope of the series

The series 'Atlantis Computational Intelligence Systems' aims at covering state-of-the-art research and development in all fields where computational intelligence is investigated and applied. The series seeks to publish monographs and edited volumes on foundations and new developments in the field of computational intelligence, including fundamental and applied research as well as work describing new, emerging technologies originating from computational intelligence research. Applied CI research may range from CI applications in the industry to research projects in the life sciences, including research in biology, physics, chemistry and the neurosciences.

All books in this series are co-published with Springer.

For more information on this series and our other book series, please visit our website at:

www.atlantis-press.com/publications/books

ATLANTIS
PRESS

AMSTERDAM – PARIS – BEIJING

© **ATLANTIS PRESS**

Answer Set Programming For Continuous Domains: A Fuzzy Logic Approach

Jeroen Janssen

Vrije Universiteit Brussel, Department of Computer Science, Pleinlaan 2, 1050 Brussels, Belgium

Steven Schockaert

School of Computer Science & Informatics, Queen's Buildings, 5 The Parade, Roath, Cardiff CF24 3AA, United Kingdom

Dirk Vermeir

Vrije Universiteit Brussel, Department of Computer Science, Pleinlaan 2, 1050 Brussels, Belgium

Martine De Cock

Ghent University, Dept. of Applied Mathematics and Computer Science (WE02), Krijgslaan 281 (S9), 9000 Gent, Belgium

ATLANTIS
PRESS

AMSTERDAM – PARIS – BEIJING

Atlantis Press

8, square des Bouleaux
75019 Paris, France

For information on all Atlantis Press publications, visit our website at: *www.atlantis-press.com*

Copyright

This book is published under the Creative Commons Attribution-Non-commercial license, meaning that copying, distribution, transmitting and adapting the book is permitted, provided that this is done for non-commercial purposes and that the book is attributed.

This book, or any parts thereof, may not be reproduced for commercial purposes in any form or by any means, electronic or mechanical, including photocopying, recording or any information storage and retrieval system known or to be invented, without prior permission from the Publisher.

Atlantis Computational Intelligence Systems

Volume 1: Linguistic Values Based Intelligent Information Processing: Theory, Methods, and Applications - Da Ruan
Volume 2: Computational Intelligence in Complex Decision Systems - Da Ruan (Editor)
Volume 3: Intelligence for Nonlinear Dynamics and Synchronisation - K. Kyamakya, A. Bouchachia, J.C. Chedjou
Volume 4: Trust Networks for Recommender Systems - P. Victor, C. Cornelis, M. De Cock

ISBNs
Print: 978-94-6239-041-6
E-Book: 978-94-91216-59-6
ISSN: 1875-7650

© 2012 ATLANTIS PRESS
Softcover reprint of the hardcover 1st edition 2012

Preface

Answer set programming (ASP) is a form of logic programming that originated at the end of the 1980s and the beginning of the 1990s. It is especially tailored towards solving hard search problems, which it allows to encode concisely. In the past two decades it has known great success and has – among others – been applied to planning problems, musical composition, biological modeling and decision support systems for the space shuttle. Unfortunately, ASP is not very well equipped for modeling problems in continuous domains. In this book we attempt to augment ASP with the capability of expressing continuous problems by creating an answer set programming framework based on fuzzy logic. The resulting language is called fuzzy answer set programming (FASP). After two introductory chapters, also introducing the necessary technical background, we study FASP and its extensions in Chapters 3 and 4. Then we focus on the question of whether the many extensions of FASP can be compiled to a core language in Chapter 5 and succeedingly study an implementation method for a subset of FASP in Chapter 6. As such, we focus both on theoretical aspects of the language as on more practical aspects such as implementation.

This book originated from the doctoral thesis of the first author, which was successfully defended in June 2011. Encouraged by the enthusiastic reports of the committee members, we have decided to publish this book, and make the obtained results available to a larger audience. We are grateful to the external members of the doctoral jury, Umberto Straccia and Wolfgang Faber, for their useful suggestions and remarks on the first version of this thesis. Our special thanks go to Da Ruan, the former editor of the Atlantis Computational Intelligence Systems book series, who initiated the publication process of this book shortly before he passed away very unexpectedly in the Summer of 2011. For us, this book will always be associated with dear memories of Da's friendship and his enthusiasm and help to publish our work. We would also like to thank the new series editors Jie Lu and Javier Montero for their valued contributions in continuing Da Ruan's work, and for guiding us through the final publication stages of this book. Finally, we would like to thank the Research Foundation - Flanders (FWO) for the financial support.

Contents

Chapter 1

Introduction

Language is one of the most important tools that exist. It allows humans to communicate efficiently and to transfer knowledge between generations. According to Benjamin Whorf, language even shapes views and influences thoughts[1]. Unfortunately, while human language is useful for communication between humans, it is not as efficient for communicating with our modern day devices. Therefore, ever since the rise of computers, the need has grown for languages that enable us to tell these machines what we expect them to do. Such languages are called *programming languages*. Their foundations can be dated back to the 1800s, where Joseph Marie Jacquard used punched cards to encode cloth patterns for his textile machine, called the "Jacquard loom"[2]. Charles Babbage improved on this idea when designing his "analytical engine" by allowing the machine to be reprogrammed using punched cards[3]. Hence, instead of merely using the punched cards as data, the analytical engine could perform arbitrary computations that were encoded in the punched cards. As such, we can consider this the first real programmable machine.

The 1940s witnessed the birth of the first machines that resemble our modern day electrical computers. Initially these machines were programmed using patched cables that encoded specific machine-instructions. Input and output was done using punched cards. Since the (re)programming of these computers was a laborious task requiring many people, the idea arose to unify programs with data and store them in memory. This led to the creation of stored-program computers, such as EDVAC (Electronic Discrete Variable Automatic Computer, successor of ENIAC[4]) and SSEM (Small-Scale Experimental Machine[5]). Contrary to the earlier designs, these systems could read programs from punched cards and store

---

[1] Source: http://en.wikipedia.org/wiki/Benjamin_Lee_Whorf. Retrieved on March 29, 2011
[2] Source: http://en.wikipedia.org/wiki/Jacquard_loom. Retrieved on Feb 25, 2011.
[3] Source: http://en.wikipedia.org/wiki/Analytical_Engine. Retrieved on Feb 25, 2011.
[4] Source: http://en.wikipedia.org/wiki/Edvac. Retrieved on Feb 25, 2011.
[5] Source: http://en.wikipedia.org/wiki/Ssem. Retrieved on Feb 25, 2011.

them in memory, thereby making (re)programming them as easy as inserting a new stack of punched cards.

While the creation of stored-program computers eliminated the physical burden of programming, the mental activity required was still high due to the use of machine-specific codes. These low-level languages allowed the programmer to greatly optimize their programs for specific machines, but also made it hard to express complex problems due to their poor readability and the fact that they are far removed from natural language. To solve these problems, so called "higher-level" programming languages were developed. One of the first such languages was "Plankalkül" ("planning calculus"). It was described by Konrad Zuse in 1943 [Zuse (1943, 1948–1949); Bauer and Wössner (1972)], but was only implemented in 1998[6] and independently in 2000 [Rojas *et al.* (2000)]. In the 1950s the first high-level programming languages with working implementations were created. The most important among them are Fortran (Formula Translator), COBOL (Common Business Oriented Language) and LISP (List Processor). Fortran was mostly oriented towards scientific computing, COBOL towards business and finance administration systems and LISP towards artificial intelligence systems. Though they focused on different domains, each of them could be used to write general purpose programs. In 1960 computer scientists from Europe and the United States developed a new language, called ALGOL 60 (algorithmic language). Though the language, and especially its formulation, contained many innovations, it did not gain widespread use. Its ideas influenced many of the languages created later, however.

In the 1960s through the 1970s many of the major programming language paradigms that are still in use today were developed. For example, Simula (end of the 1960s) was the first language supporting *object-oriented programming*, Smalltalk (mid 1970s) the first fully object-oriented programming language, Prolog (1972) the first *logic programming* language and ML (1973) the first *statically typed functional programming* language[7]. Most of our modern languages have clear influences from these languages and can thus be categorized in one of the associated paradigms. Other important programming languages created in this period were Logo (1968, a LISP offspring developed for teaching), PASCAL (1970, an ALGOL offspring) and C (1972, a systems programming language).

The 1980s mostly saw the creation of languages that recombined and improved upon the ideas from the paradigms and languages invented in the 1960s and 1970s. For example, C++ (1980) combined C with object-oriented programming, Objective-C (1983) combined

---

[6] Source: http://en.wikipedia.org/wiki/Plankalkul. Retrieved on Feb 25, 2011.
[7] Note that LISP was the first *dynamically* typed functional programming language.

C with Smalltalk-style messaging and object-oriented programming and Erlang (1986) combined functional programming with provisions for programming distributed systems. Next to these languages, a subparadigm of functional programming, called *purely* functional programming, was also created. Notable examples of the latter are Miranda (1985) and Haskell (1990).

In the 1990s general interest arose in programming languages that improve programmer productivity, so called *rapid development languages*[8]. Most of these languages incorporated object-oriented features or were fully object-oriented and had garbage-collection utilities to relieve the programmer of manual memory management. Examples are Python (1991), Visual Basic (1991), Ruby (1993), Java (1995) and Delphi (1995). The rise of the internet also spurred the development of scripting languages such as JavaScript (1995) and PHP (1995), which enabled the fast creation of interactive and dynamic websites. Due to the occurrence of computers with multiple cores, in the 2000s languages tailored for these machines were created, such as Clojure (2007) and Go (2009).

All programming languages mentioned above are *general-purpose* programming languages. This means they can be used to write software for many different application domains. While such languages have the advantage of only needing to learn one language for writing a variety of software, most of these languages do not support special constructs for specific application domains. This makes the translation of the requirements of a new software package into code much harder. *Domain-specific languages* are languages that are tailored towards one specific problem domain. Notable examples are regular expressions for handling text, SQL for describing database interactions and Yacc for creating compiler front-ends. Since the 1990s interest in domain-specific languages has increased. In fact, a new programming methodology, called language-oriented programming, has arisen that proposes to create a new language describing the domain first, and then use this language to write the final program [Ward (1994)].

Answer set programming is a declarative domain-specific language tailored towards solving combinatorial optimization problems. It has roots in logic programming and non-monotonic reasoning. In this book, we study a new domain-specific language, called *fuzzy answer set programming*, that is aimed towards solving continuous optimization problems. It combines answer set programming with *fuzzy logic* – a mathematical logic which can describe continuous concepts in an intuitive manner. In the next two sections we describe the history and general idea of these two cornerstones in more detail.

---

[8]Source: `http://en.wikipedia.org/History_of_programming_languages`. Retrieved on Mar 1, 2011

1.1   Answer Set Programming

To create systems that are capable of human-like reasoning, we need languages that are tailored towards representing knowledge and a method for reasoning over this knowledge. An idea that immediately comes to mind is to use logic to describe our knowledge and use model-finding algorithms (e.g. SAT solving) for the reasoning part. One of the limitations of classical logic when mimicking human reasoning is that it works *monotonically*: when new knowledge is added, the set of conclusions that can be inferred using classical logic grows. In contrast humans constantly revise their knowledge when new information becomes available. For example if we know that Pingu is a bird, we assume that he can fly. If we afterwards are told that he is a penguin, however, we need to revise our belief, as we know that penguins can't fly.

During the last decades, researchers have studied *non-monotonic* logics as a way to overcome this limitation of classical logic. Several such logics have been proposed, such as circumscription [McCarthy (1980)], default logic [Reiter (1980); Lukaszewicz (1984); Brewka (1991); Przymusińska and Przymusiński (1994)], auto-epistemic logic [Moore (1985)], non-monotonic modal logics in general [McDermott (1982)] and logic programming with negation-as-failure [Clark (1977); Van Gelder *et al.* (1991); Gelfond and Lifschitz (1988)]. In this book, we will focus on the latter.

Non-monotonicity in logic programming is obtained using a special construct called *negation-as-failure*, which is denoted as "not a" and intuitively means that the negation of a is true when we fail to derive a. Defining the semantics of this construct proved to be a challenge, however. The most important proposed definitions are the Clark completion [Clark (1977)], the stable model semantics [Gelfond and Lifschitz (1988)] and the well-founded semantics [Van Gelder *et al.* (1991)]. The stable model semantics refine the conclusions of the Clark completion in the presence of positive mutual dependencies between predicates [Fages (1994)]. The well-founded semantics on the other hand are more cautious in their conclusions than both the stable models and the Clark completion when there are mutual dependencies between predicates with the negation-as-failure construct. It has been shown that the well-founded semantics are an approximation of the stable model semantics [Baral and Subrahmanian (1993)]. A lot of research has also been devoted to the relationships between stable model semantics and other non-monotonic logic formalisms. For a good overview of these links we refer the reader to [Baral (2003)]. Attention has also been given to studying extensions of these semantics. In [Lifschitz and Woo (1991)] the stable model semantics is extended to programs with disjunctions, which has been shown to make the language capable of modeling a larger class of problems [Eiter *et al.* (1994)]. Another important extension is the addition of a second form of negation, called *classical negation* [Gelfond and Lifschitz (1991)]. Whereas negation-as-failure denotes that the negation follows from a failure to derive a proof term, classical negation denotes that the negation of the proof term can explicitly be derived.

At the end of the 1990s researchers began to notice that the stable model semantics gives rise to a certain logic programming paradigm that is different from the proof-derivation based approach of languages such as Prolog [Marek and Truszczyński (1999); Niemelä (1999)]. Vladimir Lifschitz named this new paradigm *"answer set programming"* (ASP) in [Lifschitz (2002, 1999)]. The basic idea of answer set programming is that a programmer translates a certain problem into an answer set program (a logic program under the stable model semantics) such that the *answer sets* (stable models) of the program correspond to the problem solutions. This program is then given as input to an *answer set solver* which computes the answer sets of the program. This solver has three possible outputs:

(1) No answer set exists. In this case, the modeled problem does not have a solution.
(2) One answer set exists. In this case, the answer set corresponds to the solution of the modeled problem.
(3) Multiple answer sets exist. In this case, the modeled problem has multiple solutions. The user can ask the answer set solver to compute all answer sets, or only a single one if this suffices.

For example, consider the problem of finding a large clique, i.e. a subset V of an undirected graph such that: (i) there is an edge between every pair of vertices in V; (ii) the cardinality of V is greater than or equal to a given l. If we take $l = 3$, for example, we can solve this using the following answer set program P_{clique} (from [Lifschitz (2002)])[9]:

$$in(X) \leftarrow not\, out(X) \tag{1.1}$$

$$out(X) \leftarrow not\, in(X) \tag{1.2}$$

$$sizeOk \leftarrow in(X), in(Y), in(Z), X \neq Y, X \neq Z, Y \neq Z \tag{1.3}$$

$$joined(X,Y) \leftarrow edge(X,Y) \tag{1.4}$$

$$joined(X,Y) \leftarrow edge(Y,X) \tag{1.5}$$

---

[9]Note that existing answer set solvers support an extension that allows to write the combination of rules (1.1)–(1.3) and (1.7) as the single rule "3 $\{in(X)\}$". Since we do not consider these extensions in this book, we opted to remove this syntactic sugar.

$$\leftarrow in(X), in(Y), X \neq Y, \text{not } joined(X,Y) \tag{1.6}$$

$$\leftarrow \text{not } sizeOk \tag{1.7}$$

In this program, rules (1.1) and (1.2) state that a vertex of the graph should either be in the clique or out of the clique. Rule (1.3) ensures that $sizeOk$ is only true when there are at least three vertices in the clique. The (1.4) and (1.5) rules declare that two vertices are joined if there is an edge between them. Last, rules (1.6) and (1.7) are *constraint* rules. Intuitively such rules remove solutions that make the right-hand side true. In the case of P_{clique}, rule (1.6) prohibits solutions where two vertices in the clique are not joined, whereas rule (1.7) stops solutions that do not have the right clique size.

Given the above program, the ASP programmer does not compile or run it using an interpreter, but *solves* it by means of an answer set solver. For this solver to work, the above program also needs to be supplemented with *fact* rules describing a graph. For example, consider the graph G with vertex set $V = \{v_1, v_2, v_3, v_4, v_5\}$ and edge set $E = \{(v_1, v_2), (v_1, v_3), (v_2, v_3), (v_4, v_5)\}$ that is depicted in Figure 1.1. This graph is encoded using the following set F_{clique} of ASP rules:

$$edge(v_1, v_2) \leftarrow$$
$$edge(v_1, v_3) \leftarrow$$
$$edge(v_2, v_3) \leftarrow$$
$$edge(v_4, v_5) \leftarrow$$

If we hand program $P_{clique} \cup F_{clique}$ as input to an ASP solver, it computes an *answer set* of the program. For our above program the resulting answer set is

$$A = \{edge(v_1, v_2), edge(v_1, v_3), edge(v_2, v_3), edge(v_4, v_5), in(v_1), in(v_2), in(v_3),$$
$$out(v_4), out(v_5), sizeOk, joined(v_1, v_2), joined(v_2, v_1), joined(v_1, v_3),$$
$$joined(v_3, v_1), joined(v_2, v_3), joined(v_3, v_2), joined(v_4, v_5), joined(v_5, v_4)\}$$

As expected, this corresponds to the clique $\{v_1, v_2, v_3\}$ of size 3 that exists for G.

Due to the creation of (relatively) fast answer set solvers such as Smodels [Simons and Niemelä (2000)] and DLV [Faber and Pfeifer (2005)], ASP was successfully applied to problems occurring in planning [Lifschitz (2002); Eiter *et al.* (2000, 2002)], configuration and verification [Soininen and Niemelä (1999); Soininen *et al.* (2001)], diagnosis [Eiter *et al.* (1999)], database repairs [Arenas *et al.* (1999)], game theory [De Vos and Vermeir (1999)] and bio-informatics [Baral *et al.* (2004)]. Furthermore it has been used to provide decision support for the space shuttle [Nogueira *et al.* (2001)].

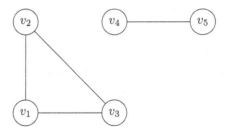

Fig. 1.1: Graph G

1.2 Fuzzy Logic

History Besides monotonicity, there are other aspects of classical logic that have been questioned throughout history. One of the most important ones is the principle of *bivalence*, i.e. the fact that propositions are either *true* or *false*. This principle was already a source of controversy among the old Greeks. While the school of Chrisippus defended it strongly, it was questioned by the Epicureans [Dubois *et al.* (1999)]. The main motivation for the rejection of bivalence was due to the perceived incapability of classical logic to handle propositions that refer to future contingencies. For example, consider the following proposition p: "Belgium will have a new government tomorrow". When stating this proposition, we cannot say that p is false, since this would mean that this is impossible. Likewise we cannot say that p is true, since this would mean that this is necessary. Classical logic dictates that p should be either true or false, however[10]. In the 4th century BC this already led Aristotle to believe that a *third logical status* of propositions exists [Gabbay and Woods (2007)]. While there has been some interest in examining this third truth value during the Middle Ages, it was only at the turn of the 19th century that more serious attempts were constructed. Notable efforts are the ones by Hugh MacColl, Charles S. Peirce and Nicolai A. Vasil'ev, who grouped propositions as either *affirmative*, *negative* and *indifferent* using considerations dealing with temporal or modal concepts [Gabbay and Woods (2007)]. The era of many-valued logic only started with the works of Jan Łukasiewicz [Łukasiewicz (1920)] and Emil L. Post [Post (1921)] in 1920, however. They built successful formulations of many-valued logic by adapting the truth-table method that was applied to classical logic by Frege, Peirce and others [Gabbay and Woods (2007)]. Łukasiewicz initially considered a logic with three truth values, where next to *true* and *false* propositions could be *possible*. In 1922 he generalized this work to a logic with an infinite number of truth values

---

[10]Note that probability theory can model this situation while preserving the bivalence of classical logic. However, this was not yet realized when philosophers first started to question the principle of bivalence.

[Borkowski (1970)]. Post applied his many-valued logic to problems of the representability of functions[11].

In the beginning of the 1930s Gödel used multiple truth values to understand intuitionistic logic [Gödel (1932)]. This led to the family of Gödel systems, which were extended to infinite truth values by Jaskowski in 1936 [Jaskowski (1936)]. In the late 1930s many-valued logics were applied to paradoxes by Bochvar [Bochvar (1938)] and to partial functions and relations by Kleene [Kleene (1938)].

In the 1950s and 1960s important work on the completeness of infinite-valued logics was done. Chang showed the relations between algebraic structures and many-valued systems [Chang (1958)] and proved a completeness result for infinite-valued Łukasiewicz logic [Chang (1959)]. Dummett proved a completeness result for infinite-valued Gödel logic [Dummet (1959)] and McNaughton created an analytical characterization of the class of truth degree functions that are definable in infinite-valued Łukasiewicz logic [McNaughton (1951)]. This time period furthermore saw proofs of the completeness of first-order infinite-valued Łukasiewicz logic [Hay (1963); Chang (1959)] and Gödel logic [Horn (1969)]. It was also shown that the former system is not (recursively) axiomatizable [Scarpellini (1962)].

Of significant importance for this book is the introduction of *fuzzy sets* by Lotfi Zadeh in 1965 [Zadeh (1965)]. Fuzzy set theory is a generalization of classical set theory with many-valued characteristic functions. Its introduction was motivated by the incapability of sets to model concepts that are not properly delineated. For example, if we say that the sky is *blue*, we do not mean that the sky has exactly the RGB value $0000FF$, but rather that the color we perceive of the sky is similar to this RGB value. The question then arises how we can define the set of colors that are similar to $0000FF$. It is easy to find examples that clearly are contained in this set (e.g. a light shade of blue) and examples that clearly are not contained in this set (e.g. red), but there are also colors that live on the boundary of these two sets, such as "greenish blue". Fuzzy sets take a graded approach: an element is not necessarily either fully contained in a set or not contained at all, but rather it can be contained to a certain *degree*. For example, for colors such as "greenish blue" we could say that it belongs to the set of colors similar to blue to a degree of 0.8, whereas red is contained in this set to a degree of 0 and a light shade of blue to a degree of 1. Note that fuzzy sets can thus be seen as mappings from a universe of discourse X to values in $[0, 1]$. From the 1970s and onwards the study of the foundations of fuzzy set theory was one of

---

[11] Source: http://plato.stanford.edu/entries/logic-manyvalued/. Retrieved on March 29, 2011.

the driving motivations behind further research into many-valued logics. Notable works include the extension of many-valued logics with a graded notion of inference and entailment by Pavelka [Pavelka (1979)], the first complexity results of infinite-valued Łukasiewicz logic in [Ragaz (1983)] and a detailed study of infinite-valued logics based on *triangular norms* [Hájek (1998)]. The latter systems have the same importance to fuzzy set theory as classical logic has to set theory. Therefore they are often called *fuzzy logics*.

The intuition of truth values Łukasiewicz proposed his many-valued logic as a method for modeling sentences referring to future contingencies, such as proposition p introduced above. His main idea was to add a third truth value *possible* and assign this value to such propositions, thereby rejecting the bivalence property. However, a couple of years after the publication of the works by Łukasiewicz, researchers in the foundations of probability theory became aware that probabilities differ from truth-values [Dubois *et al.* (1999)]. De Finetti pointed out that uncertainty is a meta-concept with respect to truth degrees and that it is still based on the idea of bivalence:

> "Even if, in itself, a proposition cannot be but true or false, it may occur that a given person does not know the answer, at least at a given moment. Hence for this person, there is a third attitude in front of a proposition. This third attitude does not correspond to a third truth-value distinct from yes or no, but to the doubt between the yes and the no (as people, who, due to incomplete or undecipherable information, appear as of *unknown sex* in a given statistics, do not constitute a third sex. They only form the group of people whose sex is unknown.)" [De Finetti (1936)] (translation from [Dubois *et al.* (1999)]).

De Finetti furthermore pointed out that many-valued logics do not reject the principle of bivalence, but are only compact representations of several ordinary propositions [De Finetti (1936)]. Gonseth moreover remarked that Łukasiewicz' original interpretation of the third truth value neglects the mutual dependence of *possible* propositions [Gabbay and Woods (2007)]. For example consider proposition p from above. If p is possible, so is $\neg p$. In the original Łukasiewicz system this leads us to conclude that $p \wedge \neg p$ is possible. However, this runs counter to our intuition as $p \wedge \neg p$ should always be false, independent from the truth value p.

The above shows that many-valued logics have nothing to do with uncertainty or probability, but instead deal with capturing the idea of *partial truth*, i.e. the fact that the compatibility of an object w.r.t. a certain concept is a matter of degree. Hence, the fuzzy answer set programming framework we create in this book does not capture uncertainty or probability, but deals with this graded truth.

1.3   Overview

While ASP allows to model combinatorial optimization problems in a concise and declarative manner, it is not suitable for expressing continuous optimization problems. These problems arise in many different domains, such as scheduling and designing gas and electricity networks [Osiadacz and Górecki (1995)], computer vision [Horn and Schunck (1981)] and investment portfolios [Hanqing (2004)]. *Fuzzy answer set programming* (FASP) combines ASP and fuzzy logic. The resulting language is capable of expressing continuous optimization problems in the same declarative manner as ASP allows the modeling of combinatorial optimization problems.

In this book we study the semantics and properties of extensions for FASP, as well as some implementation methods. We begin by recalling some preliminary notions regarding answer set programming and fuzzy logic in Chapter 2, followed by an introduction to fuzzy answer set programming in Chapter 3.

In Chapter 4 we investigate the use of allowing FASP rules to be partially fulfilled. This is often useful when modeling problems for which no perfect solution exists, or for which we are only interested in the best solution that can be found in a given time frame. Previous proposals for FASP supported partial rule satisfaction with weights. This is not ideal, however, as it puts the burden of finding the right weights on the programmer, a task that might not always be so straightforward. We improve upon these approaches by making the weights of a rule dynamic and by aggregating the value a prospective solution attaches to these weights into a global suitability score.

While users of a programming language often want the language to contain many features, implementers and theoreticians prefer a small, core language that is easy to implement and reason about. In Chapter 5 we create a bridge between these two wishes by proposing a simple core language for FASP that we show is capable of expressing many of its common extensions.

In Chapter 6 we research whether FASP can be translated to a fuzzy SAT problem. This provides the theoretical foundations for the creation of FASP solvers that rely on fuzzy SAT solving techniques such as mixed integer programming and other forms of mathematical programming. However, to build a real solver additional research on the efficient grounding of programs and the translation of functions other than t-norms is also needed. Our results are furthermore interesting on a theoretical level, as they show us where the use of FASP over fuzzy SAT is advantageous.

Chapter 2

Preliminaries

In this chapter we introduce some preliminary notions from order theory, answer set programming and fuzzy logic. Note that all notations that are frequently used in this book are included in a list of symbols at the back of the book.

2.1 Order Theory

Definition 2.1 (from [Birkhoff (1973)]). *A binary relation $\leqslant$ on a set P is a **preorder** iff for each x, y, z in P the relation obeys the following conditions:*

(1) Reflexivity: $x \leqslant x$

(2) Transitivity: $(x \leqslant y) \wedge (y \leqslant z) \Rightarrow (x \leqslant z)$

If the binary relation $\leqslant$ furthermore satisfies the anti-symmetry condition

$$(x \leqslant y) \wedge (y \leqslant x) \Rightarrow (x = y)$$

*then $\leqslant$ is called an **order relation**.*

A set P together with a preorder $\leqslant$ on P is called a **preordered set** and is denoted as $(P, \leqslant)$. For a given preorder $\mathscr{P} = (P, \leqslant_{\mathscr{P}})$ we denote $\leqslant_{\mathscr{P}}$ by $\leqslant$ if no confusion is possible. Furthermore for a preordered set $(P, \leqslant)$ the notation $y \geqslant x$ is equivalent to $x \leqslant y$. Last, a preordered set $(P, \leqslant)$ is called finite if P consists of a finite number of elements.

A set P together with an order relation $\leqslant$ is called a **partially ordered set** (short: **poset**). For an order relation $\leqslant$ we abbreviate $(x \leqslant y) \wedge (x \neq y)$ as $x < y$ (or sometimes $y > x$).

Definition 2.2 (from [Birkhoff (1973)]). *Let $(P, \leqslant)$ be a poset, let A be a subset of P and let x be an element of P. Then we define:*

$$x \text{ is a } \textbf{lower bound} \text{ for } A \text{ iff } \forall y \in A \cdot x \leqslant y$$

$$x \text{ is an } \textbf{upper bound} \text{ for } A \text{ iff } \forall y \in A \cdot y \leqslant x$$

Definition 2.3 (from [Birkhoff (1973)]). *Let $(P, \leqslant)$ be a poset, let A be a subset of P and let x be an element of P. Then we define:*

> x is the **least element** of A iff x is a lower bound for A and $x \in A$
>
> x is the **greatest element** of A iff x is an upper bound for A and $x \in A$

The least element and greatest element of A are commonly referred to as the **minimum**, resp. **maximum** of A. Note that if they exist, they must be unique [Birkhoff (1973)]. A poset $\mathscr{P}$ is called **bounded** if it contains a minimum and a maximum. We denote these elements with $0_{\mathscr{P}}$, resp. $1_{\mathscr{P}}$. If the poset used is clear from the context we denote them with 0, respectively 1. For a given set A we denote the minimum and maximum as $\min A$, resp. $\max A$, if they exist.

Definition 2.4 (from [Birkhoff (1973)]). *Let $(P, \leqslant)$ be a poset, let A be a subset of P and let x be an element of P. Then we define:*

> x is the **infimum** of A iff x is the greatest lower bound for A
>
> x is the **supremum** of A iff x is the least upper bound for A

If the infimum of A exists we denote this with $\inf A$. Likewise we denote the supremum of A with $\sup A$, if it exists.

Definition 2.5 (from [Birkhoff (1973)]). *A poset $(P, \leqslant)$ is called a **lattice** iff each pair $\{x, y\} \subseteq P$ has an infimum and supremum. If every subset of P has an infimum and supremum we call P a **complete lattice**.*

Note that every finite lattice must necessarily be complete. Furthermore every complete lattice is bounded. Last we would like to remark that $\inf\{x, y\}$ and $\sup\{x, y\}$ are commonly denoted as $x \sqcap y$, respectively $x \sqcup y$. The operation $\sqcap$ is called the **meet** operator and $\sqcup$ the **join** operator.

Definition 2.6 (from [Tarski (1955)]). *Let $(P_1, \leqslant_1)$ and $(P_2, \leqslant_2)$ be two posets and let f be a $P_1 \rightarrow P_2$ mapping. Then we define*

> f is increasing iff $\forall x, y \in P_1 \cdot x \leqslant_1 y \Rightarrow f(x) \leqslant_2 f(y)$
>
> f is decreasing iff $\forall x, y \in P_2 \cdot x \leqslant_2 y \Rightarrow f(x) \geqslant_2 f(y)$

Note that increasing functions are also commonly called **monotonic**. Tarski proved the following theorem on fixpoints of increasing functions on complete lattices.

Proposition 2.1 (from [Tarski (1955)]). *Let $\mathscr{L}$ be a complete lattice and let $f : \mathscr{L} \rightarrow \mathscr{L}$ be an increasing function. Then f has a least fixpoint, i.e. there is an $x \in \mathscr{L}$ such that*

$f(x) = x$ and for all $y \in \mathscr{L}$ such that $f(y) = y$ we have that $x \leqslant y$. We denote the least fixpoint of f as f^*.

It turns out that the least fixpoint of an increasing function f on a complete lattice $\mathscr{L}$ can be computed by iteratively applying f, starting from the least element in the lattice, until a fixpoint is found. We call this an **iterated fixpoint computation**.

Definition 2.7 (from [Baral (2003)]). *Let $\mathscr{L}$ be a complete lattice and let $f : \mathscr{L} \to \mathscr{L}$ be an increasing function. Then*

$$f^0 = 0_{\mathscr{L}}$$
$$f^n = f(f^{n-1}) \text{ if } n \text{ is a successor ordinal}$$
$$f^{\alpha} = \sup\{f^{\beta} \mid \beta < \alpha\} \text{ if } \alpha \text{ is a limit ordinal}$$

Proposition 2.2 (from [Baral (2003)]). *Let $\mathscr{L}$ be a complete lattice and let $f : \mathscr{L} \to \mathscr{L}$ be an increasing function. Then $f^* = f^{\alpha}$, where α is a limit ordinal.*

2.2   Answer Set Programming

In this section we introduce answer set programming. The section is structured as follows. First we begin by introducing the syntax & semantics in 2.2.1. This is followed by a discussion on the the two types of negation that can be considered in answer set programming in 2.2.2. Finally, in 2.2.3, we conclude by discussing the relations between answer set programming and the satisfiability problem in propositional logic.

2.2.1   Definitions

In this section we define the syntax and semantics of ASP. The terminology is based on material from [Van Nieuwenborgh (2005)].

2.2.1.1   Language

Answer set programming (**ASP**) is built from a language containing terms, atoms and (extended) literals as basic building blocks. A **term** is a **variable** or a **constant**. In this book we adopt the usual convention that variables (constants) are denoted by a symbol starting with an upper-case (lower-case) character. An **atom** is an expression of the form $p(t_1, \ldots, t_n)$, where p is a **predicate** of arity n and $t_1, \ldots, t_n$ are terms. An atom is called **grounded** if it does not contain any variables.

A **literal** is either an atom a or a negated atom $\neg a$ (called a classically or strongly negated literal). An **extended literal** is either a literal or an expression of the form $not\,l$ (called a **negation-as-failure literal** or **naf-literal**), where l is a literal. An (extended) literal is called **grounded** if its underlying atom is grounded.

For a set of literals L we use $not\,L$ to denote the set $\{not\,l \mid l \in L\}$ and $\neg L$ to denote the set $\{\neg l \mid l \in L\}$, where $\neg(\neg l) = l$. With L^+ we denote the positive part of L, i.e. $L^+ = \{a \in L \mid a$ is an atom$\}$. Furthermore, for a set of extended literals L we denote with L^- the set of literals underlying the naf-literals in L, i.e. $L^- = \{l \mid not\,l \in L\}$. For a set of grounded literals L, we say that L is **consistent** iff $L \cap \neg L = \emptyset$. Last, for a set of grounded atoms A, we denote the set of all literals over A as Lit_A, i.e. $Lit_A = A \cup \neg A$.

Definition 2.8. A **normal rule** r is an expression of the form

$$a \leftarrow \beta$$

where a is either the empty set or a singleton containing a literal and β is a set of extended literals. The left-hand side a is called the **head** of the rule, denoted as r_h, whereas the right-hand side β is called the **body** of the rule, and is denoted as r_b.

Rules can be divided in certain classes, depending on conditions satisfied by a and/or β:

(1) A **constraint** is a rule where a is empty.
(2) A **fact** is a rule where β is empty.
(3) A **simple rule** is a rule where $\beta^- = \emptyset$, i.e. a rule with no negation-as-failure literals.
(4) A **positive rule** is a rule where $\beta^- = \emptyset$, $\beta^+ = \beta$ and a is either an atom or empty, i.e. a rule containing only atoms.

Definition 2.9. An **answer set program** (**ASP program**) is a countable set of rules.

Example 2.1. Consider the following program $P_{ex2.1}$.

$$rightOf(john, chris) \leftarrow \qquad\qquad (2.1)$$

$$rightOf(chris, cathy) \leftarrow \qquad\qquad (2.2)$$

$$rightOf(X,Y) \leftarrow rightOf(X,Z), rightOf(Z,Y) \qquad\qquad (2.3)$$

In this program rules (2.1)–(2.2) are facts stating who is sitting immediately on the right of whom. For example rule (2.1) states that *john* is sitting immediately on the right of *chris*. Rule (2.3) then describes that the relation "right of" is transitive. Note that all rules in this program are positive (and thus also simple).

Using the types of rules introduced above we can consider the following types of programs:

(1) A **positive program** contains only positive rules.

(2) A **simple program** contains only simple rules.

(3) A **normal program** can contain any rule.

A positive, simple or normal program is called **constraint-free** if it does not contain any constraints.

2.2.1.2   *Grounding*

In the formulation of the semantics of ASP programs we assume that programs do not contain variables. In the following we explain how we can obtain a grounded version, $gnd(P)$, from a normal program P that contains variables.

Definition 2.10 (from [Van Nieuwenborgh (2005)]). *Let P be a program. The set of all constants appearing in P is called the **Herbrand universe**, denoted $\mathcal{U}_P$. The **Herbrand base** $\mathcal{B}_P$ of P is the set containing all grounded atoms that can be constructed from the predicates in P and the terms in $\mathcal{U}_P$.*

Consider now a rule r in a program P. A **grounded instance** of r is any rule obtained from r by replacing every variable X in r by $\sigma(X)$, where σ is a mapping from the variables occurring in r to the terms in $\mathcal{U}_P$. We denote the set of all ground instances of a rule $r \in P$ by $gnd_{\mathcal{U}_P}(r)$. The **grounded program** P is then defined as

$$gnd(P) = \bigcup_{r \in P} gnd_{\mathcal{U}_P}(r)$$

Example 2.2. Consider the following program $P_{ex2.2}$:

$$p(X,Y) \leftarrow q(X), r(Y)$$
$$q(a) \leftarrow$$
$$r(b) \leftarrow$$

Its grounding is the following program $gnd(P_{ex2.2})$:

$$p(a,a) \leftarrow q(a), r(a)$$
$$p(a,b) \leftarrow q(a), r(b)$$
$$p(b,a) \leftarrow q(b), r(a)$$
$$p(b,b) \leftarrow q(b), r(b)$$

$$q(a) \leftarrow$$
$$r(b) \leftarrow$$

Note that the grounding process can be exponential in the size of the program. Therefore researchers have recently started to devote their attention to the study of more efficient grounding methods (see e.g. [Syrjänen (2001, 2004); Leone *et al.* (2004); Gebser *et al.* (2007)]). In the remainder of this book we assume that all programs are grounded, unless stated otherwise.

2.2.1.3 *Semantics*

In this section we define the *meaning* of ASP programs constructed in the language introduced above. Intuitively, if we model certain knowledge or a certain problem with an ASP program, we want the semantics of the program to capture the knowledge that can be derived.

Formally, the meaning of a program is represented by *interpretations*. If P is a program, then any consistent set $I \subseteq Lit_{\mathscr{B}_P}$ is an **interpretation** of P. For programs without classical negation interpretations are subsets of $\mathscr{B}_P$. An interpretation I is **total** if $\mathscr{B}_P = I \cup \neg I$. An extended literal is true w.r.t. an interpretation I, denoted $I \models l$, iff $l \in I$ if l is not a naf-literal and $I \not\models a$ if l is a naf-literal of the form $not\, a$. If L is a set of (extended) literals we define $I \models L$ iff $\forall l \in L \cdot I \models l$.

For a rule $r \in P$ of the form $a \leftarrow \beta$ we say that r is **satisfied** by I, denoted $I \models r$, iff $I \not\models \beta$ or $I \models a$.

Definition 2.11. Let P be a program. An interpretation I of P is called a **model** of P iff $\forall r \in P \cdot I \models r$. Furthermore, I is a **minimal model** of P iff I is a model of P and no model J of P exists such that $J \subset I$.

For constraint-free positive programs the minimal model is guaranteed to exist and can be computed using the following monotonic operator.

Definition 2.12 (from [Van Emden and Kowalski (1976)]). *Let P be a constraint-free positive program and let I be an interpretation of P. The **immediate consequence operator** Π_P of P is a $\mathscr{P}(\mathscr{B}_P) \rightarrow \mathscr{P}(\mathscr{B}_P)$ function defined as*
$$\Pi_P(I) = \{a \mid a \leftarrow \beta \in P \wedge \beta \subseteq I\}$$

It is easy to see that this operator is monotonic, and due to Proposition 2.1 and Proposition 2.2, that it has a least fixpoint that can be computed using an iterated fixpoint computation. Define $\Pi_P^0 = \emptyset$ and $\Pi_P^i = \Pi_P(\Pi_P^{i-1})$ for $i \geq 1$, then Π_P^j is the least fixpoint of Π_P, denoted as $\Pi_P^\star$, iff $\Pi_P(\Pi_P^j) = \Pi_P^j$. In other words, the least fixpoint of Π_P can be computed by iteratively applying Π_P, starting from the empty interpretation, until a fixpoint is found. Note that this computation always ends if $\mathscr{B}_P$ is finite, which we will assume in the remainder of this book. The following proposition shows that this least fixpoint coincides with the minimal model of P, hence the procedure explained above gives us a procedural method for computing the minimal model of a program.

Proposition 2.3 (from [Van Nieuwenborgh (2005)]). *Let P be a constraint-free positive program. Then I is a model of P iff $\Pi_P(I) \subseteq I$. Furthermore, the unique minimal model of P equals the least fixpoint of Π_P.*

Note that from the former it follows that for positive programs the minimal model, if it exists, must be unique. The above definitions can easily be extended to simple programs with constraints. Let us denote by P' the program consisting of the rules in P where we (i) consider classically negated atoms $\neg a$ as fresh atoms and (ii) replace constraint rules of the form $\leftarrow \beta$ by rules of the form $\bot \leftarrow \beta$. Furthermore we extend the definition of inconsistency by saying that a set $I \subseteq \mathscr{B}_P$ is inconsistent iff $\{a, \neg a\} \subseteq I$ for some $a \in \mathscr{B}_P$ or $\bot \in I$. Note that since interpretations (and thus also models) are by definition consistent, they can never contain $\bot$.

Proposition 2.4 (from [Van Nieuwenborgh (2005)]). *Let P be a simple program. An interpretation I is the unique minimal model of P iff I is the unique minimal model of P'.*

Now we can introduce the semantics of answer set programs. We do this in two steps. First we define the answer sets for programs without negation-as-failure.

Definition 2.13. Let P be a simple program. An interpretation A is called an **answer set** of P iff A is the minimal model of P.

For normal programs, i.e. programs containing negation-as-failure, we have to define the semantics differently because the minimal models of these programs do not always correspond to our intuition regarding negation-as-failure.

Example 2.3. Consider the following program $P_{ex2.3}$:

$$person(john) \leftarrow$$
$$suitable\_for\_job(X) \leftarrow person(X), not\, criminal\_record(X)$$

It is easy to verify that this program has two minimal models, namely $M_1 = \{person(john),$ $criminal\_record(john)\}$ and $M_2 = \{person(john), suitable\_for\_job(john)\}$. Both of these minimal models contain knowledge that was not explicitly stated in our program, i.e. in M_1 we assume that John has a criminal record, whereas in M_2 we suppose the opposite. Only M_2 is intuitively acceptable, however, since the extra knowledge it includes can be inferred using negation-as-failure: due to our failure to deduct that John has a criminal record, we assume that he doesn't.

The above example illustrates that we need a way of selecting the right minimal models of a program. Formally this can be done by starting from a candidate answer set A of P and construct a reduct program P^A that does not contain negation-as-failure. Then, the candidate answer set is a real answer set if it is an answer set of the reduct (i.e. if it is the minimal model of the reduct).

Definition 2.14 (from [Gelfond and Lifschitz (1988)]). *Let P be a normal program and let I be an interpretation of P. The **reduct** of P w.r.t. I, denoted as P^I, is the program*

$$\{a \leftarrow (\beta \setminus not\,\beta^-) \mid a \leftarrow \beta \in P \land (I \models not\,\beta^-)\}$$

In other words, P^I is obtained by removing all naf-literals $not\,l$ for which $l \notin I$ from the bodies of the rules in P and removing all rules containing $not\,l$ for which $l \in I$. Intuitively this means we remove the naf-literals of rules that could be satisfied by I, judged only by looking at the negative information in I, and discard the rules that can never be satisfied by I.

Definition 2.15 (from [Van Nieuwenborgh (2005)]). *Let P be a normal program. An interpretation A is called an **answer set** of P iff A is the minimal model of P^A.*

The following example illustrates that this definition indeed eliminates the unintuitive minimal models.

Example 2.4. Consider again program $P_{ex2.3}$ from Example 2.3 together with its two minimal models M_1 and M_2. Computing the reducts gives us the program $P_{ex2.3}^{M_1}$:

$$person(john) \leftarrow$$

and $P_{ex2.3}^{M_2}$:

$$person(john) \leftarrow$$
$$suitable\_for\_job(john) \leftarrow person(john)$$

It is easy to see that the minimal model of $P_{ex2.3}^{M_1}$ is $\{person(john)\}$, which is not equal to M_1, hence M_1 is not an answer set of $P_{ex2.3}$. The minimal model M_2 is an answer set of $P_{ex2.3}$, however, as M_2 is the minimal model of $P_{ex2.3}^{M_2}$.

In general, the answer sets of a program will be a subset of the minimal models.

Proposition 2.5 (from [Baral (2003)]). *Let P be a normal program. Any answer set of P is a minimal model of P.*

The reverse does not hold, as Example 2.4 shows. Note that a program can have multiple answer sets or even no answer sets, as shown in the following examples.

Example 2.5. Consider program P_{nondet}:

$$a \leftarrow not\, b$$

$$b \leftarrow not\, a$$

This program has two answer sets: $A_1 = \{a\}$ and $A_2 = \{b\}$.

Example 2.6. Consider program P_{empty}:

$$p \leftarrow not\, p$$

This program has no answer sets. Indeed, its only minimal model is $M = \{p\}$, but $P^M = \emptyset$, which has $\emptyset \neq M$ as its answer set.

The fact that programs can have multiple answer sets or no answer sets forms the basis for the **answer set programming paradigm**[Marek and Truszczyński (1999); Niemelä (1999)]. In this paradigm, we solve a certain combinatorial problem by writing an ASP program such that the answer sets of the program correspond to the solutions of the problem. Most often this is done by writing a program in a generate-define-test style, as shown in the following example:

Example 2.7. Consider the problem of coloring the vertices of a graph in either black or white, such that adjacent nodes are colored differently. We can model this problem using the ASP program P_{gc}:

$$black(X) \leftarrow not\, white(X) \tag{2.4}$$

$$white(X) \leftarrow not\, black(X) \tag{2.5}$$

$$sim(X,Y) \leftarrow white(X), white(Y) \tag{2.6}$$

$$sim(X,Y) \leftarrow black(X), black(Y) \tag{2.7}$$

$$\leftarrow edge(X,Y), sim(X,Y) \qquad\qquad (2.8)$$

In this program rules (2.4) and (2.5) are the so-called **generate part**, which generate an arbitrary graph coloring. One can see that the possibility of having two answer sets thus allows us to state non-deterministic choice in our program. Rules (2.6) and (2.7) form the **defining part** of our program, which defines certain concepts that will be used in the **constraint part** consisting of rule (2.8). The latter rule eliminates solutions (i.e. answer sets) in which adjacent nodes are similarly colored.

Note that in the above program there are no rules defining what $edge(X,Y)$ means. This is because an ASP program consists of two parts: a general part describing a solution, as above, and an input part defining a specific instance of the problem. For our graph coloring we can e.g. describe the graph depicted in Fig. 2.1a on the facing page by the following set of facts $F_{2.1a}$:

$$node(a) \leftarrow$$
$$node(b) \leftarrow$$
$$node(c) \leftarrow$$
$$edge(a,b) \leftarrow$$
$$edge(b,a) \leftarrow$$
$$edge(a,c) \leftarrow$$
$$edge(c,a) \leftarrow$$

It is easy to verify that the answer sets of $P_{gc} \cup F_{2.1a}$ are

$$A_1 = I \cup \{black(a), white(b), white(c), sim(b,c)\}$$

and

$$A_2 = I \cup \{white(a), black(b), black(c), sim(b,c)\}$$

where

$$I = \{node(a), node(b), node(c), edge(a,b), edge(b,a), edge(a,c), edge(c,a),$$
$$edge(b,c), edge(c,b), sim(a,a), sim(b,b), sim(c,c)\}$$

Hence the answer sets correspond to the two admissible graph colorings.

If we consider the graph depicted in Fig. 2.1b, however, we find that $P_{gc} \cup F_{2.1b}$ has no answer sets, where $F_{2.1b}$ consists of the input facts encoding this graph.

The above example shows that ASP can be used as a problem solving tool, much in the same vein as constraint satisfaction solvers.

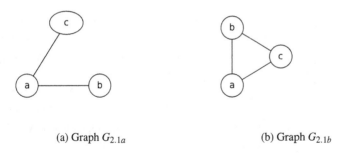

(a) Graph $G_{2.1a}$ (b) Graph $G_{2.1b}$

Fig. 2.1: Input Graphs

2.2.2 *Classical negation vs negation-as-failure*

As mentioned before, in ASP we have two types of negation: classical negation and negation-as-failure. The former states that the negation of an atom a can be explicitly derived, whereas $\text{not}\,a$ is true if we cannot derive a. The important difference between these two constructs is perhaps best illustrated by an example:

Example 2.8. Suppose we are building an ASP program for controlling a car. To ensure safety this car must abide by the traffic rules and so we need to express the usual rule of giving way to the right, i.e. that we have to yield to cars coming from the right. Doing this with negation-as-failure we obtain the rule

$$driveon \leftarrow \text{not}\,carOnRight$$

However, this rule states that if we fail to derive that there is a car on the right, we can drive on. So if it is foggy and our sensors cannot determine whether there is a car on the right, we will drive on, which can have some fatal consequences. Writing this rule with classical negation we obtain

$$driveon \leftarrow \neg carOnRight$$

This rule states that we only drive on when the sensors on the car have derived that no car is coming. Hence in the case of foggy weather we stay safe, though it can take a while until we get to our destination.

Classical negation can be eliminated from the program by introducing for each literal $\neg a$ a new atom a' and adding the constraint $\leftarrow a, a'$ to the program. The constraint ensures that any model will be consistent, and thus ensures that the semantics are preserved. For more details see [Baral (2003)]. Unless stated otherwise, for all programs in the remainder of this chapter we assume that classical negation has been eliminated in this way.

2.2.3 *Links to SAT*

There exist important links between ASP and the boolean satisfiability problem (SAT), which we highlight in this section. We begin by illustrating that the graph coloring program introduced above can be translated into an equivalent and equally concise SAT problem.

Example 2.9. Consider program $P_{gc} \cup F_{2.1a}$ from Example 2.7. Its corresponding SAT problem, denoted as $comp(P_{gc} \cup F_{2.1a})$, is obtained by replacing $\leftarrow$ by $\equiv$, replacing $not\,l$ by $\neg l$ for any literal l, replacing empty bodies by *True*, replacing empty heads by *False* and grouping rule bodies of rules with the same heads by disjunction:

$$node(a) \equiv True$$
$$node(b) \equiv True$$
$$node(c) \equiv True$$
$$edge(a,b) \equiv True$$
$$edge(b,a) \equiv True$$
$$edge(a,c) \equiv True$$
$$edge(c,a) \equiv True$$
$$black(a) \equiv \neg white(a)$$
$$white(a) \equiv \neg black(a)$$
$$black(b) \equiv \neg white(b)$$
$$white(b) \equiv \neg black(b)$$
$$black(c) \equiv \neg white(c)$$
$$white(c) \equiv \neg black(c)$$
$$sim(a,a) \equiv (white(a) \wedge white(a)) \vee (black(a) \wedge black(a))$$
$$sim(a,b) \equiv (white(a) \wedge white(b)) \vee (black(a) \wedge black(b))$$
$$sim(a,c) \equiv (white(a) \wedge white(c)) \vee (black(a) \wedge black(c))$$
$$sim(b,a) \equiv (white(b) \wedge white(a)) \vee (black(b) \wedge black(a))$$
$$sim(b,b) \equiv (white(b) \wedge white(b)) \vee (black(b) \wedge black(b))$$
$$sim(b,c) \equiv (white(b) \wedge white(c)) \vee (black(b) \wedge black(c))$$
$$sim(c,a) \equiv (white(c) \wedge white(a)) \vee (black(c) \wedge black(a))$$
$$sim(c,b) \equiv (white(c) \wedge white(b)) \vee (black(c) \wedge black(b))$$
$$sim(c,c) \equiv (white(c) \wedge white(c)) \vee (black(c) \wedge black(c))$$

$$False \equiv edge(a,a) \wedge sim(a,a)$$

$$False \equiv edge(a,b) \wedge sim(a,b)$$

$$False \equiv edge(a,c) \wedge sim(a,c)$$

$$False \equiv edge(b,a) \wedge sim(b,a)$$

$$False \equiv edge(b,b) \wedge sim(b,b)$$

$$False \equiv edge(b,c) \wedge sim(b,c)$$

$$False \equiv edge(c,a) \wedge sim(c,a)$$

$$False \equiv edge(c,b) \wedge sim(c,b)$$

$$False \equiv edge(c,c) \wedge sim(c,c)$$

One can easily verify that answer sets A_1 and A_2 from Example 2.7 are models of the above translation to SAT.

Formally this translation is called the **completion** of an ASP program. It is also commonly called **Clark's completion** after Keith Clark, who originally proposed this correspondence as a method for describing the semantics of negation-as-failure [Clark (1977)].

Definition 2.16 (from [Clark (1977)]). *Let P be a normal program. The **completion** of P, denoted comp(P), is defined as the following set of propositions:*

$$comp(P) = \{a \equiv \bigvee\{comp(\beta) \mid a \leftarrow \beta \in P\} \mid a \in \mathcal{B}_P, \beta \neq \emptyset\}$$
$$\cup \{a \equiv True \mid (a \leftarrow) \in \mathcal{B}_P\}$$
$$\cup \{False \equiv comp(\beta) \mid (\leftarrow \beta) \in \mathcal{B}_P\}$$

where $\bigvee(\emptyset) = False$ *and* $comp(\beta) = b_1 \wedge \ldots \wedge b_n \wedge \neg c_1 \wedge \ldots \wedge \neg c_m$ *for* $\beta = \{b_1, \ldots, b_n, not\, c_1, \ldots, not\, c_m\}$.

In [Fages (1994)], Fages showed that under certain conditions the answer sets of an ASP program and the models of its completion coincide. The question then arises why we need ASP at all and why we cannot just write our problems directly as their SAT encodings? After all, the completion of the graph coloring program introduced above is almost as concise as the grounded program. There are ASP programs for which the models of the completion do not coincide with the answer sets, however. This occurs when there are atoms that positively depend on other atoms, as shown in the following example.

Example 2.10. Consider the following program $P_{ex2.10}$:

$$a \leftarrow a$$

The answer set of $P_{ex2.10}$ is $\emptyset$. However, its completion $comp(P_{ex2.10})$ has two models: $\emptyset$ and $\{a\}$.

From the above example one might think that answer sets correspond to the minimal models of the completion. This turns out to be false, however, as one can see from the following example.

Example 2.11. Consider the following program $P_{ex2.11}$:

$$a \leftarrow a$$

$$p \leftarrow \text{not } p, \text{not } a$$

One can easily verify that $P_{ex2.11}$ has no answer sets. However, its completion has the single (and therefore trivially minimal) model $\{a\}$.

While the above shows that in general minimal models of the completion are not answer sets, the reverse does hold: answer sets are minimal models of the completion.

Proposition 2.6 (from [Gelfond and Lifschitz (1988)]). *Let P be a normal answer set program. Then any answer set A of P is a minimal model of the completion* $comp(P)$ *of P.*

We can now answer the question why we need ASP. While the graph coloring example could be concisely encoded in SAT, this does not hold in general. For example, programs incorporating recursion require a more involved translation [Lin and Zhao (2004)]. However, in many application domains it is quite convenient to define predicates recursively, such as the transitive closure defined by the *rightOf* predicate in Example 2.1. The following program illustrates the use of recursion on the problem of finding Hamilton cycles in a graph.

Example 2.12. Consider the problem of determining Hamilton cycles of a graph, i.e. finding a path in the graph that visits every vertex exactly once. In [Marek and Truszczyński (1999)] the authors propose to encode this problem with the following program P_{hc}:

$$in(U,V) \leftarrow edge(U,V), \text{not } out(U,V) \tag{2.9}$$

$$out(U,V) \leftarrow edge(U,V), \text{not}\, in(U,V) \tag{2.10}$$

$$reachable(V) \leftarrow in(v_0,V) \tag{2.11}$$

$$reachable(V) \leftarrow reachable(U), in(U,V) \tag{2.12}$$

$$\leftarrow in(U,V), in(U,W), V \neq W \tag{2.13}$$

$$\leftarrow in(U,W), in(V,W), U \neq V \tag{2.14}$$

$$\leftarrow vertex(U), \text{not}\, reachable(U), in(U,V) \tag{2.15}$$

where in rules (2.13) and (2.14) $V \neq W$ and $U \neq V$ are extensions of the ungrounded ASP language which denote that the grounded instances of these rules where $V = W$, resp. $U = V$ holds should not be included in the grounding of the program. Rules (2.9) and (2.10) are the generate rules, where $in(U,V)$ means edge (U,V) is included in the cycle, and $out(U,V)$ means the edge (U,V) is *not* included in the cycle. Rules (2.11) and (2.12) are the defining part, encoding when a vertex is reachable. Note that we have to explicitly state the starting vertex v_0 for this program to work. Furthermore note that we do not state that $reachable(v_0)$ is necessarily true. This is to ensure that the program adds an edge to v_0, and thus creates a cycle rather than a path. Last, rules (2.13)–(2.15) are the constraints eliminating answer sets in which a vertex is visited twice or a certain node is never visited.

Note that the *reachable* predicate is defined recursively. This can lead to counterintuitive results for the models of the completion. Consider the following input rules I from [Babovich et al. (2000)]:

$$vertex(v_0) \leftarrow$$

$$vertex(v_1) \leftarrow$$

$$edge(v_0,v_0) \leftarrow$$

$$edge(v_1,v_1) \leftarrow$$

The grounded program $gnd(P_{gc} \cup I)$ will have no answer sets, as no Hamilton cycle exists in this graph. The set $\{vertex(v_0), vertex(v_1), edge(v_0,v_0), edge(v_1,v_1), in(v_0,v_0), in(v_1,v_1), reachable(v_0), reachable(v_1)\}$ is a model of $comp(gnd(P_{gc} \cup I))$, however.

2.3 Fuzzy Logic

In this section we introduce fuzzy sets and fuzzy logic. We begin by introducing fuzzy sets in Section 2.3.1, then turn our attention to the common operators of fuzzy logic in Section 2.3.2 and conclude by discussing formal fuzzy logics in Section 2.3.3.

2.3.1 Fuzzy Sets

We briefly introduce the concepts from fuzzy set theory that we will use throughout this book.

Definition 2.17. Consider a complete lattice $\mathscr{L}$. An $\mathscr{L}$-**fuzzy set** in a universe X is a mapping from X to $\mathscr{L}$.

We will refer to $([0,1], \leqslant)$-fuzzy sets as just **fuzzy sets**. The *inclusion* of two fuzzy sets is defined as follows:

Definition 2.18. Given two $\mathscr{L}$-fuzzy sets A and B in a universe X we define the **Zadeh inclusion** $A \subseteq B$ of A and B as follows:

$$A \subseteq B \equiv \forall x \in X \cdot A(x) \leqslant B(x)$$

It is often important to denote the elements of a fuzzy set that are contained to a degree that is higher than 0. The *support* of a fuzzy set is the set of elements that have this property.

Definition 2.19. Consider an $\mathscr{L}$-fuzzy set A in a universe X. The **support** of A is the set $supp(A)$ that is defined by $supp(A) = \{x \mid x \in X, A(x) > 0\}$.

2.3.2 Logical Operators on Bounded Lattices

In this section we recall the generalizations of classical logical operators in fuzzy logic.

Negators, Triangular Norms and Triangular Conorms

The negation $\neg$ of classical logic can be generalized as follows:

Definition 2.20. A **negator** $\mathscr{N}$ on a bounded lattice $\mathscr{L}$ is a decreasing $\mathscr{L} \to \mathscr{L}$ mapping that satisfies $\mathscr{N}(0) = 1$ and $\mathscr{N}(1) = 0$. The negator $\mathscr{N}$ is called **involutive** iff for each $x \in \mathscr{L}$ we have $\mathscr{N}(\mathscr{N}(x)) = x$.

Note that if we take *True* $= 1$ and *False* $= 0$, the boundary conditions $\mathscr{N}(0) = 1$ and $\mathscr{N}(1) = 0$ ensure that any negator behaves as the negation $\neg$ of classical logic on the lattice $(\{0,1\}, \leqslant)$. The generalizations of other logical operators will similarly need certain boundary conditions to ensure that the classical behavior is recovered for the lattice $(\{0,1\}, \leqslant)$.

Example 2.13. We introduce two common negators over $([0,1], \leqslant)$, the lattice most commonly associated with fuzzy logic.

(1) The **Gödel negator** $\mathcal{N}_M$ (also known as **drastic negator**) on a bounded lattice $\mathcal{L}$ is the $\mathcal{L} \to \mathcal{L}$ mapping defined as

$$\mathcal{N}_M(x) = \begin{cases} 1 & \text{if } x = 0 \\ 0 & \text{otherwise} \end{cases}$$

(2) The **standard negator** $\mathcal{N}_W$ (also known as **Łukasiewicz negator**) is the $[0,1] \to [0,1]$ mapping defined as $\mathcal{N}_W(x) = 1 - x$. Note that this negator is involutive.

Conjunction is usually generalized by *t-norms* and disjunction by *t-conorms*.

Definition 2.21 (from [Klement *et al.* (2002)]). *A **triangular norm** $\mathcal{T}$ (short: **t-norm**) on a bounded lattice $\mathcal{L}$ is an increasing, associative and commutative $\mathcal{L}^2 \to \mathcal{L}$ mapping that satisfies the boundary condition $\mathcal{T}(1,x) = x$ for any $x \in \mathcal{L}$.*

Definition 2.22 (from [Klement *et al.* (2002)]). *A **triangular conorm** $\mathcal{S}$ (short: **t-conorm**) on a bounded lattice $\mathcal{L}$ is an increasing, associative and commutative $\mathcal{L}^2 \to \mathcal{L}$ mapping that satisfies the boundary condition $\mathcal{S}(0,x) = x$ for any $x \in \mathcal{L}$.*

Hence t-norms and t-conorms only differ in their boundary conditions. Due to the associativity and commutativity we can extend them to an arbitrary number of arguments, i.e. $\mathcal{T}(x_1,\ldots,x_n) = \mathcal{T}(x_1,\mathcal{T}(x_2,\mathcal{T}(\ldots,x_n)))$ and likewise $\mathcal{S}(x_1,\ldots,x_n) = \mathcal{S}(x_1,\mathcal{S}(x_2,\mathcal{S}(\ldots,x_n)))$. From the above definitions we also obtain two other boundary conditions: $\mathcal{T}(0,x) = 0$ and $\mathcal{S}(1,x) = 1$ for any $x \in \mathcal{L}$.

Example 2.14 (from [De Cooman and Kerre (1994)]). *The following two t-norms and t-conorms are well-known.*

(1) Consider a bounded lattice $\mathcal{L} = (L, \leqslant)$. One can immediately see that $\sqcap$ is a triangular norm on $\mathcal{L}$, which we will denote as $\mathcal{T}_M$. Likewise $\sqcup$ is a triangular t-conorm on $\mathcal{L}$ which we will denote as $\mathcal{S}_M$.

*(2) Consider a bounded lattice $\mathcal{L} = (L, \leqslant)$. The **drastic t-norm** $\mathcal{T}_Z$ is a $\mathcal{L}^2 \to \mathcal{L}$ mapping defined by*

$$\mathcal{T}_Z(x,y) = \begin{cases} x & \text{if } y = 1 \\ y & \text{if } x = 1 \\ 0 & \text{otherwise} \end{cases}$$

t-norm	t-conorm
$\mathscr{T}_M(x,y) = \min(x,y)$	$\mathscr{S}_M(x,y) = \max(x,y)$
$\mathscr{T}_W(x,y) = \max(0,x+y-1)$	$\mathscr{S}_W(x,y) = \min(1,x+y)$
$\mathscr{T}_P(x,y) = x \cdot y$	$\mathscr{S}_P(x,y) = x+y-x \cdot y$

Table 2.1: T-norms and t-conorms on $([0,1],\leqslant)$

*Likewise we can define the **drastic t-conorm** $\mathscr{S}_Z$ as the following $\mathscr{L}^2 \to \mathscr{L}$*

$$\mathscr{S}_Z(x,y) = \begin{cases} x & \text{if } y = 0 \\ y & \text{if } x = 0 \\ 1 & \text{otherwise} \end{cases}$$

The above example shows that for any bounded lattice $\mathscr{L}$ we can construct at least two t-norms and t-conorms. It is interesting to note that any other t-norm (t-conorm) that can be constructed on $\mathscr{L}$ must necessarily be in between the drastic and minimum (maximum) t-norms (t-conorms).

Proposition 2.7 (from [De Cooman and Kerre (1994)]). *For any t-norm $\mathscr{T}$ and t-conorm $\mathscr{S}$ on a bounded lattice $\mathscr{L} = (L, \leqslant)$ we have that for any $x,y \in \mathscr{L}$.*

$$\mathscr{T}_Z(x,y) \leqslant \mathscr{T}(x,y) \leqslant \mathscr{T}_M(x,y)$$

$$\mathscr{S}_M(x,y) \leqslant \mathscr{S}(x,y) \leqslant \mathscr{S}_Z(x,y)$$

It is well-known that in classical logic $\wedge$ and $\vee$ satisfy the De Morgan properties, hence they are often called *dual*. The following definition generalizes this property to arbitrary negators and binary functions on a bounded lattice.

Definition 2.23. Let $\mathscr{N}$ be a negator on a bounded lattice $\mathscr{L}$. The **dual image** of a $\mathscr{L}^2 \to \mathscr{L}$ mapping f w.r.t. $\mathscr{N}$ is the $\mathscr{L}^2 \to \mathscr{L}$ mapping $f^{\leftrightarrow \mathscr{N}}$ defined as

$$f^{\leftrightarrow \mathscr{N}}(x,y) = \mathscr{N}(f(\mathscr{N}(x),\mathscr{N}(y)))$$

It turns out that if $\mathscr{N}$ is involutive the dual of a t-norm (resp. t-conorm) is a t-conorm (resp. t-norm) and vice versa [De Cooman and Kerre (1994)].

Example 2.15. In Table 2.1 we have defined the well known t-norms $\mathscr{T}_M$, $\mathscr{T}_W$ and $\mathscr{T}_P$ on the complete lattice $([0,1],\leqslant)$. They are respectively called the **minimum t-norm**, **Łukasiewicz t-norm** and **product t-norm**. The t-conorms $\mathscr{S}_M$, $\mathscr{S}_W$ and $\mathscr{S}_P$ defined in this same table are respectively called the **maximum t-conorm, Łukasiewicz t-conorm** (also known as the **bounded sum**) and **product t-conorm** (also known as the **probabilistic sum**).

Each t-norm is dual with the t-conorm on the same line, w.r.t. the standard negator $\mathcal{N}_W$. Specifically we have that $\mathcal{T}_M^{\overset{\leftrightarrow}{\mathcal{N}_W}} = \mathcal{S}_M$, $\mathcal{T}_W^{\overset{\leftrightarrow}{\mathcal{N}_W}} = \mathcal{S}_W$ and $\mathcal{T}_P^{\overset{\leftrightarrow}{\mathcal{N}_W}} = \mathcal{S}_P$ and $\mathcal{S}_M^{\overset{\leftrightarrow}{\mathcal{N}_W}} = \mathcal{T}_M$, $\mathcal{S}_W^{\overset{\leftrightarrow}{\mathcal{N}_W}} = \mathcal{T}_W$ and $\mathcal{S}_P^{\overset{\leftrightarrow}{\mathcal{N}_W}} = \mathcal{T}_P$.

Note that different t-norms have different properties. For example, consider the t-norms introduced in Example 2.15 on the preceding page. The minimum t-norm $\mathcal{T}_M$ is the only t-norm that satisfies idempotency (i.e. $\mathcal{T}_M(x,x) = x$ for every x [Klement *et al.* (2002)]), whereas the Łukasiewicz t-norm $\mathcal{T}_W$ is the only t-norm in Table 2.1 that satisfies the law of contradiction[1] w.r.t. the standard negator $\mathcal{N}_W$. Which t-norm to use is thus greatly dependent on the application and especially on the properties of classical conjunction that are important in the problem at hand. A thorough discussion of the logical properties that remain valid for the three t-norms $\mathcal{T}_M$, $\mathcal{T}_W$ and $\mathcal{T}_P$ can be found in [Kerre (1993)].

Implicators

Definition 2.24. An **implicator** $\mathcal{I}$ on a bounded lattice $\mathcal{L}$ is a $\mathcal{L}^2 \to \mathcal{L}$ mapping that is increasing in its first partial mapping and decreasing in its second partial mapping and furthermore satisfies the boundary conditions $\mathcal{I}(0,0) = 0$ and $\mathcal{I}(1,x) = x$ for each $x \in \mathcal{L}$.

It turns out that any implicator $\mathcal{I}$ on a bounded lattice $\mathcal{L}$ also satisfies the boundary conditions $\mathcal{I}(0,x) = 0$ and $\mathcal{I}(x,1) = 1$, for any $x \in \mathcal{L}$ [De Cock (2002)].

Now the question arises how implicators can be constructed. Since we already constructed t-conorms and negators, a natural idea is to start from a generalization of the classical logic tautology $p \Rightarrow q \equiv \neg p \vee q$.

Definition 2.25. Let $\mathcal{L}$ be a bounded lattice, let $\mathcal{S}$ be a t-conorm on $\mathcal{L}$ and let $\mathcal{N}$ be a negator on $\mathcal{L}$. The $\mathcal{L}^2 \to \mathcal{L}$ mapping $\mathcal{I}_{\mathcal{S},\mathcal{N}}$ defined as $\mathcal{I}_{\mathcal{S},\mathcal{N}}(x,y) = \mathcal{S}(\mathcal{N}(x),y)$ is called the **S-implicator** induced by $\mathcal{S}$ and $\mathcal{N}$.

Using an involutive negator and the dual of the t-conorm we can also define S-implicators w.r.t. a t-norm and a negator.

Definition 2.26. Let $\mathcal{L}$ be a bounded lattice, let $\mathcal{T}$ be a t-norm on $\mathcal{L}$ and let $\mathcal{N}$ be an involutive negator on $\mathcal{L}$. The $\mathcal{L}^2 \to \mathcal{L}$ mapping $\mathcal{I}_{\mathcal{T},\mathcal{N}}$ defined as $\mathcal{I}_{\mathcal{T},\mathcal{N}}(x,y) =$

---

[1] In classical logic the law of contradiction states that $p \wedge \neg p = False$.

S-implicator	Residual implicator
$\mathscr{I}_{\mathscr{T}_M,\mathscr{N}_W}(x,y) = \max(1-x,y)$	$\mathscr{I}_M(x,y) = \begin{cases} 1 & \text{if } x \leqslant y \\ y & \text{otherwise} \end{cases}$
$\mathscr{I}_{\mathscr{T}_W,\mathscr{N}_W}(x,y) = \min(1-x+y,1)$	$\mathscr{I}_W(x,y) = \min(1-x+y,1)$
$\mathscr{I}_{\mathscr{T}_P,\mathscr{N}_W}(x,y) = 1-x+x\cdot y$	$\mathscr{I}_P(x,y) = \begin{cases} 1 & \text{if } x \leqslant y \\ \frac{y}{x} & \text{otherwise} \end{cases}$

Table 2.2: Implicators on $([0,1],\leqslant)$

$\mathscr{N}(\mathscr{T}(x,\mathscr{N}(y)))$ is called the **S-implicator** induced by $\mathscr{T}$ and $\mathscr{N}$.

Example 2.16. In the first column of Table 2.2 one can find the S-implicators on $[0,1]$ that are induced by the t-norms from Table 2.1 and the involutive negator $\mathscr{N}_W$. The implicator $\mathscr{I}_{\mathscr{T}_M,\mathscr{N}_W}$ is called the **Kleene-Dienes implicator**, $\mathscr{I}_{\mathscr{T}_W,\mathscr{N}_W}$ the **Łukasiewicz implicator** and $\mathscr{I}_{\mathscr{T}_P,\mathscr{N}_W}$ the **Reichenbach implicator**.

While S-implicators are useful, they do not preserve some important properties of classical implication such as modus ponens (i.e. $p \wedge (p \Rightarrow q) \Rightarrow q$), transitivity (i.e. $(p \Rightarrow q) \wedge (q \Rightarrow r) \Rightarrow (p \Rightarrow r)$ and shunting (i.e. $p \Rightarrow (q \Rightarrow r) \equiv p \wedge q \Rightarrow r$). For example, generalizing the modus ponens formula $p \wedge (p \Rightarrow q) \Rightarrow q$ can be done by stating that for any $x,y \in [0,1]$ we must have that $\mathscr{T}(x,\mathscr{I}(x,y)) \leqslant y$. However, one can easily see that some S-implicators violate this requirement:

$$\mathscr{T}_M(0.5,\mathscr{I}_{\mathscr{T}_M,\mathscr{N}_W}(0.5,0.3)) = 0.5 > 0.3$$

It turns out that for certain t-norms one can construct implicators that do satisfy these properties.

Definition 2.27. Let $\mathscr{L}$ be a complete lattice and let $\mathscr{T}$ be a t-norm on $\mathscr{L}$. The **residual implicator** (short: **R-implicator**) of $\mathscr{T}$ is the $\mathscr{L}^2 \to \mathscr{L}$ mapping

$$\mathscr{I}_{\mathscr{T}}(x,y) = \sup\{\lambda \mid \lambda \in \mathscr{L} \wedge \mathscr{T}(x,\lambda) \leqslant y\}$$

The following proposition shows that R-implicators are indeed implicators as defined by Definition 2.24.

Proposition 2.8 (from [De Cock (2002)]). *Let $\mathscr{L}$ be a complete lattice and let $\mathscr{T}$ be a t-norm on $\mathscr{L}$. Then the residual implicator of $\mathscr{T}$ is an implicator on $\mathscr{L}$.*

For a specific class of t-norms we also obtain the following important property.

Proposition 2.9 (from [De Cock (2002)]). *Let $\mathscr{L}$ be a complete lattice and let $\mathscr{T}$ be a t-norm on $\mathscr{L}$. If for each $\lambda \in \mathscr{L}$ and family $(x_i)_{i \in I}$ we have that $\mathscr{T}(\sup_{i \in I} x_i, \lambda) = \sup_{i \in I} \mathscr{T}(x_i, \lambda)$, i.e. all partial mappings of $\mathscr{T}$ are supmorphisms, it holds that*

$$\mathscr{T}(x,y) \leqslant z \text{ iff } x \leqslant \mathscr{I}(y,z)$$

*for all $x,y,z \in \mathscr{L}$. This property is called the **residuation principle**.*

The residuation principle is also commonly referred to as the **Galois connection** or **adjoint property**. In [De Baets (1995)] it is shown that for a t-norm $\mathscr{T}$ that satisfies the condition in Proposition 2.9, we have that $\mathscr{T}(x, \mathscr{I}_{\mathscr{T}}(y,z)) \leqslant y$ for each $x,y,z \in \mathscr{L}$, i.e. the generalization of the modus ponens, introduced above, holds. For this reason we will limit our attention to t-norms satisfying this condition in the remainder of this book.

Example 2.17. In the second column of Table 2.2 we listed some common residual implicators on $([0,1], \leqslant)$. The implicator $\mathscr{I}_M$ is called the **Gödel implicator**, $\mathscr{I}_W$ the **Łukasiewicz implicator**, $\mathscr{I}_P$ the **Goguen implicator**. Note that the Łukasiewicz implicator is both a residual implicator and an S-implicator.

An important property of residual implicators is the following.

Proposition 2.10 (from [De Baets (1995)]). *Let $\mathscr{I}$ be a residual implicator on $\mathscr{L}$. For any $x,y \in \mathscr{L}$ it holds that $\mathscr{I}(x,y) = 1$ iff $x \leqslant y$.*

In classical logic it is well-known that $a \wedge (a \Rightarrow b) \equiv a \wedge b$. For t-norms and implicators this does not hold in general, but for specific t-norms on $([0,1], \leqslant)$ a similar property can be shown to hold.

Proposition 2.11 (from [Klement *et al.* (2002)]). *Let $\mathscr{T}$ be a continuous t-norm on $([0,1], \leqslant)$. Then for any $x,y \in [0,1]$ it holds that $\mathscr{T}(x, \mathscr{I}_{\mathscr{T}}(x,y)) = \min(x,y)$. This property is called **divisibility**.*

Usually the equivalence $a \equiv b$ in classical logic is defined as $((a \Rightarrow b) \wedge (b \Rightarrow a))$. A similar concept can be defined in fuzzy logic using a residual implicator and t-norm.

Definition 2.28. Consider a residual implicator $\mathscr{I}$ and t-norm $\mathscr{T}$ on $\mathscr{L}$. The **biresiduum** of $\mathscr{I}$ and $\mathscr{T}$ is the $\mathscr{L}^2 \to \mathscr{L}$ mapping $\approx$ defined for all $x,y \in \mathscr{L}$ as:

$$x \approx y = \mathscr{T}(\mathscr{I}(x,y), \mathscr{I}(y,x))$$

Finally, one can show that for any implicator $\mathscr{I}$ on a bounded lattice $\mathscr{L}$, the partial mapping $\mathscr{I}(.,0)$ is a negator on $\mathscr{L}$.

Definition 2.29. Let $\mathscr{L}$ be a bounded lattice and let $\mathscr{I}$ be an implicator on $\mathscr{L}$. The **induced negator** of $\mathscr{I}$ is then the $\mathscr{L} \to \mathscr{L}$ mapping $\mathscr{N}_\mathscr{I}$ defined as $\mathscr{I}(x) = \mathscr{I}(x,0)$, for each $x \in \mathscr{L}$.

Example 2.18. The Gödel negator $\mathscr{N}_M$ is the induced negator of the Gödel implicator; the Łukasiewicz negator $\mathscr{N}_W$ is the induced negator of the Łukasiewicz implicator.

2.3.3   Formal Fuzzy Logics

In [Hájek (1998)] it is shown that for the minimum t-norm, Łukasiewicz t-norm and product t-norm a propositional calculus capable of describing their properties can be constructed. The author of [Hájek (1998)] furthermore identifies a propositional calculus that captures the properties shared by all continuous t-norms on $([0,1], \leqslant)$. We briefly discuss this in this section.

Definition 2.30 (from [Hájek (1998)]). *The **propositional calculus** PC$(\mathscr{T})$ given by the continuous t-norm $\mathscr{T}$ on $([0,1], \leqslant)$ has propositional variables $p_1, \ldots, p_n$, the connectives $\wedge$ and $\to$ and the truth constant $\overline{0}$ for 0. **Formulas** are defined as usual: each propositional variable is a formula; $\overline{0}$ is a formula; if φ, ψ, are formulas, then $\varphi \wedge \psi$ and $\varphi \to \psi$ are formulas. Further connectives are defined as follows:*

(1) $\varphi \triangle \psi = \varphi \wedge (\varphi \to \psi)$

(2) $\varphi \triangledown \psi = ((\varphi \to \psi) \to \psi) \wedge ((\psi \to \varphi) \to \varphi)$

(3) $\neg \varphi = \varphi \to \overline{0}$

(4) $\varphi \leftrightarrow \psi = (\varphi \to \psi) \wedge (\psi \to \varphi)$

*An **evaluation** of propositional variables is a mapping e assigning to each propositional variable p a truth value $e(p) \in [0,1]$. This evaluation is extended to formulas as follows:*

(1) $e(\overline{0}) = 0$

(2) $e(\varphi \to \psi) = \mathscr{I}_\mathscr{T}(e(\varphi), e(\psi))$

(3) $e(\varphi \wedge \psi) = \mathscr{T}(e(\varphi), e(\psi))$

*A formula φ is a 1-**tautology** of PC$(\mathscr{T})$ iff $e(\varphi) = 1$ for each evaluation e. A set of formulas is called a **theory**. Given a theory Θ we say that an evaluation e is a **model** of Θ, denoted $e \models \Theta$, if and only if $e(\theta) = 1$ for each $\theta \in \Theta$.*

One can see that 1-tautologies are formulas that are absolutely true under any evaluation. Furthermore note that from Proposition 2.11 we know that the definition of $\triangle$ corresponds to the minimum, which is one of the reasons why the calculus is restricted to continuous t-norms. Now a logic can be constructed that captures the properties that are common to all continuous t-norms on $([0,1], \leqslant)$.

Definition 2.31 (from [Hájek (1998)]). *The following formulas are axioms of the **basic logic** **BL**:*

(A1) $(\varphi \to \psi) \to ((\psi \to \chi) \to (\varphi \to \chi))$

(A2) $(\varphi \wedge \psi) \to \varphi$

(A3) $(\varphi \wedge \psi) \to (\psi \wedge \varphi)$

(A4) $(\varphi \wedge (\varphi \to \psi)) \to (\psi \wedge (\psi \to \varphi))$

(A5) $(\varphi \to (\psi \to \chi)) \to ((\varphi \wedge \psi) \to \chi)$

(A6) $((\varphi \wedge \psi) \to \chi) \to (\varphi \to (\psi \to \chi))$

(A7) $((\varphi \to \psi) \to \chi) \to (((\psi \to \varphi) \to \chi) \to \chi)$

(A8) $\bar{0} \to \varphi$

*The deduction rule of **BL** is modus ponens. Proof and a provable formula in **BL** are defined similar to proof, respectively provable formula in classical logic.*

The above axioms all have intuitive meanings and correspond to properties in classical logic. Axiom 1 is transitivity of implication. Axiom 2 is sometimes called *weakening* of conjunction in classical logic. Axioms 3 and 4 express the commutativity of $\wedge$, respectively $\triangle$. Axioms 5 and 6 are commonly called the *shunting* rules in classical logic. Axiom 7 is a variant of proof by cases: if χ follows from $\varphi \to \psi$ then if χ also follows from $\psi \to \varphi$ we have χ is true. Finally Axiom 8 states that anything can be proven from a false proposition. The axioms of **BL** are all 1-tautologies in each $\mathbf{PC}(\mathcal{T})$, where $\mathcal{T}$ is a continuous t-norm on $([0,1], \leqslant)$. Hence these properties are true for all continuous t-norms on $([0,1], \leqslant)$. It can be shown that **BL** is *sound*, i.e. that each provable formula in **BL** is a 1-tautology in each $\mathbf{PC}(\mathcal{T})$. Two types of completeness are distinguished: *standard completeness* and *general completeness*. The former states that every 1-tautology in each $\mathbf{PC}(\mathcal{T})$ can be proven in **BL** and has been shown to hold in [Cignoli *et al.* (2000)]. The latter defines completeness with respect to a more general semantics for **BL**, called BL-algebras. The general completeness theorem states that a formula φ is provable in **BL** if it is a general BL-tautology, i.e. a tautology for each BL-algebra [Hájek (1998)]. We can thus conclude

t-norm	logic name	extra axiom(s)
$\mathscr{T}_M$	Gödel logic	$\varphi \to (\varphi \wedge \varphi)$
$\mathscr{T}_W$	Łukasiewicz logic	$\neg\neg\varphi \to \varphi$
$\mathscr{T}_P$	product logic	$\neg\neg\chi \to ((\varphi \wedge \chi \to \psi \wedge \chi) \to (\varphi \to \psi))$
		$\varphi \triangle \neg\varphi \to \overline{0}$

Table 2.3: Propositional logics for the common continuous t-norms on $([0,1], \leqslant)$ (from [Hájek (1998)])

that the logic **BL** captures all properties that are common to the continuous t-norms on $([0,1], \leqslant)$.

If we now consider specific t-norms, it is also possible to construct a logic that exactly captures the 1-tautologies for this specific t-norm. Note that these logics can be characterized by extending **BL** with certain axioms. In Table 2.3 we illustrate the logics one obtains by considering the minimum, Łukasiewicz and product t-norm, as well as the axiom(s) that need to be added to **BL** to create this logic.

An interesting extension of Łukasiewicz logic is **Rational Pavelka Logic** (short: **RPL**). The language of RPL is constructed by extending the language of $\textbf{PC}(\mathscr{T}_W)$ with truth constants $\overline{r}$ for each *rational number* $r \in [0,1] \cap \mathbb{Q}$. The formulas in this logic are defined as for $\textbf{PC}(\mathscr{T}_W)$, where we also consider the truth constants as formulas. Evaluations e are extended such that for any rational $r \in [0,1] \cap \mathbb{Q}$ we have that $e(\overline{r}) = r$. The axioms of RPL are the axioms of Łukasiewicz logic plus two bookkeeping axioms for the truth constants: $(\overline{r} \to \overline{s}) \leftrightarrow \overline{\mathscr{T}_W(r,s)}$ and $\neg\overline{r} \leftrightarrow \overline{1-r}$ for all r and s in $[0,1] \cap \mathbb{Q}$. Hence the set of axioms is countable, but not finite. The deduction rule, theories, proofs, provability and models are defined as for Łukasiewicz logic.

Finally, reasoning in the above logics can be done using existing methods. For Gödel logic we can use boolean SAT solvers, for Łukasiewicz and rational Pavelka logic we can use mixed integer programming (MIP) [Hähnle (1994)] or constraint satisfaction [Schockaert *et al.* (2009)] and for product logic we can use bounded mixed integer quadratically constrained programming (bMICQP), as is used for fuzzy description logics [Bobillo and Straccia (2007)]. Similar to the boolean case, checking whether a set of formulas Θ is **satisfiable**, i.e. whether some model exists for Θ, is NP-complete [Hájek (1998)].

Chapter 3

Fuzzy Answer Set Programming

3.1 Introduction

In the previous chapter we introduced ASP, a language that allows to model combinatorial problems in a declarative manner. Unfortunately, ASP is limited to expressing problems in boolean logic. Many interesting applications require different logics, however. For example, suppose we want to write an ASP program that finds the disease from which a patient is suffering, given a set of his symptoms as the input. Obviously the output of this program will be uncertain, as certain symptoms may occur in 80% of the patients, while others may only occur in about 30%. Hence, the answer sets and the computation of the answer sets should reflect this in some way. This can be done by extending the ASP semantics with a theory of uncertainty, such as possibility or probability theory.

Another interesting application domain for which ASP has no direct support is modeling continuous optimization problems. For example, suppose we wish to optimally place ATMs somewhere along the roads connecting different cities, such that each city has an ATM nearby. Modeling this problem using ASP requires the semantics to cope with defining the "nearness" degree of an ATM and a town. This can be done by extending the ASP semantics with fuzzy logic.

In recent years, researchers have extended ASP and, more general, logic programming to handle the aforementioned problem domains. Most notable are the probabilistic [Damásio and Pereira (2000); Fuhr (2000); Lukasiewicz (1998, 1999); Ng and Subrahmanian (1993, 1994); Straccia (2008)] and possibilistic [Alsinet et al. (2002); Bauters et al. (2010); Nicolas et al. (2005, 2006)] extensions to handle uncertainty; the fuzzy extensions [Cao (2000); Ishizuka and Kanai (1985); Lukasiewicz (2006); Lukasiewicz and Straccia (2007a,b); Madrid and Ojeda-Aciego (2008, 2009); Saad (2009a); Straccia (2008); Van Nieuwenborgh et al. (2007b); Vojtás (2001); Wagner (1998)] which allow to encode the intensity to which the predicates are satisfied, and, more generally, many-valued extensions [Damásio *et al.* (2004); Damásio *et al.* (2007); Damásio and Pereira (2001a,b, 2004); Emden (1986); Fitting (1991); Kifer and Li (1988); Kifer and Subrahmanian (1992); Lakshmanan (1994); Lakshmanan and Sadri (1994a, 1997); Lakshmanan and Shiri (2001); Lakshmanan (1997); Loyer and Straccia (2002, 2003); Nerode *et al.* (1997); Shapiro (1983); Straccia (2005, 2006a); Straccia *et al.* (2009); Subrahmanian (1994)].

In this book we focus on **fuzzy answer set programming (FASP)**. This ASP extension bases its semantics on fuzzy logic (in the narrow sense). It is capable of encoding continuous optimization problems in a concise manner, similar to how ASP is able to encode discrete optimization problems. Currently, there exist a multitude of different fuzzy answer set programming languages which extend the basic idea with various enhancements. In Chapter 4 we provide a detailed comparison of these frameworks. In this chapter we distill from previous proposals the FASP language that will be used for presenting our contributions in the succeeding chapters. We begin by introducing the necessary definitions in Section 3.2. The syntax is introduced in Section 3.2.1, followed by the semantics in Section 3.2.2. Afterwards, in Section 3.3, we illustrate the main ideas of the language with a fuzzy variant of the graph coloring problem. Interestingly the example has the same structure as the ASP program for graph coloring introduced in Example 2.7 on page 19. This shows that FASP preserves the declarative advantage of ASP, while adding the power to model continuous problems.

3.2 Definitions

In this section we define the syntax and semantics of fuzzy answer set programming.

3.2.1 *Language*

Fuzzy answer set programming (FASP) is built from a language containing terms, atoms, truth values and function symbols as basic building blocks. A **term** is either a **constant** or a **variable**. Similar as for ASP we adopt the convention that constants (variables) are denoted by a symbol starting with a lower-case (upper-case) character. An **atom** is an expression of the form $p(t_1, \ldots, t_n)$, where p is a **predicate** symbol of arity n and t_i, for $1 \leqslant i \leqslant n$, are terms. A term or an atom is called **grounded** if it does not contain any variables.

Definition 3.1. A FASP **rule** on a complete lattice $\mathscr{L}$ is an expression of the form

$$r:a \leftarrow f(b_1,\ldots,b_n;c_1,\ldots,c_m) \tag{3.1}$$

where r is the **label** of the rule, a is either an atom or a value from $\mathscr{L}$, b_i, for $1 \leqslant i \leqslant n$, and c_j, for $1 \leqslant j \leqslant m$, are either atoms or values from $\mathscr{L}$, and f is a (total) $\mathscr{L}^{n+m} \rightarrow \mathscr{L}$ mapping that is increasing in its n first and decreasing in its m last arguments. Furthermore we require that f is computable in finite time. When there is no cause for confusion, we will use the label of the rule to denote the rule itself. For a rule as (3.1), the left-hand side a is called the **head** of the rule, denoted r_h, the right-hand side $f(b_1,\ldots,b_n;c_1,\ldots,c_m)$ is called the **body** of the rule, denoted r_b.

In the remainder of this book we implicitly assume all lattices to be complete. For convenience we will often shorten the notation of a general rule such as (3.1) using $r : a \leftarrow \alpha$. The **Herbrand base** of a rule r, denoted $\mathscr{B}_r$, is defined as the set of atoms occurring in r. Similar to ASP, FASP rules can be divided in certain classes, depending on the conditions satisfied by their head and body.

(1) A rule $r:a \leftarrow f(b_1,\ldots,b_n;c_1,\ldots,c_m)$ on a lattice $\mathscr{L}$ is called a **constraint** if $a \in \mathscr{L}$.
(2) A rule $r:a \leftarrow f(b_1,\ldots,b_n;c_1,\ldots,c_m)$ on a lattice $\mathscr{L}$ is called a **fact** if all b_i, for $1 \leqslant i \leqslant n$, and c_j, for $1 \leqslant j \leqslant m$, are elements from $\mathscr{L}$.
(3) A rule $r:a \leftarrow f(b_1,\ldots,b_n;c_1,\ldots,c_m)$ on a lattice $\mathscr{L}$ is called **positive** if $m = 0$ or $c_j \in \mathscr{L}$ for $1 \leqslant j \leqslant m$.
(4) A rule $r:a \leftarrow f(b_1,\ldots,b_n;c_1,\ldots,c_m)$ on a lattice $\mathscr{L}$ is called **simple** if it is positive and not a constraint.

For convenience we will write any FASP rule $r:a \leftarrow f(b_1,\ldots,b_n;c_1,\ldots,c_m)$ with f the identity function, $n = 1$ and $m = 0$ as $r:a \leftarrow b_1$.

Definition 3.2. A **fuzzy answer set program (FASP program)** on a complete lattice $\mathscr{L}$ is a finite set of FASP rules on $\mathscr{L}$.

Given a FASP program P, the **Herbrand base** $\mathscr{B}_P$ is defined as $\mathscr{B}_P = \bigcup\{\mathscr{B}_r \mid r \in P\}$. The grounding $gnd(P)$ of a FASP program P is defined as in Section 2.2.1.2. Unless stated otherwise, we assume all programs to be grounded. Furthermore, for an atom $a \in \mathscr{B}_P$ we denote with P_a the set of rules in P with atom a in the head. The lattice on which P is defined is denoted as $\mathscr{L}_P$. We also adopt the convention that the lattice used in examples is $([0,1], \leqslant)$, unless stated otherwise.

Similar to ASP, FASP programs can be divided in certain classes, depending on the rules they contain.

(1) A FASP program is called **constraint-free** if it does not contain constraints.

(2) A FASP program is called **positive** if all rules occurring in it are positive rules.

(3) A FASP program is called **simple** if all rules occurring in it are simple rules.

Note that all simple programs are positive.

Example 3.1. Consider the following FASP program $P_{ex3.1}$:

$$f: white(b) \leftarrow 0.4$$
$$r: black(a) \leftarrow \mathscr{N}_W(white(b))$$
$$c: \qquad 0 \leftarrow \mathscr{T}_W(white(b), white(a))$$

Rule f is a *fact*, r is a regular rule and c is a constraint.

3.2.2 Semantics

An **interpretation** of a FASP program P is a $\mathscr{B}_P$ to $\mathscr{L}_P$ mapping. For ease of presentation we write $I = \{a_1^{l_1}, \ldots, a_n^{l_n}\}$ for the interpretation I defined by $I(a_i) = l_i$ if $1 \leqslant i \leqslant n$ and $I(a) = 0$ otherwise. We extend interpretations to lattice values and expressions of the form $f(b_1, \ldots, b_n; c_1, \ldots, c_m)$ as follows. Suppose I is an interpretation of a FASP program P then

(1) $I(l) = l$ if $l \in \mathscr{L}$

(2) $I(f(b_1, \ldots, b_n; c_1, \ldots, c_m)) = f(I(b_1), \ldots, I(b_n); I(c_1), \ldots, I(c_m))$

For a rule $(r: a \leftarrow \alpha) \in P$ we say that it is **satisfied** by an interpretation I of P iff $I(a) \geqslant I(\alpha)$. Intuitively we can regard rules as residual implicators. Due to Proposition 2.10 r is then satisfied by I iff $\mathscr{I}(I(\alpha), I(a)) \geqslant 1$, where $\mathscr{I}$ is the residual implicator corresponding to r.

Definition 3.3. Let P be a FASP program. An interpretation I of P is a **model** of P iff every rule $r \in P$ is satisfied by I.

To define *minimal models* we need an ordering on interpretations. Given two interpretations I and J of a FASP program P we define $I \subseteq J$ iff $\forall a \in \mathscr{B}_P \cdot I(a) \leqslant J(a)$ and $I \subset J$ iff $(\forall a \in \mathscr{B}_P \cdot I(a) \leqslant J(a)) \wedge (I \neq J)$. Now an interpretation I of a FASP program P is called a **minimal model** of P iff I is a model of P and no model J of P exists such that $J \subset I$.

Similar to ASP, minimal models of simple FASP programs can be characterized as the least fixpoints of a monotonic operator that captures **forward chaining**.

Definition 3.4 (from [Damásio and Pereira (2001a)]). *Let P be a FASP program. The* ***immediate consequence operator*** Π_P *is the* $(\mathcal{B}_P \to \mathcal{L}_P) \to (\mathcal{B}_P \to \mathcal{L}_P)$ *mapping defined for an interpretation I of P and a* $\in \mathcal{B}_P$ *as*

$$\Pi_P(I)(a) = \sup\{I(r_b) \mid r \in P_a\}$$

Example 3.2. Consider the following FASP program $P_{ex3.2}$:

$$r_1 : a \leftarrow 0.8$$
$$r_2 : c \leftarrow 0.5$$
$$r_3 : b \leftarrow \mathcal{T}_M(a,c)$$
$$r_4 : b \leftarrow 0.2$$

Now consider the interpretation $\emptyset$ that attaches to each atom $a \in \mathcal{B}_{P_{ex3.2}}$ the value 0. If we apply Π_P to this interpretation we obtain:

(1) For a: $\Pi_P(\emptyset)(a) = 0.8$
(2) For b: $\Pi_P(\emptyset)(b) = \max(\mathcal{T}_M(\emptyset(a), \emptyset(c)), 0.2) = 0.2$
(3) For c: $\Pi_P(\emptyset)(c) = 0.5$

Proposition 3.1 (from [Damásio and Pereira (2001a)]). *Let P be a FASP program. If P is positive, the immediate consequence operator of P is monotonic, i.e. if* $I \subseteq I'$ *then* $\Pi_P(I) \subseteq \Pi_P(I')$.

Due to the Tarski theorem introduced in Proposition 2.1 on page 12, the least fixpoint of the immediate consequence operator for simple FASP programs exists and is unique. For a given FASP program P the least fixpoint of Π_P is denoted as $\Pi_P^\star$.

Proposition 3.2 (from [Damásio and Pereira (2001a)]). *Let P be a simple FASP program. The least fixpoint of* Π_P *exists and coincides with the unique minimal model of P.*

Due to Proposition 2.2 on page 13 this least fixpoint can be computed using an iterated fixpoint computation.

Definition 3.5. Let P be a positive FASP program. Formally, we define the sequence $\mathcal{S}\langle P \rangle = \langle J_i \mid i \text{ an ordinal}\rangle$ by

$$J_i = \begin{cases} \emptyset & \text{if } i = 0 \\ \Pi_P(J_{i-1}) & \text{if } i \text{ is a successor ordinal} \\ \bigcup_{j<i}(J_j) & \text{if } i \text{ is a limit ordinal} \end{cases} \tag{3.2}$$

where for all $a \in \mathcal{B}_P$ we have that $\bigcup_{i \in I}(J_i)(a) = \sup_{i \in I} J_i(a)$.

The first element J_i in the sequence $\mathcal{S}\langle P \rangle$ for which $\Pi_P(J_i) = J_i$ then coincides with the least fixpoint of Π_P.

Example 3.3. Consider program $P_{ex3.2}$ from Example 3.2. In Example 3.2 we computed that $\Pi_P(\emptyset) = \Pi_P(J_0) = J_1 = \{a^{0.8}, b^{0.2}, c^{0.5}\}$. For J_2 we obtain:

(1) For a: $J_2(a) = \Pi_P(J_1)(a) = 0.8$
(2) For b: $J_2(b) = \Pi_P(J_1)(b) = \max(\mathcal{T}_M(J_1(a), J_1(c)), 0.2) = \max(0.5, 0.2) = 0.5$
(3) For c: $J_2(c) = \Pi_P(J_1)(c) = 0.5$

Hence, $J_2 = \{a^{0.8}, b^{0.5}, c^{0.5}\}$. Since $J_1 \neq J_2$, J_1 is not the least fixpoint. Hence, we continue and compute J_3:

(1) For a: $J_3(a) = \Pi_P(J_2)(a) = 0.8$
(2) For b: $J_3(b) = \Pi_P(J_2)(b) = \max(\mathcal{T}_M(J_2(a), J_2(c)), 0.2) = \max(0.5, 0.2) = 0.5$
(3) For c: $J_3(c) = \Pi_P(J_2)(c) = 0.5$

Hence $J_3 = J_2$, which means that J_2 is the least fixpoint of Π_P.

Note that, unlike ASP, the computation of this fixpoint may never end. This is illustrated in the next example.

Example 3.4 (from [Straccia (2006a)]). *Consider the following FASP program Inf:*

$$r : a \leftarrow \delta(a)$$

Where $\delta(x) = x + (1-x)/2$. Obviously, δ is increasing and, moreover, $\forall x \in [0,1] \cdot 0 < \delta(x) \leqslant 1$. Consider $\mathcal{S}\langle P \rangle$. The first steps of the computation of the least fixpoint of Π_{Inf} are shown below:

$$J_0 = \{a^0\}$$
$$J_1 = \Pi_P(J_0) = \{a^{0.5}\}$$
$$J_2 = \Pi_P(J_1) = \{a^{0.75}\}$$
$$J_3 = \Pi_P(J_2) = \{a^{0.875}\}$$
$$J_4 = \Pi_P(J_3) = \{a^{0.9375}\}$$
$$J_5 = \Pi_P(J_4) = \{a^{0.96875}\}$$
$$J_6 = \Pi_P(J_5) = \{a^{0.984375}\}$$
$$\ldots = \ldots$$

Clearly, $\forall i \in \mathbb{N} \cdot J_i \subset \{a^1\}$, but $J_\omega = \bigcup_{i \in \mathbb{N}} J_i = \{a^1\}$, which is the least fixpoint $\Pi_p^\star$.

In [Damásio *et al.* (2007)] termination conditions for this operator are studied.

Using the above, we can introduce the semantics of FASP programs. Similar to ASP, the semantics of a FASP program P are given by a certain subset of the models of P. Important to note is that we will view the truth values that are attached to atoms by these models as *lower bounds*. Rules in FASP then implement the intuition of (non-deterministic) forward chaining. In practice, we are therefore interested in those models that are in accordance with this intuition. Effectively, there are two types of models we wish to exclude from our solution.

The first problem is the occurrence of atoms with a value above the one warranted by the rules. Consider the rule $r: a \leftarrow \alpha$. This rule will be satisfied by an interpretation I whenever $I(a) \geqslant I(\alpha)$. Examples are the two models M and M', satisfying $M(a) = 1$, $M(\alpha) = 0.5 = M'(\alpha)$ and $M'(a) = 0.5$. However, the first model attaches a higher value to a than what the rule actually supports (viz. 0.5) and is therefore unwanted. In other words, we do not want to conclude anything more than what is needed to satisfy the rule.

The second problem arises when atoms are "self-motivating", i.e. their truth value is supported by some rule, but that support is ultimately based on the value of the atom itself. An illustration of this can be seen in the following two-rule program P:

$$r_1 : a \leftarrow b$$
$$r_2 : b \leftarrow a$$

Both the models $M = \{a^1, b^1\}$ and $M' = \{a^0, b^0\}$ are free from the first problem we mentioned, but the support given to the value of b is derived from the support for the value of a, which is itself derived from the value of b. Hence, only model M' is free from knowledge not supported by the program.

The models that do not suffer from these defects will be called **answer sets**, and correspond to particular minimal models, as we will show later on. As the definition of answer sets for non-positive programs is an extension of the one for positive programs, we introduce them separately.

3.2.2.1 *Positive Programs*

Definition 3.6. Let P be a positive FASP program. An interpretation A is called the **answer set** of P iff A is the minimal model of P.

Intuitively the answer set of a positive FASP program corresponds to the maximal information we can derive by successively applying the immediate consequence operator, until no
new knowledge can be discovered anymore, i.e. until a fixpoint is found. Note that not all
positive programs have an answer set, as illustrated in the following example.

Example 3.5. Consider the following positive FASP program $P_{ex3.5}$:

$$r_1 : a \leftarrow 1$$
$$r_2 : 0 \leftarrow a$$

One can easily see that $I = \{a^1\}$ is the least fixpoint of $\Pi_{P_{ex3.5}}$. However, I is not an answer
set of P as $I(a) > 0$, meaning that it does not satisfy rule r_2. In fact, no models exist for
this program as no interpretation I' can satisfy both $I'(a) \geqslant 1$ and $0 \geqslant I'(a)$.

3.2.2.2   General Programs

In this section, we extend the definition of answer sets to cover arbitrary programs, similar
to [Lukasiewicz and Straccia (2007a)]. One might think that the semantics of non-positive
programs could again be given by minimal models, but it turns out that minimal models are
not at all suitable. For example, consider the following program:

$$r_1 : a \leftarrow a$$
$$r_2 : 0 \leftarrow \mathcal{N}_W(a)$$

The minimal model is $\{a^1\}$, but the motivation for a depends on a itself and thus $\{a^1\}$ is
not acceptable. The underlying reason is that constraints should not be used as support of
an atom, i.e. in (F)ASP, stating that a is true is not at all the same as stating that solutions
in which a is false are not allowed.

To solve this problem, we reduce the semantics of such a program P to that of a positive
program P^I, which is called the reduct w.r.t. a candidate answer set I, similar to [Damásio
and Pereira (2001a); Lukasiewicz and Straccia (2007a)]. Note that this generalizes the
well-known Gelfond-Lifschitz transformation from [Gelfond and Lifschitz (1988)].

Definition 3.7. Let P be a FASP program. The **reduct** of a rule $(r : a \leftarrow f(b_1,\ldots,b_n;$
$c_1,\ldots,c_m)) \in P$ w.r.t. an interpretation I of P is the positive rule r^I defined as

$$r^I = r : a \leftarrow f(b_1,\ldots,b_n; I(c_1),\ldots,I(c_m))$$

The reduct of P is the set of rules P^I defined as

$$P^I = \{r^I \mid r \in P\}$$

In other words, the reduct of a program w.r.t. an interpretation I is obtained by replacing all negatively occurring atoms by their value in I.

Example 3.6. Consider program $P_{ex3.1}$ from Example 3.1 on page 38. The reduct of $P_{ex3.1}$ w.r.t. an interpretation $I = \{white(b)^{0.4}, black(a)^1\}$ is the following program $P_{ex3.1}^I$:

$$f: white(b) \leftarrow 0.4$$
$$r: black(a) \leftarrow 0.6$$
$$c: \qquad 0 \leftarrow \mathscr{T}_W(white(b), white(a))$$

To see that the above reduction generalizes the traditional Gelfond-Lifschitz (GL) transformation, it suffices to note that in traditional logic programming the only way to have a negative occurrence of an atom a in a rule body is via a negation-as-failure literal not a. The GL transformation then essentially replaces such literals with their values in the intended stable model interpretation, yielding a positive program.

The semantics of a FASP program can now be defined in terms of the semantics of the positive reduct program.

Definition 3.8. Let P be a FASP program. An interpretation A of P is an **answer set** of P iff A is the answer set of P^A.

Note that, in the boolean case, the idea of negation-as-failure is that not a is true for an atom a if during the application of forward chaining we fail to establish the truth of a. Here, we generalize this taking as truth value for $f(b_1, \ldots, b_n; c_1, \ldots, c_m)$ the highest possible value, i.e. by assuming for a candidate answer set A the lower bounds in A for $\{c_1, \ldots, c_m\}$. Intuitively, A is then an answer set if under the above assumption, applying forward chaining again delivers A.

Note that in general, FASP programs can have multiple answer sets or no answer sets, as shown in the following examples.

Example 3.7. Consider the following program $P_{ex3.7}$:

$$r_1: a \leftarrow \mathscr{N}_W(b)$$
$$r_2: b \leftarrow \mathscr{N}_W(a)$$

It is easy to see that for any $l \in [0,1]$ we have that $\{a^l, b^{1-l}\}$ is an answer set of $P_{ex3.7}$. Hence, this program has an infinite number of answer sets (and therefore also models).

Example 3.8. Consider the following program $P_{ex3.8}$:

$$r: p \leftarrow \mathscr{N}_M(p)$$

Now consider an interpretation $I = \{p^l\}$ with $l \in]0,1]$. By definition of $\mathcal{N}_M$ we know that the reduct of $P_{ex3.8}$ is

$$r^I : p \leftarrow 0$$

Since the answer set of $P^I_{ex3.8}$ is $\emptyset$, we know that I is not an answer set of $P_{ex3.8}$. Similarly we obtain that $\emptyset$ is not an answer set, meaning that this program has no answer sets.

Similar to ASP, the answer sets of a FASP program form a subset of the minimal models.

Proposition 3.3. *Let P be a FASP program. If A is an answer set of P it is a minimal model of P.*

Proof.   Suppose A is an answer set of P, but not a minimal model of P. Then there must be some $M \subset A$ such that M is a model of P.

Since $M \subset A$ we can easily see by definition of the reduct that for each $(r : a \leftarrow \alpha) \in P$ we have $M(\alpha^A) \leqslant M(\alpha)$. Since M is a model of P we however know that $M(a) \geqslant M(\alpha)$. From the foregoing it then follows that $M(a) \geqslant M(\alpha^A)$. Hence M is a model of P^A. This contradicts the assumption that A is an answer set of P, from which the stated follows. $\square$

The reverse does not hold, as shown in the following example.

Example 3.9. Consider the following FASP program $P_{ex3.9}$:

$$r_1 : a \leftarrow a$$
$$r_2 : p \leftarrow \mathcal{T}_W(\mathcal{N}_W(p), \mathcal{N}_W(a))$$

Now consider the interpretation $I = \{a^{0.2}, p^{0.4}\}$. We will show that it is a minimal model of $P_{ex3.9}$. First, it is clear that rule r_1 is trivially satisfied by I. Second, consider rule r_2. To satisfy this rule we need to have that $I(p) \geqslant \mathcal{T}_W(\mathcal{N}_W(I(p)), \mathcal{N}_W(I(a)))$. By definition of $\mathcal{N}_W$ and $\mathcal{T}_W$ this means $I(p) \geqslant \max(1 - I(p) + 1 - I(a) - 1, 0)$, which does indeed hold. Hence, I is a model of $P_{ex3.9}$. Now suppose there is some model I' such that $I' \subset I$. Obviously r_1 is again trivially satisfied by I'. From the foregoing we know that for rule r_2 this interpretation then needs to satisfy the following inequation

$$I'(p) \geqslant \max(-I'(p) + 1 - I'(a), 0) \tag{3.3}$$

We consider three cases:

(1) Suppose $I'(p) = I(p)$ and $I'(a) < I(a)$. Then (3.3) becomes $0.4 \geqslant \max(-0.4 + (1 - I'(a)), 0)$. Since $I'(a) \in [0, 0.2[$ we know that $(1 - I'(a)) \in]0.8, 1]$ and thus $(-0.4 + (1 - I'(a))) \in]0.4, 0.6]$, meaning (3.3) is not satisfied.

(2) Suppose $I'(p) < I(p)$ and $I'(a) = I(a)$. Then (3.3) becomes $I'(p) \geqslant \max(-I'(p) + 0.8, 0)$. Since $I'(p) \in [0, 0.4[$ we know that $(-I'(p) + 0.8) \in]0.4, 0.8]$, meaning (3.3) is not satisfied.

(3) Suppose $I'(p) < I(p)$ and $I'(a) < I(a)$. Then (3.3) becomes $I'(p) \geqslant \max(-I'(p) + (1 - I'(a)), 0)$. Since $I'(a) \in [0, 0.2[$ we know that $(1 - I'(a)) \in]0.8, 1]$. From this and the fact that $I'(p) \in [0, 0.4[$ it follows that $(-I'(p) + (1 - I'(a))) \in]0.4, 1]$, meaning (3.3) is not satisfied.

From the above it follows that no $I' \subset I$ exists that is a model of $P_{ex3.9}$, hence I is a minimal model of $P_{ex3.9}$. Now let us check whether I is an answer set of P. Consider the reduct $P^I_{ex3.9}$:

$$r^I_1 : a \leftarrow a$$
$$r^I_2 : p \leftarrow \mathcal{T}_W(0.6, 0.8)$$

The minimal model of the reduct is $M = \{p^{0.4}\} \neq I$, hence I is not an answer set of $P_{ex3.9}$.

It turns out that for constraint-free programs there is a correspondence with minimal fix-points of the immediate consequence operator.

Proposition 3.4. *Let P be a constraint-free FASP program. If M is an answer set of P, it is a minimal fixpoint of Π_P.*

Proof. Suppose M is an answer set of P. First we show that it must be a fixpoint of Π_P and then that it must be a minimal fixpoint.

(1) For any $a \in \mathcal{B}_P$ we have:

$$
\begin{aligned}
M(a) &= \langle \text{Def. 3.8, Prop. 3.4} \rangle \; \Pi_{P^M}(M)(a) \\
&= \langle \text{Def. 3.4, Def. 3.7} \rangle \; \sup\{M(\alpha^M) \mid (r : a \leftarrow \alpha) \in P\} \\
&= \langle M(\alpha^M) = M(\alpha) \rangle \; \sup\{M(\alpha) \mid (r : a \leftarrow \alpha) \in P\} \\
&= \quad \langle \text{Def. 3.4} \rangle \quad \Pi_P(M)(a)
\end{aligned}
$$

where the fact that for any interpretation M and rule $r : a \leftarrow \alpha \in P$ we have that $M(\alpha^M) = M(\alpha)$ can easily be seen from the construction of the reduct in Definition 3.7. Hence, we can conclude that M is a fixpoint of Π_P.

(2) Suppose M is not a minimal fixpoint of Π_P. Then there must be some $N \subset M$ such that

$N = \Pi_P(N)$. We can show that N is then a model of P:

$$N = \Pi_P(N)$$

$$\equiv \quad \langle\text{Def. 3.4}\rangle \quad \forall a \in \mathscr{B}_P \cdot N(a) = \sup\{N(\alpha) \mid (r{:}a \leftarrow \alpha) \in P\}$$

$$\Rightarrow \quad \langle(*)\rangle \quad \forall a \in \mathscr{B}_P \cdot \forall (r{:}a \leftarrow \alpha) \in P \cdot N(a) \geqslant N(\alpha)$$

$$\equiv \quad \langle \bigcup_{a \in \mathscr{B}_P} P_a = P \rangle \quad \forall (r{:}a \leftarrow \alpha) \in P \cdot N(a) \geqslant N(\alpha)$$

$$\equiv \quad \langle\text{Def. 3.3}\rangle \quad N \text{ is a model of } P$$

where the (*) justification is that the supremum is an upper bound and $\bigcup_{a \in \mathscr{B}_P} P_a = P$ follows from the assumption that P is constraint-free. Due to Proposition 3.3 this contradicts the fact that M is an answer set of P. $\qquad\square$

As shown in the following example, the reverse does not hold, however.

Example 3.10. Consider program $P_{ex3.9}$ and its interpretation $I = \{a^{0.2}, p^{0.4}\}$ from Example 3.9 on page 44. It is not hard to see that I is a fixpoint of $\Pi_{P_{ex3.9}}$. Now, suppose there is some interpretation I' such that $I' \subset I$. Obviously $\Pi_P(I')(a) = I'(a)$. To obtain $\Pi_P(I')(p) = I'(p)$ the interpretation I' needs to satisfy $I'(p) = \mathscr{T}_W(\mathcal{N}_W(p), \mathcal{N}_W(a))$. As shown in Example 3.9, there is no I' satisfying this equation, thus I is a minimal fixpoint of Π_P. It is not an answer set, however, as was already shown in the aforementioned example.

3.3   Example: Fuzzy Graph Coloring

Consider a continuous graph coloring problem, where nodes can be colored using an infinite number of gray values, represented by a value between 0 (completely black) and 1 (completely white). The objective is to color a graph such that the colors of adjacent nodes are dissimilar to a degree that satisfies the weight of their connecting edge. We can model this problem using the following program P_{fgc}:

$$
\begin{aligned}
gen_1: \quad & white(X) \leftarrow \mathcal{N}_W(black(X)) \\
gen_2: \quad & black(X) \leftarrow \mathcal{N}_W(white(X)) \\
sim_1: \quad & sim(X,Y) \leftarrow \mathscr{T}_M(\mathscr{I}_M(white(X), white(Y)), \\
& \qquad\qquad\qquad \mathscr{I}_M(white(Y), white(X))) \\
sim_2: \quad & sim(X,Y) \leftarrow \mathscr{T}_M(\mathscr{I}_M(black(X), black(Y)), \\
& \qquad\qquad\qquad \mathscr{I}_M(black(Y), black(X))) \\
constr: \quad & 0 \leftarrow \mathscr{T}_W(edge(X,Y), sim(X,Y))
\end{aligned}
$$

Similar to the ASP program modeling the black-and-white graph coloring in Example 2.7 on page 19, this program is written in a generate-define-test style. Rules gen_1 and gen_2 are the *generate* part, which create an arbitrary coloring of the graph. Rules sim_1 and sim_2 define the similarity degree of the colors of two nodes. Note that $\mathcal{I}_M(\mathcal{I}_M(x,y), \mathcal{I}_M(y,x))$ is a generalization of the classical logic equivalence $x \Leftrightarrow y \equiv (x \Rightarrow y) \wedge (y \Rightarrow x)$. Rule *constr* is a constraint that eliminates solutions where $sim(X,Y) + edge(X,Y) \leqslant 1$, i.e. where adjacent nodes are too similarly colored.

Consider now graphs $G_{(a)}$ and $G_{(b)}$ depicted in Figure 3.1 on the following page. To find a coloring of these graphs, we add facts to P_{fgc} that describe the graph and find the answer sets of the resulting program (after grounding). The facts $F_{(a)}$, respectively $F_{(b)}$ corresponding to these graphs are

$$n_a: node(a) \leftarrow 1 \qquad\qquad f_{a,b}: edge(a,b) \leftarrow 0.5$$
$$n_b: node(b) \leftarrow 1 \qquad\qquad f_{b,a}: edge(b,a) \leftarrow 0.5$$

and

$$
\begin{aligned}
n_a: &\quad node(a) \leftarrow 1 & f_{a,c}: edge(a,c) \leftarrow 1 \\
n_b: &\quad node(b) \leftarrow 1 & f_{c,a}: edge(c,a) \leftarrow 1 \\
n_c: &\quad node(c) \leftarrow 1 & f_{b,c}: edge(b,c) \leftarrow 1 \\
f_{a,b}: &\; edge(a,b) \leftarrow 1 & f_{c,b}: edge(c,b) \leftarrow 1 \\
f_{b,a}: &\; edge(b,a) \leftarrow 1 &
\end{aligned}
$$

An answer set for program $gnd(P_{fgc} \cup F_{(a)})$ is

$$A^{(a)} = \{node(a)^1, node(b)^1, edge(a,b)^{0.5}, edge(b,a)^{0.5}, white(a)^1, white(b)^{0.5},$$
$$black(b)^{0.5}, sim(a,b)^{0.5}, sim(b,a)^{0.5}\}$$

This corresponds to a coloring where node a is white and node b is exactly gray (i.e. right in between entirely white and black). Of course, many other solutions are possible, and thus many more answer sets exist for this program. For example, the answer sets of the crisp graph coloring problem given in Example 2.7 on page 19 will also be answer sets of $gnd(P)_{fgc} \cup F_{(a)}$.

Now if we consider the program $gnd(P_{fgc}) \cup F_{(b)}$, we find that no answer sets exist. This is because the weights are very strict and prohibit any solution where $sim(x,y) = 0$ for any two nodes x and y (i.e. where two nodes are entirely dissimilar in color). In the next chapter we show how we can find approximate solutions for such problems and how we can model preference among the edges in other ways than by using weights.

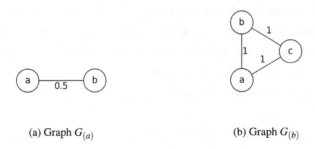

(a) Graph $G_{(a)}$ (b) Graph $G_{(b)}$

Fig. 3.1: Example instances for the graph coloring problem

To summarize, in this chapter we introduced the basic elements of fuzzy answer set programming (FASP). We showed how FASP can be used to model continuous problems in
an elegant manner, similar to how ASP is capable of declaratively modeling combinatorial
problems. We illustrated this on a fuzzy graph coloring problem, but also found that the
language misses flexibility: sometimes no solutions could be found, whereas intuitively
certain approximate solutions would certainly be admissible. In the next chapter we show
how we can alleviate this problem.

Chapter 4

Aggregated Fuzzy Answer Set Programming

4.1 Introduction

In the previous chapter we introduced FASP, an extension of ASP that allows to solve continuous problems in a concise, declarative manner. We have also shown that FASP can sometimes be limited in its flexibility, however. For example, the fuzzy graph coloring program P_{fgc} introduced in Section 3.3 on page 46 allowed a continuous range of gray values as colors, but was unable to find a suitable graph coloring for graph $G_{(b)}$ depicted in Figure 3.1 on the preceding page. This is not ideal, as a coloring that colors node a white, node b black, and node c gray may be better than having no solution at all. The inadmissibility is due to the constraint $constr$, which for $G_{(b)}$ removes solutions in which nodes have a similarity that is strictly greater than 0. A possible alternative is to allow solutions in which the similarity degree of two adjacent nodes may be greater than 0. Of course, solutions in which this degree is as small as possible are still preferred. This idea can be implemented by allowing that the last rule, $constr$, may not always be completely satisfied.

Many of the current approaches (for example [Damásio *et al.* (2004); Damásio *et al.* (2007); Emden (1986); Lakshmanan and Shiri (2001); Lakshmanan (1997); Loyer and Straccia (2002, 2003); Lukasiewicz (2006); Lukasiewicz and Straccia (2007a); Madrid and Ojeda-Aciego (2008, 2009); Shapiro (1983)]) that allow such *partial rule satisfaction* do so by coupling a residual implicator $\mathcal{I}$ and weight w to each rule $r: a \leftarrow \alpha$. A rule is then *satisfied* by an interpretation I if $\mathcal{I}(I(\alpha), I(a)) \geqslant w$. This means that the degree to which a rule should be satisfied is predefined.

Attaching weights to rules is not an entirely satisfactory solution, however. First of all, having weights puts an additional burden on the programmer, who, moreover, may not always be aware of which weights are suitable. Second, we are not only interested in finding any solution: if multiple solutions can be found, we are especially interested in the solution modeling the rules best. Hence, based on the degree to which the rules of the program are satisfied, it is of interest to define an ordering on the solutions, which cannot be meaningfully done using fixed weights. In [Van Nieuwenborgh *et al.* (2007b)] the proposed solution is to attach an aggregator expression to a program. This aggregator expression maps each prospective solution to a score, based on the satisfaction degrees of the rules. The latter is obtained by attaching an implicator to each rule, similar to the weighted approaches. We call this **aggregated fuzzy answer set programming (AFASP)**. In this chapter, we further develop this approach. In particular, the main contribution of the chapter is two-fold. First, we decouple the order structure used by the aggregator expression from the lattice underlying the truth values. This ensures that we can define preference orderings on answer sets which may not correspond to complete lattices. Second, our approach is based on a fixpoint semantics, rather than unfounded sets. As we show below, the approach from [Van Nieuwenborgh *et al.* (2007b)] does not correctly generalize to arbitrary truth lattices, an issue which is solved by our proposed fixpoint semantics. In addition, the fixpoint semantics are also more general, as they are not restricted to formulas that are built from t-norms. Last, the fixpoint semantics (more clearly) reveal the link between FASP with an aggregator expression and FASP with weighted rules.

The structure of the chapter is as follows. In Section 4.2 we develop a fixpoint theory for fuzzy answer set programming with aggregators and investigate its main properties. While many of the properties we find are unsurprising, in the sense that they have a direct counterpart in fixpoint theory for (F)ASP, there are some notable differences as well. For instance, while one of the central properties of (F)ASP is that programs without negation have unique answer sets, it turns out that such programs can have several non-trivial answer sets in our setting, depending on the aggregator that is chosen. We apply AFASP on the reviewer assignment problem in Section 4.3, followed by a detailed overview of the relationship between AFASP and existing approaches in Section 4.4.

4.2   Aggregated Fuzzy Answer Set Programming

In this section we introduce the concepts of AFASP. We begin by introducing the notion of approximate models, which do not satisfy all rules completely. Afterwards we define the semantics of AFASP programs.

4.2.1 *Models*

Normally, given a FASP program P, one is interested in the interpretations I satisfying $I(a) \geqslant I(\alpha)$ for each $(r : a \leftarrow \alpha) \in P$. Such interpretations are called *models*. In the present framework, however, we recognize that rules cannot always be completely fulfilled. This has two main advantages: first, we can tackle problems lacking a "perfect" solution (i.e. a solution satisfying all rules) and second, we can find satisfactory solutions faster if we do not need a "perfect" solution.

The first situation can occur when problems are *overconstrained*. For example, consider the graph coloring problem introduced in Section 3.3 on page 46. For the graph depicted in Fig. 3.1b on page 48, we found that no perfect coloring exists. Hence the problem is overconstrained and we must make some compromises, adhering more strictly to rules that are considered more important. The second situation occurs when approximate solutions can be computed substantially faster and when having a perfect solution is not crucial.

To define what it means for a rule of a FASP program P to be satisfied to a degree, we attach to each FASP rule $(r : a \leftarrow \alpha) \in P$ a residual implicator, denoted $\mathscr{I}_r$. We also denote the t-norm of which $\mathscr{I}_r$ is the residual implicator with $\mathscr{T}_r$. An interpretation I of P is then said to **satisfy** r **to the degree** $k \in \mathscr{L}_P$ iff $\mathscr{I}_r(I(\alpha), I(a)) \geqslant k$. Note that by Proposition 2.10 r is satisfied to degree 1 iff $I(\alpha) \leqslant I(a)$, i.e. iff r is satisfied by I according to the definition of a satisfied FASP rule on page 38. Throughout this book we use $r : a \leftarrow_m \alpha$, $r : a \leftarrow_l \alpha$ and $r : a \leftarrow_p \alpha$ to denote a rule $r : a \leftarrow \alpha$ that is respectively associated with the Gödel, Łukasiewicz and product implicator. If no subscript is attached to $\leftarrow$ either the associated implicator will be clear from the context, or will not be important in the given context.

The behavior of rules that are only partially satisfied depends crucially on the choice of the residual implicator. For example, rule $r : a \leftarrow \alpha$ is satisfied exactly to degree $k < 1$ for $I(a) = k$ when the Gödel implicator is used, for $I(a) = k \cdot I(\alpha)$ when the Goguen implicator is used and for $I(a) = I(\alpha) - (1 - k)$ when the Łukasiewicz implicator is used. Thus, depending on the chosen implicator, the degree to which the head should be satisfied, depends 1) not at all on $I(\alpha)$; 2) proportionally on $I(\alpha)$; or 3) linearly on $I(\alpha)$. Depending on the context, each of these three situations may be required.

To construct the AFASP theory, we first extend interpretations to rules.

Definition 4.1. Let P be a FASP program and let $r : a \leftarrow \alpha$ be a rule in P. We extend interpretations I of P to r as follows:

$$I(r) = \mathscr{I}_r(I(\alpha), I(a))$$

To make the presentation clearer, we will often write $I(a \leftarrow \alpha)$ to denote $I(r)$ for a FASP rule $r:a \leftarrow \alpha$. Now we can use this extension to define *rule interpretations*, which are functions that map *rules* to a truth value (i.e. a value from the considered lattice).

Definition 4.2. Given a FASP program P, a **rule interpretation** of P is a $P \rightarrow \mathscr{L}_P$ mapping. Any interpretation I of P induces a rule interpretation ρ_I defined as $\rho_I(r) = I(a \leftarrow \alpha)$ for every rule $r:a \leftarrow \alpha$ in P.

Hence, the difference between an interpretation of a program and a rule interpretation is that the former maps propositional symbols to truth values, whereas the latter maps the rules themselves to a truth value. We define $\rho_1 \leqslant_{\mathscr{L}_P} \rho_2$ iff $\forall r \in P \cdot \rho_1(r) \leqslant_{\mathscr{L}_P} \rho_2(r)$. The relative importance of rules is encoded in an *aggregator* function.

Definition 4.3. An **aggregator** over a program P is an order-preserving $(P \rightarrow \mathscr{L}_P) \rightarrow \mathscr{P}$ function, where $(\mathscr{P}, \leqslant_{\mathscr{P}})$ is a preordered set.

Hence, an aggregator maps rule interpretations to preference scores from some preorder. As it is order-preserving, we guarantee that rule interpretations which map the rules to a higher degree receive a higher score. The aggregator typically encodes which rules are deemed more important by the designer, who may be more reluctant to accept solutions that do poorly on some rules while not caring much about failing to fully satisfy others.

Example 4.1. Consider the fuzzy graph coloring program P_{fgc} and the graph from Fig. 3.1b introduced in Section 3.3 on page 46. Now, suppose that the dissimilarity of the colors of a and c is more important than the dissimilarity between the colors of b and c, which is more important than the dissimilarity between the colors of a and b. In terms of the graph this means that edge (a,c) is more important than edge (b,c), which is more important than edge (a,b). If the generate rules or similarity rules are not satisfied to degree 1, the score of an interpretation of the rules should always be 0 since this means we are underestimating the similarity or color value, which is unwanted. If the generate rules and similarity rules are satisfied to degree 1 we can use the weighted sum of the constraint rules to represent the edge preference. Let us denote by $constr_{(x,y)}$ the grounding of the $constr$ rule where variable X is replaced by constant x and variable Y by constant y. The following aggregator function over the preorder $\mathscr{P} = (\mathbb{R}, \leqslant)$ models this:

$$\mathscr{A}(\rho) = \beta(\rho) \cdot \left(1.4 \cdot \rho(constr_{(a,c)}) + 1 \cdot \rho(constr_{(b,c)}) + 0.8 \cdot \rho(constr_{(a,b)})\right)$$

where

$$\beta(\rho) = crisp\Bigg(\Big(n_a \cdot n_b \cdot n_c \cdot f_{(a,b)} \cdot f_{(b,a)} \cdot f_{(a,c)} \cdot f_{(c,a)} \cdot f_{(b,c)} \cdot f_{(c,b)} \Big)$$

$$\cdot \Big(\prod_{a \in Nodes} \rho((gen_1)_a) \cdot \rho((gen_2)_a) \cdot \rho(n_a) \Big)$$

$$\cdot \Big(\prod_{(a,b) \in Nodes^2} \rho((sim_1)_{(a,b)}) \cdot \rho((sim_2)_{(a,b)}) \Big) \Bigg)$$

where $crisp(x) = 0$ if $x < 1$ and $crisp(x) = 1$ otherwise. Note that since $constr_{(x,y)} = constr_{(y,x)}$, for any $x,y \in Nodes$, we doubled the weights of the constraints to take the symmetry into account. Now consider two rule interpretations ρ_1 and ρ_2 of this program such that $\beta(\rho_1) = \beta(\rho_2) = 1$ and with the following values for the constraints:

	$constr_{(a,b)}$	$constr_{(a,c)}$	$constr_{(b,c)}$
ρ_1	0.3	0.7	0.7
ρ_2	1	0.5	0.5

Computing $\mathscr{A}(\rho_1)$ and $\mathscr{A}(\rho_2)$ we obtain $\mathscr{A}(\rho_1) = 1.92$ and $\mathscr{A}(\rho_2) = 2$. Hence according to this aggregator, a solution satisfying the rules to the degrees specified by rule interpretation ρ_2 is better than a solution satisfying the rules to the degrees specified by rule interpretation ρ_1. This corresponds to our intended semantics of the aggregator, since ρ_2 satisfies the most important edge (a,b) to a much higher degree than ρ_1, whereas ρ_1 satisfies the lesser important edge (a,c) only slightly better than ρ_2 and satisfies the least important edge (b,c) a bit worse than ρ_2.

However, depending on the application, this might not be what we want. For example, the fact that edge (a,c) is more important can also mean that ρ_1 should be more preferred than ρ_2, since it satisfies this rule better. This can be encoded using an aggregator over the partial order $\mathscr{P}' = ([0,1]^3, \leqslant_{lex})$ where by definition $(a_1,a_2,a_3) \leqslant_{lex} (a_1',a_2',a_3')$ iff

$$(a_1 < a_1') \vee (a_1 = a_1' \wedge a_2 < a_2') \vee (a_1 = a_1' \wedge a_2 = a_2' \wedge a_3 < a_3')$$

$$\vee (a_1 = a_1' \wedge a_2 = a_2' \wedge a_3 = a_3')$$

The corresponding aggregator is

$$\mathscr{A}'(\rho) = \begin{cases} (0,0,0) & \text{if } \beta(\rho) = 0 \\ (\rho(constr_{(a,c)}), \rho(constr_{(b,c)}), \rho(constr_{(a,b)})) & \text{otherwise} \end{cases} \quad (4.1)$$

Note that due to the symmetry between the constraints we do not need to take the constraints $constr_{(b,a)}$, $constr_{(c,b)}$ and $constr_{(c,a)}$ into account. Using $\mathscr{A}'$, we obtain $\mathscr{A}'(\rho_1) = (0.7, 0.7, 0.3)$ and $\mathscr{A}'(\rho_2) = (0.5, 0.5, 1)$, from which we obtain that $\mathscr{A}'(\rho_2) \leqslant_{lex} \mathscr{A}'(\rho_1)$, i.e. ρ_1 is strictly preferred over ρ_2.

Many aggregation strategies have been proposed over the years (for an overview see [Detyniecki (2001)]). Formally, an aggregation operator $\mathscr{A}$ is defined as a function mapping vectors over $\mathscr{L}^n$, with $\mathscr{L}$ a complete lattice, to a preordered set $\mathscr{P}$. It can easily be seen that the aggregator defined in Definition 4.3 above fits this definition as rule interpretations correspond to vectors in $\mathscr{L}^n$, with n the number of rules in a program. In the following, let $u = (u_1, \ldots, u_n)$ and $v = (v_1, \ldots, v_n)$ be two vectors in $\mathscr{L}^n$. The main task of an aggregation operator is to define an ordering over the vectors in $\mathscr{L}^n$, which we call the **induced ordering** of an aggregation operator $\mathscr{A}$. Formally for an aggregation operator $\mathscr{A}$ it is defined as

$$u \leqslant_{\mathscr{A}} v \equiv \mathscr{A}(u) \leqslant_{\mathscr{P}} \mathscr{A}(v)$$

We can distinguish two types of aggregators. In the first case the aggregator maps vectors in $\mathscr{L}^n$ to a single value in $\mathscr{L}$ or $\mathbb{R}$. Well-known aggregation operators of this form are the minimum, maximum, median, product and sum. Though these operators are useful, sometimes, we may consider the satisfaction of some rules to be more important, e.g. expressed using priority levels for each rule. To cope with such priority levels, weighted versions of the basic operators have been proposed, such as the weighted sum used in Example 4.1. For weighted minimum and maximum we refer the reader to [Dubois and Prade (1986); Fagin and Wimmers (1998); Yager (1981)]. A particularly interesting class of operators with weights are the Ordered Weighted Average (OWA) operators (see e.g. [Yager (1988); Yager and Kacprzyk (1997)]), which encompass a wide range of aggregation operators over vectors in $[0, 1]^n$, including the minimum, maximum and median. Formally, given a vector $u = (u_1, \ldots, u_n) \in [0, 1]^n$, a collection of weights $(w_1, \ldots, w_n) \in [0, 1]^n$ such that $\sum_i w_i = 1$ and a permutation σ of u such that $u_{\sigma(1)} \leqslant \ldots \leqslant u_{\sigma(n)}$, an OWA operator is defined by

$$OWA(u) = \sum_{j=1}^{n} w_j u_{\sigma(j)} \tag{4.2}$$

By manipulating the weights of the OWA operator, particular aggregation operators are obtained, with the minimum and the maximum as extreme cases, corresponding to the weight vectors $(1, 0, \ldots, 0)$ and $(0, \ldots, 0, 1)$ respectively. Note that the aggregated value will always be in between the minimum and the maximum of their arguments. Interestingly, the weights of an OWA operator are not associated to a component of the vector, but to an ordered position. This makes it ideal for applications where certain outliers should not be taken into account, such as for example in the judging of some Olympic sports, where the most extreme scores do not count for the final score. Furthermore OWAs can be used to model the demand that most of the rules should be fulfilled, or at least a few rules should be fulfilled.

Two other families of aggregation operators allow to model interaction between values, viz. the discrete **Sugeno** integral [Sugeno (1974)] and the **Choquet** integral [Choquet (1954)]. The difference between these aggregators is that the Sugeno integral is more suitable for ordinal aggregation (where only the order of elements is important) while the Choquet integral is suitable for cardinal aggregation (where the distance between the numbers has a meaning) [Detyniecki (2001)]. Interestingly, the Sugeno integral generalizes the weighted minimum and the weighted maximum, and the Choquet integral generalizes the weighted mean and the OWA operators. The downside of using these operators is the high number of weights that need to be provided by the user. To aggregate n values, in principle, the user needs to supply 2^n weights, which clearly is rather cumbersome. However, in some cases one can reduce the number of required weights; see for example [Nguyen *et al.* (1995); Grabisch (1996)].

One can also use **t-norms** and **t-conorms** for aggregation. However, the aggregated value of these operators is not in between the minimum and the maximum, though this can be useful in certain applications. Two classes of operators that do have this feature can be constructed based on t-norms and t-conorms, viz. the **exponential compensatory operators** [Turksen (1992)] and the **convex-linear compensatory operators** [Luhandjula (1982); Turksen (1992)]. Another related class of operators are **uninorms** [Fodor *et al.* (1997)], which generalize t-norms and t-conorms. Contrary to the two aforementioned compensatory operators, uninorms satisfy the full reinforcement property, i.e. the tendency that when we collect a number of high scores, the aggregated value will be greater than the maximum of these scores, and similarly when we collect a number of low scores, the aggregated value will be lower than the minimum of these scores. In some cases this follows the human aggregation process more closely.

The second type of aggregators are those where the aggregator function is the identity function, and thus $u \leqslant_{\mathscr{A}} v \equiv u \leqslant_{\mathscr{P}} v$, with $\leqslant_{\mathscr{P}}$ an ordering over vectors in $\mathscr{L}^n$. This is for example the case with the **Pareto aggregator** and **lexicographical aggregator**. Formally the former orders the vectors of $\mathscr{L}^n$ with $\leqslant_{par}$ defined as

$$u \leqslant_{par} v \equiv \forall i \in \{1, \ldots, n\} \cdot u_i \leqslant_{\mathscr{L}} v_i$$

The latter orders the vectors of $\mathscr{L}^n$ with the preorder $\leqslant_{lex}$ defined as

$$u \leqslant_{lex} v \equiv (u \leqslant_{par} v) \vee (\exists i \in \{1, \ldots, n\} \cdot (u_i <_{\mathscr{L}} v_i) \wedge (\forall j < i \cdot u_j = v_j))$$

Although the min and max operators are useful because they work in a strictly ordinal manner, the ordering induced by these operators can sometimes be too coarse. For example, using the minimum, the vectors $(0.1,0.5)$ and $(0.1,0.1)$ would be equally preferred, as $\min(0.1,0.5) = \min(0.1,0.1)$. However, the first vector clearly has a better score for the second value to be aggregated. To cope with this, refinements of the induced ordering have been proposed, namely the **discrimin** and the **leximin** (see e.g. [Dubois and Prade (2001)]). Formally the discrimin aggregator orders vectors in $\mathscr{L}^n$ using $\leqslant_{disc}$ defined as

$$u \leqslant_{disc} v \equiv \min\{u_i \mid i \in \mathscr{D}(u,v)\} \leqslant \min\{v_i \mid i \in \mathscr{D}(u,v)\}$$

where $\mathscr{D}(u,v) = \{i \mid i \in \{1,\ldots,n\}, u_i \neq v_i\}$. Intuitively, this ordering is based on the idea that the values on which the two vectors agree are of no importance when comparing them. Decisions are thus based on the least satisfied discriminating value. The idea of the leximin aggregator is to represent vectors of satisfaction levels by ranked multi-sets of satisfaction degrees. Formally it maps a vector in $\mathscr{L}^n$ to the corresponding element in the structure $(\mathscr{L}^n, \leqslant_{lexi})$ defined as

$$u \leqslant_{lexi} v \equiv \exists k \leqslant n \cdot \forall i < k \cdot \left(u_{\sigma(i)} = v_{\pi(i)}\right) \wedge \left(u_{\sigma(k)} < v_{\pi(k)}\right)$$
$$\vee \forall j \in \{1,\ldots,n\} \cdot u_j = v_j$$

where σ and π are permutations of u, resp. v such that $u_{\sigma(1)} \leqslant \ldots \leqslant u_{\sigma(n)}$ and $v_{\pi(1)} \leqslant \ldots \leqslant v_{\pi(n)}$. Hence, two vectors are indifferent if the corresponding reordered vectors are the same. The leximin ordering is a refinement of both the minimum and the discrimin [Dubois *et al.* (1996)]. Similarly two refinements of the maximum, called *discrimax* and *leximax*, can be defined.

Of course it is also possible to combine a non-trivial aggregation function $\mathscr{A}$ with a non-trivial ordering, as we have for example done in Example 4.1.

An *aggregated FASP program* then consists of a FASP program and an aggregator function over this program.

Definition 4.4. An **aggregated FASP program (AFASP program)** P is a tuple $\langle \mathscr{R}, \mathscr{A} \rangle$, where $\mathscr{R}$ is a FASP program over a lattice $\mathscr{L}$, called the **rule base**, and $\mathscr{A}$ is an aggregator function over $\mathscr{R}$. Given an AFASP program P we denote its rule base as $\mathscr{R}_P$, its aggregator as $\mathscr{A}_P$, the lattice over which $\mathscr{R}_P$ is defined as $\mathscr{L}_P$ and the preorder used by the aggregator as $\mathscr{P}_P$. The set $\mathscr{B}_P = \mathscr{B}_{\mathscr{R}_P}$ is called the **Herbrand base** of P. Furthermore, we define the set P_a, for $a \in \mathscr{B}_P$, as $P_a = \{r \mid r \in \mathscr{R}_{P_a}\}$. Last, a **rule interpretation of an AFASP program** is a rule interpretation of $\mathscr{R}_P$.

In the remainder of this chapter the term *program* always refers to an AFASP program. Furthermore, we will use the term **interpretation of a program** for the interpretation of the rule base of the program. Similar to FASP we can divide an AFASP program in different classes:

(1) An AFASP program P is called **constraint-free** if $\mathscr{R}_P$ is constraint-free.
(2) An AFASP program P is called **positive** if $\mathscr{R}_P$ is positive, i.e. if every rule body is increasing in its arguments.
(3) An AFASP program P is called **simple** if $\mathscr{R}_P$ is simple, i.e. if every rule is positive and not a constraint.

Finally, we introduce two types of *approximate models*: ρ-*rule models*, which relate interpretations of the program to rule interpretations, and k-*models*, which are interpretations that induce rule interpretations whose score is at least k.

Definition 4.5. Let $P = \langle \mathscr{R}_P, \mathscr{A}_P \rangle$ be an AFASP program. A ρ-**rule model**, with ρ a rule interpretation of P, is an interpretation I of $\mathscr{R}_P$ such that $\rho_I \geqslant \rho$. A k-**model**, $k \in \mathscr{P}_P$, of P is any interpretation I satisfying $\mathscr{A}_P(\rho_I) \geqslant k$. Lastly, we define the values $\min(P) = \mathscr{A}_P(\rho_\perp)$ and $\max(P) = \mathscr{A}_P(\rho_\top)$, where $\forall r \in \mathscr{R}_P \cdot \rho_\perp(r) = 0$ and $\forall r \in \mathscr{R}_P \cdot \rho_\top(r) = 1$. Intuitively these correspond to the minimal, resp. maximal value the aggregator expression can attain.

Obviously, any ρ_1-rule model M, with ρ_1 some rule interpretation, is also a ρ_2-rule model when $\rho_2 \leqslant \rho_1$. Similarly any k_1-model M of a program P, with $k_1 \in \mathscr{P}_P$, is also a k_2-model when $k_2 \leqslant_{\mathscr{P}_P} k_1$.

Example 4.2. Consider program P_{fgc} and the graph depicted in Fig. 3.1b on page 48, together with rule interpretations ρ_1 and ρ_2 from Example 4.1 on page 52. Furthermore, for this example we interpret the rules using the Łukasiewicz implication. To have a ρ_1-rule model, we need an interpretation I such that $\rho_I \geqslant \rho_1$. Now consider

$$I_1 = \{edge(a,b)^1, edge(b,a)^1, edge(a,c)^1, edge(c,a)^1, edge(b,c)^1, edge(c,b)^1,$$
$$white(a)^1, white(b)^{0.7}, black(b)^{0.3}, white(c)^{0.3}, black(c)^{0.7}, sim(a,b)^{0.7},$$
$$sim(b,a)^{0.7}, sim(a,c)^{0.3}, sim(c,a)^{0.3}, sim(b,c)^{0.3}, sim(c,b)^{0.3}, sim(a,a)^1,$$
$$sim(b,b)^1, sim(c,c)^1\}$$

Clearly $I_1(r) = 1$ for every rule not in $\{constr_{(x,y)} \mid x,y \in Nodes\}$, hence $I_1(r) \geqslant \rho_1(r)$. For the constraint rules we obtain:

$$I_1(constr_{(a,b)}) = \mathscr{I}_W(\mathscr{T}_W(1, 0.7), 0) = 0.3 = \rho_1(constr_{(a,b)})$$

Likewise for the other constraint rules we obtain that $I_1(constr_{(x,y)}) = \rho_1(constr_{(x,y)})$ for any $x,y \in Nodes$. Hence I_1 is a ρ_1-rule model of P_{fgc}. We can also verify that I_1 is not a

ρ_2-rule model of P_{fgc} as $I_1(constr_{(a,b)}) = 0.3 < \rho_2(constr_{(b,c)})$. Consider now

$$
\begin{aligned}
I_2 = \{ & edge(a,b)^1, edge(b,a)^1, edge(a,c)^1, edge(c,a)^1, edge(b,c)^1, edge(c,b)^1, \\
& white(a)^1, black(b)^1, white(c)^{0.5}, black(c)^{0.5}, sim(a,c)^{0.5}, sim(c,a)^{0.5}, \\
& sim(b,c)^{0.5}, sim(c,b)^{0.5}, sim(a,a)^1, sim(b,b)^1, sim(c,c)^1 \}
\end{aligned}
$$

Again one can easily verify that $I_2(r) = 1$ for any rule not in $\{constr_{(x,y)} \mid x,y \in Nodes\}$. For the constraint rules we obtain:

$$ I_2(constr_{(a,b)}) = \mathscr{I}_W(\mathscr{T}_W(1,0),0) = 1 \geqslant \rho_2(constr_{(a,b)}) $$

Likewise for every other constraint rule $constr_{(x,y)}$ with $x,y \in Nodes$ we obtain $I_2(constr_{(x,y)}) \geqslant \rho_2(constr_{(x,y)})$. Hence I_2 is a ρ_2-rule model of P_{fgc}.

Now consider the aggregators $\mathscr{A}$ and $\mathscr{A}'$ from Example 4.1 on page 52. Using $\mathscr{A}$ we obtain that I_1 is an 1.92-model and I_2 is a 2-model of P_{fgc}, hence I_2 is preferred over I_1. However, with $\mathscr{A}'$ we obtain that I_1 is an $(0.7, 0.7, 0.3)$-model of P_{fgc}, whereas I_2 is an $(0.5, 0.5, 1)$-model of P_{fgc}. This means that $\rho_{I_2} \leqslant_{lex} \rho_{I_1}$, and thus with this aggregator interpretation I_1 is preferred over I_2 since it satisfies the more important rules to a better degree.

Hence, the above example shows that by adding an aggregator function to FASP we can order models according to how well they satisfy the program rules.

4.2.2 Answer Sets

In this section we introduce k-answer sets of AFASP programs P, which are approximations of the answer sets of the FASP program $\mathscr{R}_P$. Similar to FASP the semantics of general AFASP programs is based on those of positive AFASP programs. Therefore we begin by introducing the semantics of the latter.

4.2.2.1 Positive Programs

To define the answer sets of positive programs we need to extend concepts from FASP to deal with partial rule satisfaction. First we introduce the support of a rule w.r.t. some truth value representing the minimal degree to which this rule should be satisfied. This captures the idea of partial rule application. Using the support, we then extend the immediate consequence operator in such a way that we can derive knowledge from a program in a forward chaining manner, while still allowing for partial rule satisfaction. Afterwards we define answer sets of positive programs and present a number of propositions.

Definition 4.6 (from [Van Nieuwenborgh et al. (2007b)]). *Let $r : a \leftarrow \alpha$ be a rule defined on the lattice $\mathcal{L}$ and let I be an interpretation of r. The **support** of this rule w.r.t. I and some $c \in \mathcal{L}$ is denoted as $I_s(r,c)$ and is defined by*

$$I_s(r,c) = \inf\{y \in \mathcal{L} \mid \mathcal{I}_r(I(\alpha),y) \geqslant c\}$$

In practice the weight c will mostly be determined using a rule interpretation. It turns out that a characterization of this operator is easy to find.

Proposition 4.1. *Let $r : a \leftarrow \alpha$ be a rule defined on the lattice $\mathcal{L}$, I an interpretation of r, and c a value in $\mathcal{L}$. Then $I_s(r,c) = \mathcal{I}_r(I(\alpha),c)$.*

Proof. Suppose $r : a \leftarrow \alpha$ is defined over a lattice $\mathcal{L}$, then:

$$
\begin{aligned}
I_s(r,c) = & \quad \langle \text{Def. } I_s(r,c) \rangle & \inf\{y \in \mathcal{L} \mid \mathcal{I}_r(I(\alpha),y) \geqslant c\} \\
= & \quad \langle \text{Residuation principle} \rangle & \inf\{y \in \mathcal{L} \mid y \geqslant \mathcal{I}_r(I(\alpha),c)\} \\
= & \quad \langle \text{See below} \rangle & \mathcal{I}_r(I(\alpha),c)
\end{aligned}
$$

The last step follows from the fact that $\mathcal{I}_r(I(\alpha),c)$ is an element of $\mathcal{L}$ and is a lower bound of $\{y \in \mathcal{L} \mid y \geqslant \mathcal{I}_r(I(\alpha),c)\}$. $\qquad \square$

Note that this property is only valid when the partial mappings of $\mathcal{I}_r$ are supmorphisms, which we assumed in Chapter 2.

Example 4.3. Consider the rule $r : a \leftarrow_m \alpha$ with interpretations I and I' satisfying $I(\alpha) = I'(\alpha) = 0.5$, $I(a) = 1$ and $I'(a) = 0.5$. Recall that for a rule of the aforementioned form we defined that $\mathcal{I}_r = \mathcal{I}_M$. The support of this rule w.r.t. $\rho_\top(r)$ is given by $I_s(r,\rho_\top(r)) = \mathcal{I}_M(0.5,1) = 0.5$. Likewise we can compute that $I'_s(r,\rho_\top(r)) = \mathcal{I}_M(0.5,1) = 0.5$. Hence, $I(a) > I_s(r,\rho_\top(r))$ and $I'(a) = I_s(r,\rho_\top(r))$. This means that the interpretation of a by I' is consistent with the support provided by the rule, whereas the interpretation by I is strictly greater. Hence, rule r cannot be used to justify the value of a under interpretation I. Likewise we can see that $I_s(r,0.9) < I(a)$, meaning I attaches a value to a that is higher than the support that is needed to satisfy this rule to a degree of 0.9.

The support is monotonic, as shown in the following proposition.

Proposition 4.2. *Let I_1 and I_2 be interpretations of a simple rule $r : a \leftarrow \alpha$ defined on a lattice $\mathcal{L}$. If $I_1 \leqslant I_2$ we have for any $c \in \mathcal{L}$ that $(I_1)_s(r,c) \leqslant (I_2)_s(r,c)$.*

Proof. Using Proposition 4.1 and the monotonicity of t-norms we can easily see that:

$$(I_1)_s(r,c) = \mathcal{I}_r(I_1(\alpha),c) \leqslant \mathcal{I}_r(I_2(\alpha),c) = (I_2)_s(r,c) \qquad \square$$

For simple AFASP programs, answer set semantics are based on a "forward chaining" approach, captured in the definition of an extended version of the *immediate consequence operator* (Definition 3.4 on page 39). This operator ensures that the support of a rule is propagated to its head, which means that we derive exactly the maximal amount of knowledge contained in the program.

Definition 4.7. Let P be an AFASP program with ρ a rule interpretation of P. The **immediate consequence operator** $\Pi_{P,\rho}$ derived from P and ρ is a mapping from $(\mathscr{B}_P \to \mathscr{L}_P)$ to $(\mathscr{B}_P \to \mathscr{L}_P)$ defined for any interpretation I of P and $a \in \mathscr{B}_P$ as:

$$\Pi_{P,\rho}(I)(a) = \sup\{I_s(r,\rho(r)) \mid r \in P_a\}$$

The following example illustrates the use of this operator.

Example 4.4. Let P be an AFASP program with the following rule base $\mathscr{R}_P$:

$$r_1 : a \leftarrow_m 0.8$$
$$r_2 : c \leftarrow_m 0.5$$
$$r_3 : b \leftarrow_m \mathscr{T}_M(a,c)$$
$$r_4 : b \leftarrow_m 0.2$$

and aggregator function $\mathscr{A}_P(\rho) = \inf\{\rho(r) \mid r \in \mathscr{R}_P\}$. Consider now the interpretation $\emptyset$, which attaches to each atom the value 0. When using the rule interpretation $\rho_\top$ we can compute $\Pi_{P,\rho_\top}(\emptyset)$ as follows (note that we are using Proposition 4.1 in the computation):

(1) For a: $\Pi_{P,\rho_\top}(\emptyset)(a) = \sup\{\emptyset_s(r,\rho_\top(r)) \mid r \in P_a\} = \emptyset_s(r_1,\rho_\top(r_1)) = \mathscr{T}_M(0.8,1) = 0.8$
(2) For b: $\Pi_{P,\rho_\top}(\emptyset)(b) = \sup\{\emptyset_s(r,\rho_\top(r)) \mid r \in P_b\} = \sup\{\emptyset_s(r_3,\rho_\top(r_3)),\emptyset_s(r_4,\rho_\top(r_4))\}$
$= \sup\{\mathscr{T}_W(\emptyset(\mathscr{T}_M(a,c)),1),\mathscr{T}_M(0.2,1)\} = \sup\{0,0.2\} = 0.2$
(3) For c: $\Pi_{P,\rho_\top}(\emptyset)(c) = \sup\{\emptyset_s(r,\rho_\top(r)) \mid r \in P_c\} = \mathscr{T}_M(0.5,1) = 0.5$

Hence $\Pi_{P,\rho_\top}(\emptyset) = \{a^{0.8}, b^{0.2}, c^{0.5}\}$. For rule interpretation $\rho = \{r_1^{0.5}, r_2^{0.3}, r_3^1, r_4^1\}$ the computation of $\Pi_{P,\rho}(\emptyset)$ is as follows:

(1) For a: $\Pi_{P,\rho}(\emptyset)(a) = \emptyset_s(r_1,\rho(r_1)) = \mathscr{T}_M(0.8,0.5) = 0.5$
(2) For b: $\Pi_{P,\rho}(\emptyset)(b) = \sup\{\emptyset_s(r_3,\rho(r_3)),\emptyset_s(r_4,\rho(r_4))\} = \sup\{\mathscr{T}_W(\emptyset(\mathscr{T}_M(a,c)),1),$
$\mathscr{T}_M(0.2,1)\} = \sup\{0,0.2\} = 0.2$
(3) For c: $\Pi_{P,\rho}(\emptyset)(c) = \emptyset_s(r_2,\rho(r_2)) = \mathscr{T}_M(0.5,0.3) = 0.3$

Hence $\Pi_{P,\rho}(\emptyset) = \{a^{0.5}, b^{0.2}, c^{0.3}\}$.

This immediate consequence operator is similar to the one proposed by Damásio et al. in [Damásio et al. (2007)]. The difference is that we add the weights of the program as a parameter of the operator, where in [Damásio et al. (2007)] the weights of the program are fixed in the program itself. The resulting dynamicity of the weights is crucial for our aggregation based framework. However, once we have chosen a particular rule interpretation the two operators coincide. As in [Damásio et al. (2007)], our operator is monotonic for simple programs:

Proposition 4.3. *Let P be a positive AFASP program and ρ a rule interpretation of this program. The immediate consequence operator* $\Pi_{P,\rho}$ *is monotonically increasing, i.e. for every two interpretations I_1 and I_2 it holds that*

$$I_1 \leqslant I_2 \Rightarrow \Pi_{P,\rho}(I_1) \leqslant \Pi_{P,\rho}(I_2)$$

Proof. Follows from Theorem 16 in [Damásio et al. (2007)]. □

The following proposition shows that our operator is also monotonic in the rule interpretations, something that is also illustrated in Example 4.4.

Proposition 4.4. *Let P be a positive AFASP program. The immediate consequence operator is monotonically increasing in the rule interpretations, i.e. for any two rule interpretations ρ_1 and ρ_2 and interpretation I of P it holds that*

$$\rho_1 \leqslant \rho_2 \Rightarrow \Pi_{P,\rho_1}(I) \leqslant \Pi_{P,\rho_2}(I)$$

Proof.

$$
\begin{aligned}
\Pi_{P,\rho_1}(I)(a) = & \quad \langle \text{Def. } \Pi_{P,\rho_1} \rangle & \sup\{I_s(r,\rho_1(r)) \mid r \in P_a\} \\
= & \quad \langle \text{Prop. 4.1} \rangle & \sup\{\mathscr{T}_r(I(r_b),\rho_1(r)) \mid r \in P_a\} \\
\leqslant & \quad \langle \text{Monot. t-norm} \rangle & \sup\{\mathscr{T}_r(I(r_b),\rho_2(r)) \mid r \in P_a\} \\
= & \quad \langle \text{Prop. 4.1} \rangle & \sup\{I_s(r,\rho_2(r)) \mid r \in P_a\} \\
= & \quad \langle \text{Def. } \Pi_{P,\rho_2} \rangle & \Pi_{P,\rho_2}(I)(a)
\end{aligned}
$$

□

Due to Proposition 2.1 on page 12 it follows that our immediate consequence operator has a least fixpoint $\Pi_{P,\rho}^{\star}$ for any positive AFASP program P and rule interpretation ρ. Similar to ASP and FASP, this least fixpoint can in principle be computed using the iterated fixpoint computation introduced in Definition 2.7 on page 13.

Definition 4.8. Let P be a positive AFASP program, and let ρ be a rule interpretation of P. Formally, we define the sequence $\mathscr{S}\langle P, \rho \rangle = \langle J_i \mid i \text{ an ordinal} \rangle$ by

$$J_i = \begin{cases} \emptyset & \text{if } i = 0 \\ \Pi_{P,\rho}(J_{i-1}) & \text{if } i \text{ is a successor ordinal} \\ \bigcup_{j<i}(J_j) & \text{if } i \text{ is a limit ordinal} \end{cases} \tag{4.3}$$

where $\bigcup_{i \in I}(J_i) = \sup_{i \in I} J_i$.

The least fixpoint of $\Pi_{P,\rho}$ is the first element J_i in the sequence $\mathscr{S}\langle P, \rho \rangle$ for which $\Pi_{P,\rho}(J_i) = J_i$.

Example 4.5. Consider program P from Example 4.4. If we apply $\Pi_{P,\rho_\top}$ to the interpretation $J_1 = \Pi_{P,\rho_\top}(\emptyset) = \{a^{0.8}, b^{0.2}, c^{0.5}\}$ of the sequence $\mathscr{S}\langle P, \rho_\top \rangle$ we obtain J_2:

(1) For a: $J_2(a) = \Pi_{P,\rho_\top}(J_1)(a) = \sup\{(J_1)_s(r, \rho_\top(r)) \mid r \in P_a\} = (J_1)_s(r_1, \rho_\top(r_1)) = \mathscr{T}_M(0.8, 1) = 0.8 = J_1(a)$

(2) For b: $J_2(b) = \Pi_{P,\rho_\top}(J_1)(b) = \sup\{(J_1)_s(r, \rho_\top(r)) \mid r \in P_b\} = \sup\{(J_1)_s(r_3), (J_1)_s(r_4)\}$
$= \sup\{J_1(\mathscr{T}_W(\mathscr{T}_M(a,c), 1)), \mathscr{T}_M(0.2, 1)\} = \sup\{0.5, 0.2\} = 0.5$

(3) For c: $J_2(c) = \Pi_{P,\rho_\top}(J_1)(c) = \sup\{(J_2)_s(r, \rho_\top(r)) \mid r \in P_c\} = (J_1)_s(r_2, \rho_\top(r_2)) = \mathscr{T}_M(0.5, 1) = 0.5$

Hence $J_2 = \{a^{0.8}, b^{0.5}, c^{0.5}\}$. One can readily verify that $J_3 = \Pi_{P,\rho_\top}(J_2) = J_2$. Hence J_2 is a fixpoint of $\Pi_{P,\rho_\top}$ and, as it is the first element of the sequence $\mathscr{S}\langle P, \rho_\top \rangle$ that is a fixpoint of $\Pi_{P,\rho_\top}$, it is its least fixpoint. In other words $J_2 = \Pi^\star_{P,\rho_\top}$.

Example 4.6. Consider program P from Example 4.4 with the rule interpretation $\rho = \{r_1^{0.5}, r_2^{0.3}, r_3^1, r_4^1\}$. If we apply $\Pi_{P,\rho}$ to the interpretation $J_1 = \Pi_{P,\rho}(\emptyset) = \{a^{0.5}, b^{0.2}, c^{0.3}\}$ of the sequence $\mathscr{S}\langle P, \rho \rangle$ we obtain J_2:

(1) For a: $J_2(a) = \Pi_{P,\rho}(J_1)(a) = \sup\{(J_1)_s(r, \rho(r)) \mid r \in P_a\} = (J_1)_s(r_1, \rho(r_1)) = \mathscr{T}_M(0.8, 0.5) = 0.5$

(2) For b: $J_2(b) = \Pi_{P,\rho}(J_1)(b) = \sup\{(J_1)_s(r, \rho(r)) \mid r \in P_b\} = \sup\{(J_1)_s(r_3, \rho(r_3)), (J_1)_s(r_4, \rho(r_4))\} = \sup\{J_1(\mathscr{T}_W(\mathscr{T}_M(a,c), 1)), \mathscr{T}_M(0.2, 1)\} = \sup\{0.3, 0.2\} = 0.3$

(3) For c: $J_2(c) = \Pi_{P,\rho}(J_1)(c) = \sup\{(J_1)_s(r, \rho(r)) \mid r \in P_c\} = (J_1)_s(r_2, \rho(r_2)) = \mathscr{T}_M(0.5, 0.3) = 0.3$

Again one can readily verify that $\Pi_{P,\rho}(J_2) = J_2$ and hence J_2 is the least fixpoint of $\Pi_{P,\rho}$, i.e. $J_2 = \Pi_{P,\rho}^\star$. Note that $\rho \leqslant \rho_\top$ and $\Pi_{P,\rho}^\star \leqslant \Pi_{P,\rho_\top}^\star$, i.e. rule interpretations that put stricter requirements on the satisfaction of rules will lead to greater fixpoints.

Similar to FASP, the least fixpoint may not necessarily be found after a finite number of steps, as can easily be seen by combining program *Inf* in Example 3.4 on page 40 with rule interpretation $\rho_\top$.

The following proposition shows us that smaller rule interpretations yield smaller (least) fixpoints. Hence if we increase the lower bounds imposed on the rules of a program P, the resulting knowledge that we can derive from P using forward chaining increases as well. This corresponds to our intuition, as in general derivable knowledge monotonically increases with tighter constraints.

Proposition 4.5. *Let $\rho_1 \leqslant \rho_2$ be rule interpretations of a positive AFASP program P. Then $\Pi_{P,\rho_1}^\star \leqslant \Pi_{P,\rho_2}^\star$.*

Proof. It is straightforward to show, using transfinite induction and Propositions 4.3 and 4.4, that, for any ordinal i, $J_i^1 \leqslant J_i^2$, where $\mathscr{S}\langle P, \rho_1 \rangle = \langle J_i^1 \mid i \text{ an ordinal} \rangle$ and $\mathscr{S}\langle P, \rho_2 \rangle = \langle J_i^2 \mid i \text{ an ordinal} \rangle$.

Indeed: $J_0^1 = J_0^2 = \emptyset$. Propositions 4.3 and 4.4 then ensure that, for a successor ordinal i, $J_i^1 = \Pi_{P,\rho_1}(J_{i-1}^1) \leqslant \Pi_{P,\rho_2}(J_{i-1}^2) = J_i^2$ follows from $\rho_1 \leqslant \rho_2$ and the induction hypothesis. For a limit ordinal i, $J_i^1 = \bigcup_{j<i} J_j^1 \leqslant \bigcup_{j<i} J_j^2 = J_i^2$ is immediate from the induction hypothesis. $\square$

Consider program P from Example 4.4 on page 60 and its interpretation J_2 from Example 4.6 on the preceding page. Note that for J_2 we obtain that

(1) $J_2(r_1) = \mathscr{I}_M(0.8, 0.5) = 0.5$

(2) $J_2(r_2) = \mathscr{I}_M(0.5, 0.3) = 0.3$

(3) $J_2(r_3) = \mathscr{I}_M(\mathscr{T}_M(0.5, 0.3), 0.3) = 1$

(4) $J_2(r_4) = \mathscr{I}_M(0.2, 0.3) = 1$

Hence, according to Definition 4.5, J_2 is a ρ-rule model with ρ defined as in Example 4.6, i.e. $\rho = \{r_1^{0.5}, r_2^{0.3}, r_3^1, r_4^1\}$. It turns out that this is a general property, i.e. that fixpoints of the immediate consequence operator are ρ-rule models. Note that this property holds for all constraint-free programs and thus in particular also for non-positive programs.

Proposition 4.6. *Let P be a constraint-free AFASP program, ρ a rule interpretation of P and M a fixpoint of $\Pi_{P,\rho}$. Then M is a ρ-rule model of P.*

Proof. Since P is constraint-free, we know that $\mathscr{R}_P = \bigcup_{a \in \mathscr{B}_P} P_a$. Using this property we obtain the stated as follows:

$$M = \Pi_{P,\rho}(M)$$

$\equiv \quad \langle \text{Def. } \Pi_{P,\rho}(M) \rangle \quad \forall a \in \mathscr{B}_P \cdot M(a) = \sup\{M_s(r, \rho(r)) \mid r \in P_a\}$

$\Rightarrow \quad \langle \text{sup is upper bound} \rangle \quad \forall a \in \mathscr{B}_P \cdot \forall r \in P_a \cdot M(a) \geqslant M_s(r, \rho(r))$

$\equiv \quad \langle \text{Prop. 4.1, (*)} \rangle \quad \forall r \in \mathscr{R}_P \cdot M(r_h) \geqslant \mathscr{T}_r(M(r_b), \rho(r))$

$\equiv \quad \langle \text{Residuation principle} \rangle \quad \forall r \in \mathscr{R}_P \cdot \mathscr{I}_r(M(r_b), M(r_h)) \geqslant \rho(r)$

$\equiv \quad \langle \text{Def. } \rho\text{-rule model} \rangle \quad M \text{ is a } \rho\text{-rule model of } P$

where the (*) justification is that $\mathscr{R}_P = \bigcup_{a \in \mathscr{B}_P} P_a$. □

The converse is not true in general, as one can see from the following example.

Example 4.7. Consider the following simple AFASP program:

$$r : a \leftarrow 0.5$$

with rule interpretation $\rho_\top$ and interpretation $I = \{a^1\}$. As $I(r) = 1 = \rho_\top(r)$, I is a $\rho_\top$-rule model of P. But $\Pi_{P,\rho_\top}(I)(a) = \mathscr{T}_M(0.5, 1) = 0.5 < I(a)$ and thus I is not a fixpoint of $\Pi_{P,\rho_\top}$.

However, the converse of Proposition 4.6 turns out to hold for minimal (w.r.t. Zadeh inclusion[1]) ρ-rule models and simple programs.

Proposition 4.7. *Let P be a simple AFASP program, ρ a rule interpretation of P and M a minimal ρ-rule model of P. Then M is a fixpoint of $\Pi_{P,\rho}$.*

Proof. Since P is constraint-free, we know that $\mathscr{R}_P = \bigcup_{a \in \mathscr{B}_P} P_a$. Now, suppose that M is a minimal ρ-rule model of P and not a fixpoint of $\Pi_{P,\rho}$. Then we first show that $\forall a \in \mathscr{B}_P \cdot M(a) \geqslant \sup_{r \in P_a} M_s(r, \rho(r))$ as follows:

$$M \text{ is a } \rho\text{-rule model of } P$$

$\equiv \quad \langle \text{Def. } \rho\text{-rule model} \rangle \quad \forall r \in \mathscr{R}_P \cdot \mathscr{I}_r(M(r_b), M(r_h)) \geqslant \rho(r)$

$\equiv \quad \langle \text{Residuation principle} \rangle \quad \forall r \in \mathscr{R}_P \cdot M(r_h) \geqslant \mathscr{T}_r(M(r_b), \rho(r))$

$\equiv \langle \text{Prop. 4.1, } \mathscr{R}_P = \bigcup_{a \in \mathscr{B}_P} P_a \rangle \quad \forall a \in \mathscr{B}_P \cdot \forall r \in P_a \cdot M(a) \geqslant M_s(r, \rho(r))$

$\equiv \quad \langle \text{Def. upper bound, sup} \rangle \quad \forall a \in \mathscr{B}_P \cdot M(a) \geqslant \sup_{r \in P_a} M_s(r, \rho(r))$

As M is not a fixpoint of $\Pi_{P,\rho}$, for some $a \in \mathscr{B}_P$ it must hold that $M(a) > \sup_{r \in P_a} M_s(r, \rho(r))$. Consider then the interpretation M' defined as

$$M'(x) = \begin{cases} M(x) & \text{if } x \neq a \\ \sup_{r \in P_a} M_s(r, \rho(r)) & \text{otherwise} \end{cases}$$

---

[1] See Definition 2.18 on page 26.

Clearly $M' < M$. We will show that M' is a ρ-rule model, leading to a contradiction with the minimality of M. For any $x \in (\mathscr{B}_P \setminus \{a\})$ we show that

$$\forall r \in P_x \cdot \mathscr{I}_r(M'(r_b), M'(x)) \geqslant \rho(r) \qquad (4.4)$$

Indeed:

$$
\begin{aligned}
M' < M &\Rightarrow \langle\text{Body is increasing}\rangle \ M'(r_b) \leqslant M(r_b) \\
&\Rightarrow \langle\text{Anti-monoton. } \mathscr{I}\rangle \ \mathscr{I}_r(M'(r_b), M(x)) \geqslant \mathscr{I}_r(M(r_b), M(x)) \\
&\Rightarrow \langle M \text{ is } \rho\text{-rule model}\rangle \ \mathscr{I}_r(M'(r_b), M(x)) \geqslant \rho(r) \\
&\equiv \langle\text{Def. } M', r_h = x \neq a\rangle \ \mathscr{I}_r(M'(r_b), M'(x)) \geqslant \rho(r)
\end{aligned}
$$

For a we show that

$$\forall r \in P_a \cdot \mathscr{I}_r(M'(r_b), M'(a)) \geqslant \rho(r) \qquad (4.5)$$

as follows:

$$
\begin{aligned}
& & M'(a) = \sup_{r \in P_a} M_s(r, \rho(r)) \\
&\Rightarrow \ \langle\text{sup is upper bound}\rangle & \forall r \in P_a \cdot M'(a) \geqslant M_s(r, \rho(r)) \\
&\equiv \ \langle\text{Prop. 4.1}\rangle & \forall r \in P_a \cdot M'(a) \geqslant \mathscr{T}_r(M(r_b), \rho(r)) \\
&\Rightarrow \langle M' < M, \text{Monot. } \wedge_r, (*)\rangle & \forall r \in P_a \cdot M'(a) \geqslant \mathscr{T}_r(M'(r_b), \rho(r)) \\
&\equiv \ \langle\text{Residuation principle}\rangle & \forall r \in P_a \cdot \mathscr{I}_r(M'(r_b), M'(a)) \geqslant \rho(r)
\end{aligned}
$$

The $(*)$ justification is that r_b contains an increasing function. By combining (4.4) and (4.5), we obtain that M' is a ρ-rule model, contradicting the assumption that M is a minimal ρ-rule model. Hence M must be a fixpoint of $\Pi_{P,\rho}$. $\qquad\square$

Finally, we define k-**answer sets** of a program P as those least fixpoints of the immediate consequence operator that are k-models of P.

Definition 4.9. Let P be a positive AFASP program. An interpretation M is a k-**answer set** ($k \in \mathscr{P}_P$) of P iff $M = \Pi^\star_{P,\rho_M}$ and $\mathscr{A}_P(\rho_M) \geqslant k$.

Example 4.8. Consider program P from Example 4.4 on page 60 and the least fixpoints $\Pi^\star_{P,\rho_\top}$ and $\Pi^\star_{P,\rho}$ (with ρ as in Example 4.6 on page 62) computed in Example 4.5 on page 62 and Example 4.6 on page 62 respectively. For convenience we refer to $\Pi^\star_{P,\rho_\top}$ as A_1 and to $\Pi^\star_{P,\rho}$ as A_2. Then A_1 is a 1-answer set of P as $\mathscr{A}_P(\rho_{A_1}) = \inf\{r_1, r_2, r_3, r_4\}(\rho_{A_1}) = 1$ and A_2 is an 0.3-answer set as $\mathscr{A}_P(\rho_{A_2}) = \inf\{r_1, r_2, r_3, r_4\}(\rho_{A_2}) = 0.3$. Note that A_1 is also an 0.3-answer set, since according to Definition 4.5 it is an 0.3-model, i.e. $\rho_{A_1}(\mathscr{A}_P) \geqslant 0.3$.

Similar to FASP, the idea behind this definition is that answer sets represent the knowledge inferable from a program P without resorting to external knowledge, i.e. knowledge not contained in the program. This is reflected in the definition since the least fixpoint of Π_{P,ρ_I} corresponds to the result of applying forward chaining on the minimal interpretation. Furthermore, the knowledge expressed by an answer set is also maximal as it is a fixpoint of the immediate consequence operator. Hence using forward chaining on this model will not yield new knowledge.

The k-prefix allows to distinguish between **approximate** answer sets, i.e. answer sets that do not fulfill the rules of the program completely. This allows us to handle conflicting information, or to find approximate solutions to problems encoded as fuzzy answer set programs, when the computation of perfect solutions is too costly.

Note that answer sets for simple programs, contrary to the classical case and non-aggregated FASP approaches, are not necessarily unique. This is illustrated in the following example.

Example 4.9. Consider a program $P_{ex4.9}$ with the following rules:

$$r_1 : a \leftarrow_m 1$$
$$r_2 : b \leftarrow_m 1$$

and aggregator function $\mathscr{A}_{P_{ex4.9}}(\rho) = \inf\{\rho(r) \mid r \in \mathscr{R}_{P_{ex4.9}}\}$. Consider now two interpretations of $P_{ex4.9}$, viz. $I_1 = \{a^{0.5}, b^1\}$ and $I_2 = \{a^1, b^{0.5}\}$. It is easy to see that both of them are least fixpoints of the immediate consequence operator with their induced rule interpretations. As $\rho_{I_1}(r_1) = 0.5 = \rho_{I_2}(r_2)$ and $\rho_{I_1}(r_2) = 1 = \rho_{I_2}(r_1)$, both of them are 0.5-answer sets.

There is a strong connection between minimal ρ-rule models and the answer sets we define here.

Proposition 4.8. *Let P be a simple AFASP program and ρ a rule interpretation of P. Then $\Pi^\star_{P,\rho}$ is the unique minimal ρ-rule model of P.*

Proof. First, we show that $\Pi^\star_{P,\rho}$ is a minimal ρ-rule model of P. Due to Proposition 4.6 we know that $\Pi^\star_{P,\rho}$ must be a ρ-rule model of P. Suppose M is a ρ-rule model such that $M \leqslant \Pi^\star_{P,\rho}$. Without loss of generalization, we can assume that M is a minimal ρ-rule model. Now from Proposition 4.7 we know that M must be a fixpoint of $\Pi_{P,\rho}$ and hence, as $\Pi^\star_{P,\rho}$ is the least fixpoint of $\Pi_{P,\rho}$, that $M = \Pi^\star_{P,\rho}$. Thus $\Pi^\star_{P,\rho}$ is a minimal ρ-rule model of P.

Second, we show that no other minimal ρ-rule models of P exist. Suppose M is a minimal ρ-rule model of P. From Proposition 4.7 we know that M must be a fixpoint of $\Pi_{P,\rho}$ and hence $\Pi^\star_{P,\rho} \leqslant M$ as $\Pi^\star_{P,\rho}$ is the least fixpoint of $\Pi_{P,\rho}$. From this it follows that $M = \Pi^\star_{P,\rho}$. $\square$

From this proposition we can show that our answer sets correspond to minimal rule models.

Corollary 4.1. *Let P be a simple AFASP program. Then A is a $\mathscr{A}_P(\rho_A)$-answer set of P iff A is the unique minimal ρ_A-rule model of P.*

Proof. Follows immediately from Proposition 4.8. □

One may wonder whether every rule interpretation ρ for a simple AFASP program P can be used to generate an answer set $M = \Pi_{P,\rho}^\star$ such that $\rho_M = \rho$. The answer is negative, as one can see from the following example:

Example 4.10. Consider the program P with aggregator $\mathscr{A}_P(\rho) = \inf\{\rho(r) \mid r \in \mathscr{R}_P\}$ and the following rule base $\mathscr{R}_P$:

$$r_1 : a \leftarrow_m 0.2$$

$$r_2 : a \leftarrow_m gt(a,0)$$

where $gt(x,y) = 1$ if $x > y$ and $gt(x,y) = 0$ otherwise. Computing $\Pi_{P,\rho}^\star$ for $\rho = \{r_1^{0.2}, r_2^1\}$ yields $\Pi_{P,\rho}^\star = \{a^1\} = M$, which induces $\rho_M = \{r_1^1, r_2^1\} \neq \rho$. One can easily verify that $M = \Pi_{P,\rho_M}^\star$ and $\mathscr{A}_P(\rho_M) \geq 1$, thus M is an 1-answer set of P.

As one can see, the least fixpoint of $\Pi_{P,\rho}$ from Example 4.10 turned out to be a 1-answer set of P, where $1 > \mathscr{A}_P(\rho)$, since $\mathscr{A}_P(\rho) = 0.2$. The following propositions show that in general the least fixpoint of $\Pi_{P,\rho}$ for some program P and an arbitrary rule interpretation ρ of this program will always be a k-answer set, for all $k \geq \mathscr{A}_P(\rho)$. This means that to obtain a k-answer set of a positive program P for an arbitrary $k \in \mathscr{P}_P$, we only need to compute $\Pi_{P,\rho}^\star$ for an arbitrary rule interpretation ρ satisfying $\mathscr{A}_P(\rho) \geq k$.

Lemma 4.1. *Let P be an AFASP program and I an interpretation of this program, then for each $a \in \mathscr{B}_P$ it holds that $I(a)$ is an upper bound of the set $\{I_s(r, \rho_I(r)) \mid r \in P_a\}$.*

Proof. We show that for any $a \in \mathscr{B}_P$ and $r \in P_a$ it holds that $I(a) \geq I_s(r, \rho_I(r))$, from which the stated readily follows.

$$I_s(r, \rho_I(r))$$
$$= \langle \text{Def. } I_s(r, \rho_I(r)) \rangle \ \inf\{y \in \mathscr{L}_P \mid \mathscr{I}_r(I(r_b), y) \geq \rho_I(r)\}$$
$$= \quad \langle \text{Def. } \rho_I \rangle \qquad \inf\{y \in \mathscr{L}_P \mid \mathscr{I}_r(I(r_b), y) \geq \mathscr{I}_r(I(r_b), I(a))\}$$
$$\leq \quad \langle \text{Def. inf} \rangle \qquad I(a) \qquad\qquad\qquad □$$

Proposition 4.9. *Let P be a simple AFASP program, ρ a rule interpretation of P, and $M = \Pi_{P,\rho}^\star$. Then $\Pi_{P,\rho_M}^\star = M$.*

Proof.   First, note that from Proposition 4.6 we can immediately see that $\rho \leqslant \rho_M$ as M is a fixpoint of $\Pi_{P,\rho}$. Second, we show that $\Pi_{P,\rho_M}(M) = M$:

$$M = \Pi_{P,\rho}^{\star}$$

$\Rightarrow$ $\langle$Def. fixpoint$\rangle$ $\forall a \in \mathcal{B}_P \cdot M(a) = \Pi_{P,\rho}(M)(a)$

$\Rightarrow$ $\langle \rho \leqslant \rho_M$, Prop. 4.4$\rangle$ $\forall a \in \mathcal{B}_P \cdot M(a) \leqslant \Pi_{P,\rho_M}(M)(a)$

$\equiv$ $\langle$Def. $\Pi_{P,\rho_M}\rangle$ $\forall a \in \mathcal{B}_P \cdot M(a) \leqslant \sup_{r \in P_a} M_s(r, \rho_M(r))$

$\Rightarrow$ $\langle$Lemma 4.1$\rangle$ $\forall a \in \mathcal{B}_P \cdot M(a) = \sup_{r \in P_a} M_s(r, \rho_M(r))$

$\equiv$ $\langle$Def. $\Pi_{P,\rho_M}\rangle$ $\forall a \in \mathcal{B}_P \cdot M(a) = \Pi_{P,\rho_M}(M)(a)$

By Proposition 4.5 and the fact that $\rho \leqslant \rho_M$ we obtain that $\Pi_{P,\rho}^{\star} \leqslant \Pi_{P,\rho_M}^{\star}$ and thus by definition of M that $M \leqslant \Pi_{P,\rho_M}^{\star}$. As we have shown that M is a fixpoint of Π_{P,ρ_M}, and thus $\Pi_{P,\rho_M}^{\star} \leqslant M$, this means that $M = \Pi_{P,\rho_M}^{\star}$.   □

Proposition 4.10. *Let P be a simple AFASP program and ρ a rule interpretation of P. Then $M = \Pi_{P,\rho}^{\star}$ is a $\mathscr{A}_P(\rho)$-answer set.*

Proof.   Due to Proposition 4.9 we already know that $M = \Pi_{P,\rho_M}^{\star}$. We thus only need to show that $\mathscr{A}_P(\rho_M) \geqslant \mathscr{A}_P(\rho)$. From Proposition 4.6, we know that M is a ρ-rule model, i.e. $\forall r \in \mathscr{R}_P \cdot \rho_M(r) \geqslant \rho(r)$. This implies $\mathscr{A}_P(\rho_M) \geqslant \mathscr{A}_P(\rho)$ because $\mathscr{A}_P$ is increasing.   □

We obtain two immediate corollaries, the first of which shows that a model of a simple program is a k-answer set iff it is produced by some ρ-rule interpretation with $\mathscr{A}_P(\rho) \geqslant k$.

Corollary 4.2. *M is a k-answer set of a simple AFASP program P iff there is some rule interpretation ρ for which $\mathscr{A}_P(\rho) \geqslant k$, such that $M = \Pi_{P,\rho}^{\star}$.*

Proof.   First, suppose M is a k-answer set of a simple AFASP program P. By definition of k-answer sets it must then hold that $\mathscr{A}_P(\rho_M) \geqslant k$ and that $M = \Pi_{P,\rho_M}^{\star}$, hence some rule interpretation ρ exists such that $M = \Pi_{P,\rho}^{\star}$ and $\mathscr{A}_P(\rho) \geqslant k$.

Second, suppose there is some rule interpretation ρ for which $\mathscr{A}_P(\rho) \geqslant k$ and $M = \Pi_{P,\rho}^{\star}$. From Proposition 4.10 we then know that M is a $\mathscr{A}_P(\rho)$-answer set of P, from which we know that $\mathscr{A}_P(\rho_M) \geqslant \mathscr{A}_P(\rho)$ and hence, as $\mathscr{A}_P(\rho) \geqslant k$, it follows that $\mathscr{A}_P(\rho_M) \geqslant k$. Thus M is a k-answer set.   □

The following corollary shows that it is easy to obtain a suitable rule interpretation for simple AFASP programs.

Corollary 4.3. *Every simple AFASP program P has a $max(P)$-answer set, with $max(P)$ as defined in Definition 4.5.*

Proof. Let P be a simple AFASP program. The desired answer set is obtained by applying Proposition 4.9 to the rule interpretation $\rho_\top$.   □

Hence, when constructing a k-answer set of a simple program P, with $k \in \mathscr{P}_P$ and $k \leqslant max(P)$, we can simply use $\rho_\top$ and compute $\Pi^\star_{P,\rho_\top}$. As any k_1-answer set of P is a k_2-answer set of P for $k_1 \geqslant k_2$, $\Pi^\star_{P,\rho_\top}$ is a k-answer set for any $k \leqslant max(P)$.

Example 4.11. Consider an AFASP program P with rule base $\mathscr{R}_P$:

$$r_1 : a \leftarrow_m 0.8$$
$$r_2 : b \leftarrow_m 0.4$$
$$r_3 : c \leftarrow \mathscr{T}_M(a,b)$$

The aggregator is $\mathscr{A}_P(\rho) = \rho(r_1) + \rho(r_2) + \rho(r_3)$, defined over the preorder $(\mathbb{R}, \leqslant)$. As $\mathscr{A}_P(\rho_\top) = 3$, we know that $\Pi^\star_{P,\rho_\top} = \{a^{0.8}, b^{0.4}, c^{0.4}\}$ is a 3-answer set of P. Since the least fixpoint of $\Pi_{P,\rho_\top}$ is unique we know from the aggregator definition that this is also the unique 3-answer set of P.

4.2.2.2 General programs

Recall that for a FASP program $\mathscr{R}_P$ and interpretation M we defined the reduct of $\mathscr{R}_P$ w.r.t. M, denoted as $\mathscr{R}_P^M$, in Definition 3.7 on page 42. The semantics of general AFASP programs will be based on this reduct definition. However, different to FASP we don't require answer sets to be models, but require them to be k-models. Hence they are *approximate* answer sets.

Definition 4.10. Let P be an AFASP program. An interpretation M is a k**-answer set** of P ($k \in \mathscr{P}_P$) iff $M = \Pi^\star_{\mathscr{R}_P^M, \rho_M}$ and $\mathscr{A}_P(\rho_M) \geqslant k$.

Example 4.12. Consider program P_{fgc} from Section 3.3 on page 46 together with interpretations I_1 and I_2 from Example 4.2 on page 57. It turns out that both I_1 and I_2 are approximate answer sets of this program. Indeed, for I_1 the reduct $\mathscr{R}^{I_1}_{P_{fgc}}$ is:

$$(gen_1)_a : white(a) \leftarrow 1$$
$$(gen_1)_b : white(b) \leftarrow 0.7$$
$$(gen_1)_c : white(c) \leftarrow 0.3$$
$$(gen_2)_a : black(a) \leftarrow 0$$
$$(gen_2)_b : black(b) \leftarrow 0.3$$

$$(gen_2)_c : black(c) \leftarrow 0.7$$

$$(sim_1)_{(a,a)} : sim(a,a) \leftarrow \mathscr{T}_M(\mathscr{I}_M(1, white(a)), \mathscr{I}_M(1, white(a)))$$

$$(sim_1)_{(a,b)} : sim(a,b) \leftarrow \mathscr{T}_M(\mathscr{I}_M(0.7, white(a)), \mathscr{I}_M(1, white(b)))$$

$$(sim_1)_{(a,c)} : sim(a,c) \leftarrow \mathscr{T}_M(\mathscr{I}_M(0.3, white(a)), \mathscr{I}_M(1, white(c)))$$

$$(sim_1)_{(b,a)} : sim(b,a) \leftarrow \mathscr{T}_M(\mathscr{I}_M(1, white(b)), \mathscr{I}_M(0.7, white(a)))$$

$$(sim_1)_{(b,b)} : sim(b,b) \leftarrow \mathscr{T}_M(\mathscr{I}_M(0.7, white(b)), \mathscr{I}_M(0.7, white(b)))$$

$$(sim_1)_{(b,c)} : sim(b,c) \leftarrow \mathscr{T}_M(\mathscr{I}_M(0.3, white(b)), \mathscr{I}_M(0.7, white(c)))$$

$$(sim_1)_{(c,a)} : sim(c,a) \leftarrow \mathscr{T}_M(\mathscr{I}_M(1, white(c)), \mathscr{I}_M(0.3, white(a)))$$

$$(sim_1)_{(c,b)} : sim(c,b) \leftarrow \mathscr{T}_M(\mathscr{I}_M(0.7, white(c)), \mathscr{I}_M(0.3, white(b)))$$

$$(sim_1)_{(c,c)} : sim(c,c) \leftarrow \mathscr{T}_M(\mathscr{I}_M(0.3, white(c)), \mathscr{I}_M(0.3, white(c)))$$

$$(sim_2)_{(a,a)} : sim(a,a) \leftarrow \mathscr{T}_M(\mathscr{I}_M(0, black(a)), \mathscr{I}_M(0, black(a)))$$

$$(sim_2)_{(a,b)} : sim(a,b) \leftarrow \mathscr{T}_M(\mathscr{I}_M(0.3, black(a)), \mathscr{I}_M(0, black(b)))$$

$$(sim_2)_{(a,c)} : sim(a,c) \leftarrow \mathscr{T}_M(\mathscr{I}_M(0.7, black(a)), \mathscr{I}_M(0, black(c)))$$

$$(sim_2)_{(b,a)} : sim(b,a) \leftarrow \mathscr{T}_M(\mathscr{I}_M(0, black)(b)), \mathscr{I}_M(0.3, black(a)))$$

$$(sim_2)_{(b,b)} : sim(b,b) \leftarrow \mathscr{T}_M(\mathscr{I}_M(0.3, black(b)), \mathscr{I}_M(0.3, black(b)))$$

$$(sim_2)_{(b,c)} : sim(b,c) \leftarrow \mathscr{T}_M(\mathscr{I}_M(0.7, black(b)), \mathscr{I}_M(0.3, black(c)))$$

$$(sim_2)_{(c,a)} : sim(c,a) \leftarrow \mathscr{T}_M(\mathscr{I}_M(0, black(c)), \mathscr{I}_M(0.7, black(a)))$$

$$(sim_2)_{(c,b)} : sim(c,b) \leftarrow \mathscr{T}_M(\mathscr{I}_M(0.3, black(c)), \mathscr{I}_M(0.7, black(b)))$$

$$(sim_2)_{(c,c)} : sim(c,c) \leftarrow \mathscr{T}_M(\mathscr{I}_M(0.7, black(c)), \mathscr{I}_M(0.7, black(c)))$$

$$constr_{(a,a)} : 0 \leftarrow \mathscr{T}_W(edge(a,a), sim(a,a))$$

$$constr_{(a,b)} : 0 \leftarrow \mathscr{T}_W(edge(a,b), sim(a,b))$$

$$constr_{(a,c)} : 0 \leftarrow \mathscr{T}_W(edge(a,c), sim(a,c))$$

$$constr_{(b,a)} : 0 \leftarrow \mathscr{T}_W(edge(b,a), sim(b,a))$$

$$constr_{(b,b)} : 0 \leftarrow \mathscr{T}_W(edge(b,b), sim(b,b))$$

$$constr_{(b,c)} : 0 \leftarrow \mathscr{T}_W(edge(b,c), sim(b,c))$$

$$constr_{(c,a)} : 0 \leftarrow \mathscr{T}_W(edge(c,a), sim(c,a))$$

$$constr_{(c,b)} : 0 \leftarrow \mathscr{T}_W(edge(c,b), sim(c,b))$$

$$constr_{(c,c)} : 0 \leftarrow \mathscr{T}_W(edge(c,c), sim(c,c))$$

One can easily verify that $\Pi^{\star}_{\mathscr{R}_{P_{fgc}},\rho_{I_1}} = I_1$. Hence, combining this with the observation that I_1 is an 1.92-model of P_{fgc} using aggregator $\mathscr{A}$ from Example 4.2, we obtain that I_1 is a 1.92-answer set of P. With aggregator $\mathscr{A}'$ from Example 4.2 it would be a $(0.7, 0.7, 0.3)$-answer set. Likewise we obtain that $I_2 = \Pi^{\star}_{\mathscr{R}_{P_{fgc}},\rho_{I_2}}$. This means that I_2 is a 2-answer set with aggregator $\mathscr{A}$ and a $(0.5, 0.5, 1)$-answer set with aggregator $\mathscr{A}'$.

Intuitively, answer sets need to be *self-producing*, i.e. by assuming the knowledge in the answer set and starting from the empty interpretation of a program, we should only be able to infer the same set. Note that Definition 4.10 supports programs with constraints, as these only influence the k-score obtained in the aggregator, and not the fixpoint computation of the reduct program; therefore constraints can only restrict the results and cannot add atoms to solutions. A first proposition shows that answer sets are models of a program, as we would expect.

Proposition 4.11. *Let M be a k-answer set of an AFASP program P. Then M is a k-model of P.*

Proof. From Definition 4.10, it immediately follows that $\mathscr{A}_P(\rho_M) \geqslant k$. □

A second proposition shows that answer sets are minimal rule models of a (constraint-free) program.

Proposition 4.12. *Let M be a k-answer set of a constraint-free AFASP program P. Then M is a minimal ρ_M-model of P.*

Proof. Let M be a k-answer set of P, then by definition of answer sets we know that $M = \Pi^{\star}_{\mathscr{R}^M_P,\rho_M}$. We will show by contradiction that no $M' \subset M$ can exist such that M' is a ρ_M-rule model of P. Suppose $M' \subset M$ such that M' is a ρ_M-rule model of P. From this it follows that for any rule $r \in P$ we have $M'(r_b) \geqslant M'(r_b^M)$ as only the arguments in which the body function is decreasing are replaced by their value in M. We can then proceed as follows:

$$M' \text{ is a } \rho_M\text{-rule model of } P$$
$$\equiv \langle \text{Def. } \rho_M\text{-rule model} \rangle \quad \forall r \in \mathscr{R}_P \cdot \mathscr{I}_r(M'(r_b), M'(r_h)) \geqslant \rho_M(r)$$
$$\equiv \langle \text{Property reduct} \rangle \quad \forall r \in \mathscr{R}_P \cdot \mathscr{I}_r(M'(r_b), M'(r_h)) \geqslant \rho_M(r^M)$$
$$\Rightarrow \langle M'(r_b) \geqslant M'(r_b^M) \rangle \quad \forall r \in \mathscr{R}_P \cdot \mathscr{I}_r(M'(r_b^M), M'(r_h)) \geqslant \rho_M(r^M)$$
$$\equiv \langle r_h \in \mathscr{B}_P, \text{Def. reduct} \rangle \quad \forall r \in \mathscr{R}_P \cdot \mathscr{I}_r(M'(r_b^M), M'(r_h^M)) \geqslant \rho_M(r^M)$$
$$\equiv \langle \text{Def. } \mathscr{R}^M_P \rangle \quad \forall r \in \mathscr{R}^M_P \cdot \mathscr{I}_r(M'(r_b), M'(r_h)) \geqslant \rho_M(r)$$
$$\equiv \langle \text{Def. } \rho_M\text{-rule model} \rangle \quad M' \text{ is a } \rho_M\text{-rule model of } \mathscr{R}^M_P$$

From Proposition 4.8 and the fact that $M = \Pi^\star_{\mathscr{R}^M_P, \rho_M}$ we know that M is the unique minimal ρ_M-rule model of $\mathscr{R}^M_P$, leading to a contradiction with the fact that M' is a ρ_M-rule model of $\mathscr{R}^M_P$ and $M' \subset M$. $\qquad\square$

As is the case for classical answer set programming and FASP, the reverse of this proposition does not hold:

Example 4.13. Consider the $\rho_\top$-rule model and interpretation $M = \{a^0, b^1\}$ of the following program P:

$$r : a \leftarrow_m \mathscr{N}_W(b)$$

with aggregator $\mathscr{A}_P(\rho) = \inf\{\rho(r) \mid r \in P\}$. As any $M' \subset M$ must satisfy $M'(a) = 0$ and $M'(b) < 1$, we obtain that $M'(r) = \mathscr{I}_M(1 - M'(b), M'(a)) = \mathscr{I}_M(1 - M'(b), 0)$. Since $\mathscr{I}_M(1 - M'(b), 0) \geqslant 1$ only if $1 - M'(b) = 0$, or $M'(b) = 1$, we obtain $M'(r) < 1$. This means that M is a minimal $\rho_\top$-rule model of P. M is not a 1-answer set of P, however, as $\Pi^\star_{\rho_M, \rho_\top} = \emptyset \neq M$.

Similar to Proposition 3.4 for FASP on page 45, there is a correspondence with minimal fixpoints of the immediate consequence operator and answer sets of (constraint-free) AFASP programs.

Lemma 4.2. *Let P be an AFASP program, then an interpretation I is a fixpoint of $\Pi_{P,\rho}$ iff it is a fixpoint of $\Pi_{\mathscr{R}^I_P, \rho}$.*

Proof. First, remark that for any expression α and interpretation I we have that $I(\alpha) = I(\alpha^I)$. Then we proceed as follows:

$$I = \Pi_{P,\rho}(I)$$
$$\equiv \langle \text{Equality of functions} \rangle \; \forall a \in \mathscr{B}_P \cdot I(a) = \Pi_{P,\rho}(I)(a)$$
$$\equiv \quad \langle \text{Def. } \Pi_{P,\rho} \rangle \quad \forall a \in \mathscr{B}_P \cdot I(a) = \sup_{r \in P_a} I_s(r, \rho(r))$$
$$\equiv \quad \langle \text{Prop. 4.1} \rangle \quad \forall a \in \mathscr{B}_P \cdot I(a) = \sup_{r \in P_a} \mathscr{T}_r(I(r_b), \rho(r))$$
$$\equiv \quad \langle I(\alpha) = I(\alpha^I) \rangle \quad \forall a \in \mathscr{B}_P \cdot I(a) = \sup_{r \in P_a} \mathscr{T}_r(I(r_b^I), \rho(r))$$
$$\equiv \; \langle \text{Def. } \Pi_{P,\rho}, \text{Def. } \mathscr{R}^I_P \rangle \; \forall a \in \mathscr{B}_P \cdot I(a) = \Pi_{\mathscr{R}^I_P, \rho}(I)(a)$$

Hence I is a fixpoint of $\Pi_{\mathscr{R}^I_P, \rho}$. $\qquad\square$

Proposition 4.13. *Let P be a constraint-free AFASP program with a k-answer set M. Then M is a minimal fixpoint of Π_{P,ρ_M}.*

Proof. From Lemma 4.2, we know that any answer set M must be a fixpoint of Π_{P,ρ_M}. Suppose M is not a minimal fixpoint and thus, that some N exists, $N \subset M$, such that N is a fixpoint of Π_{P,ρ_M}. We will show that any such N is also a ρ_M-rule model of $\mathscr{R}_P^M$, leading to $N \supseteq M$ due to Proposition 4.8, a contradiction.

First, as $N \subset M$ and since the reduct only substitutes negative subexpressions for their corresponding values, it follows that, for any expression α:

$$N(\alpha^N) \geqslant N(\alpha^M)$$

and thus, since $N(\alpha) = N(\alpha^N)$ that

$$N(\alpha) \geqslant N(\alpha^M)$$

We can now show that N is a ρ_M-rule model of $\mathscr{R}_P^M$ as follows:

$$N = \Pi_{P,\rho_M}(N)$$
$$\Rightarrow \quad \langle\text{Prop. 4.6}\rangle \quad \forall r \in \mathscr{R}_P \cdot \mathscr{I}_r(N(r_b), N(r_h)) \geqslant \rho_M(r)$$
$$\Rightarrow \quad \langle(*)\rangle \quad \forall r \in \mathscr{R}_P \cdot \mathscr{I}_r(N(r_b^M), N(r_h)) \geqslant \rho_M(r)$$
$$\equiv \quad \langle\text{Def. reduct}\rangle \quad \forall r \in \mathscr{R}_{\mathscr{R}_P^M} \cdot \mathscr{I}_r(N(r_b), N(r_h)) \geqslant \rho_M(r)$$
$$\equiv \quad \langle\text{Def. } N(r)\rangle \quad \forall r \in \mathscr{R}_P^M \cdot N(r) \geqslant \rho_M(r)$$

where (*) follows from the anti-monotonicity of $\mathscr{I}$ in its second argument and the fact that $N(r_b) \geqslant N(r_b^M)$. $\square$

The converse of Proposition 4.13 does not hold, however, as witnessed by the following example.

Example 4.14. Consider program $P_{ex4.14}$:

$$r_1 : a \leftarrow a$$
$$r_2 : p \leftarrow \mathscr{T}_M(gt(\mathscr{N}_W(p), 0), gt(\mathscr{N}_W(a), 0))$$

and the following aggregator over $([0,1], \leqslant)$: $\mathscr{A}_P = \mathscr{T}_M(\rho(r_1), \rho(r_2))$. Note that $gt(x,y)$ is defined as in Example 4.10. It is easy to verify that $M = \{a^1, p^0\}$, with $\rho_M = \rho_\top$, is the only, and thus minimal, fixpoint of $\Pi_{P_{ex4.14}, \rho_\top}$. However, $\mathscr{R}_{P_{ex4.14}}^M$ is

$$r_1^M : a \leftarrow a$$
$$r_2^M : p \leftarrow \mathscr{T}_M(1, gt(0,0))$$

It thus holds that $\Pi^*_{\mathscr{R}_{P_{ex4.14}}^M, \rho_\top} = \{a^0, p^0\} \neq M$. From this it follows that the minimal fixpoint of $\Pi_{P,\rho_\top}$ is not an answer set of $P_{ex4.14}$.

Note that $P_{ex4.14}$ is very similar to $P_{ex2.11}$ from Example 2.11 on page 24, which showed that answer sets do not correspond to minimal models of the completion. The above example illustrates our intuition about answer sets: the minimal interpretation M contains an atom a that is self-motivating and therefore unwanted. Hence, not every minimal fixpoint is intuitively suitable as an answer set.

Finally, we would like to point out that constraints can be simulated in the presented framework using decreasing functions, meaning the aforementioned results are generally applicable. The details of this simulation will be discussed at length in Chapter 5.

4.3   Illustrative Example

In this section we illustrate how the features of the AFASP framework can be useful for building real-life applications. The example we use is the "paper distribution" problem, which attracted quite some attention from the research community (see e.g. [Garg *et al.* (2008)]). Specifically, we assume that there is a set of papers (named *Papers*) about a certain set of topics (named *Topics*) that need to be assigned to reviewers (from the set *Reviewers*) with a certain *expertise* on the aforementioned topics. When assigning these papers, care must be taken to ensure that there are no *conflicts* between reviewers and authors; furthermore, each paper should have enough reviewers and no reviewer should be burdened with a high review workload. We assume that the expertise of reviewers, the topics of papers and the affiliations of both authors and reviewers are known and thus need not be calculated with an AFASP program, but are given by a set of fact rules $\mathscr{F}$. For example to denote that reviewer r_1 is an expert of degree 0.4 on topic t_3 we add the fact $f_{r_1,t_3}: expert(r_1,t_3) \leftarrow 0.4$. The rule base $\mathscr{R}_{P_{paper}}$ of the program P_{paper} solving this problem is defined over the lattice $([0,1], \leqslant)$ and consists of the set $\mathscr{F}$ together with the following rules:

$$confl: \quad conflict(R,P) \leftarrow_m \mathscr{S}_M(author(R,P),$$
$$\mathscr{T}_M(author(R',P), university(R,U),$$
$$university(R',U'), close(U,U')))$$

$$appr: \quad appropriate(R,P) \leftarrow_m \mathscr{T}_M(\mathscr{N}_W(conflict(R,P)),$$
$$\mathscr{T}_W(about(P,T), expert(R,T)))$$

$$inappr: inappropriate(R,P) \leftarrow_l \mathscr{N}_W(appropriate(R,P))$$

$$qualr: \quad overworked(R) \leftarrow_l f_1(\sum_{p \in Papers} assign(R,p))$$

$$enough: \quad enough(P) \leftarrow_m f_2(\sum_{r \in Reviewers} assign(r,P))$$

$$qualp: \quad 0 \leftarrow_l \mathscr{N}_W(enough(P))$$

$$assgn: \quad assign(R,P) \leftarrow_m geq(\mathscr{T}_M(\mathscr{N}_W(inappropriate(R,P)),$$
$$\mathscr{N}_W(overworked(R))),1)$$

where $geq(x,y) = 1$ if $x \geqslant y$ and $geq(x,y) = 0$ otherwise; furthermore f_1 is:

$$f_1(x) = \begin{cases} 0 & \text{if } x \leqslant 3 \\ \dfrac{x-3}{7} & \text{if } x \in [4,9] \\ 1 & \text{if } x \geqslant 10 \end{cases}$$

and f_2 is:

$$f_2(x) = \begin{cases} \dfrac{x}{4} & \text{if } x \leqslant 3 \\ 1 & \text{otherwise} \end{cases}$$

Note that the application of t-norms to more than one argument, such as in rule *confl*, poses no problem due to their associativity. Furthermore we recall that, due to the process of grounding (see e.g. [Baral (2003)]), a rule like *inappr* actually denotes the set of rules $\{inappr_{r,p}: inappropriate(r,p) \leftarrow_l (1 - appropriate(r,p)) \mid r \in Reviewers, p \in Papers\}$.

The intuition of the rules is as follows. The *confl* rules determine when there are potential conflicts-of-interest with reviewer neutrality, i.e. $conflict(R,P)$ quantifies the degree of conflict that diminishes the suitability of person R reviewing paper P. To keep the discussion simple, we opted to only consider the degree to which universities are close (by which we mean both geographical proximity and the affiliations between universities) to determine these conflicts. Furthermore we assumed that the set of authors is equivalent to the set of potential reviewers. The *appr* rules determine the degree to which an assignment is appropriate, based on the expertise of the reviewer ($expert(R,T)$), the topic of the paper ($about(P,T)$) and potential conflicts. We use the Łukasiewicz t-norm for combining the reviewer knowledge and paper topic to ensure that reviewers have enough knowledge about the paper content. The *inappr* rules determine the inappropriateness of a given paper assignment. The *qualr* rules determine when a reviewer is overworked. By our definition of f_1 the degree to which a reviewer is overworked scales linearly with the number of assigned papers, where less than three papers means that he is not overworked at all and ten or more papers means that he has too many papers to review. The combination of the *enough* rules and *qualp* constraints are used in the aggregator to score an answer set based on the number of reviews papers have. Due to our definition of f_2 the degree to which a paper is considered to have enough reviewers scales linearly, where 4 or more reviewers is considered to be optimal. Last, the *assgn* rules assign papers to reviewers based on the suitability of the match between reviewer and paper and bearing in mind the workload of reviewers.

Note that the *inappr*, *qualr*, and *qualp* rules are all evaluated with a Łukasiewicz implicator. The reason for this is that the former rules are allowed to be partially fulfilled and we want their fulfillment to change gradually, while the other rules should be completely fulfilled, hence an arbitrary residual implicator can be used for their evaluation. The effect of allowing the *inappr* to be partially satisfied is that we can underestimate the inappropriateness score when this leads to better reviewer assignments. For example, if a certain paper has a low number of reviewers, we can opt to also include a reviewer that is less familiar with the topics of the paper in this way. Furthermore, note that there is a strong interaction between the *assgn*, *inappr*, and *qualr* rules: if no reviewer is assigned a paper, the *assgn* rule is triggered for that reviewer and a paper is correspondingly assigned to him; this in turn leads to an increasing *overworked* score, leading to either fewer remaining assignments or a violation of the overworked constraint if this is needed to ensure that each paper has enough reviews for example.

One example of an aggregator function for P_{paper} is

$$\mathscr{A}_{P_{paper}}(\rho) = E_1(\rho) \cdot E_2(\rho) \cdot (E_3(\rho) + 10 \cdot E_4(\rho) + 20 \cdot E_5(\rho)) \tag{4.6}$$

where

$$E_1(\rho) = \min\{\rho(f) \mid f \in \mathscr{F}\} \geqslant 1$$
$$E_2(\rho) = \min\{\min(\rho(confl_{r,p}), \rho(appr_{r,p}), \rho(enough_p), \rho(assgn_{r,p}))$$
$$\mid r \in Reviewers, p \in Papers\} \geqslant 1$$
$$E_3(\rho) = \sum\{\rho(inappr_{r,p}) \mid r \in Reviewers, p \in Papers\}$$
$$E_4(\rho) = \sum\{\rho(qualp_p) \mid p \in Papers\}$$

$$E_5(\rho) = \sum \{\rho(qualr_r) \mid r \in Reviewers\}$$

The preorder for the aggregator is $(\mathbb{R}, \leqslant)$. The aggregation expression ensures that the *confl*, *appr*, *enough*, and *assgn* rules are completely fulfilled and allows partial fulfillment of the *inappr*, *qualr*, and *qualp* rules. The weights in the expression state that solutions in which reviewers are not overworked are better than solutions in which some reviewer is assigned a paper about a topic the reviewer is not familiar with or where papers do not have a lot of reviews. This can be seen from the fact that the *qualr* rules are satisfied to a lower degree when we underestimate *overworked*(R), i.e. when we attach a lower value to *overworked*(R) than the one warranted, when this allows us to find a solution in which papers have an appropriate number of reviewers. Thus the *qualr* rules are less fulfilled when reviewers are actually more overworked, meaning that giving the highest weight to these rules in the aggregator makes it more important to estimate the *overworked*(R) values correctly.

As an example, suppose *Papers* = $\{p_1, \ldots, p_{10}\}$, *Authors* = $\{a_1, \ldots, a_{10}\}$ such that $author(a_i, p_i) = 1$ for any $i \in 1 \ldots 10$ and *Universities* = $\{u_1, \ldots, u_{10}\}$ such that $university(a_i, u_i) = 1$ for any $i \in 1 \ldots 10$. Furthermore, suppose *Reviewers* = $\{r_1, \ldots, r_5\}$, *Universities'* = $\{u'_1, \ldots, u'_5\}$ such that $university(r_i, u'_i) = 1$ for any $i \in 1 \ldots 5$. Tables 4.1 to 4.3 on page 93 then respectively give the *about*, *expert* and *close* scores. Note that for any answer set of this program, the value of these atoms must be those from the afore-mentioned tables as they are added to the program as fact rules that must be completely satisfied, i.e. things that must be true in any answer set. In Tables 4.4 to 4.5 on page 94 the corresponding conflict and appropriateness scores are shown. Note that the degree of conflict $confl(r_i, p_j)$ of reviewer r_i and paper p_j is equivalent to the degree of closeness $close(u'_i, u_j)$ of the affiliation u_i of r_i and the affiliation u_j of the author of paper p_j. Further-more note that, as the *confl* and *appr* scores directly depend on the atoms given as facts and since the rules defining these atoms always need to be completely satisfied, these atoms must also have the same score in any answer set of P_{paper}. Although the *inappropriate* scores are also only dependent on the *appropriate* atoms, the rules defining these atoms can be partially satisfied, meaning the *inappropriate* scores can be lower than the corre-sponding $\mathcal{N}_W(appropriate)$ scores. Hence the difference between answer sets will be in the *overworked*, *inappropriate*, *enough* and *assign* scores.

Now, consider an approximate answer set A_1 with assignments as given in Table 4.6. The corresponding *inappropriate* scores can be found in Table 4.7 on page 95. One can check that A_1 indeed is an answer set by checking whether $\Pi^{\star}_{P^{A_1},\rho_{A_1}} = A_1$. For example, for $inappropriate(r_1,p_1)$ we can see that there is only one rule with $inappropriate(r_1,p_1)$ in its head, viz. $inappr_{r_1,p_1}$. Now the reduct of this rule is

$$inappr^{A_1}_{r_1,p_1} : inappropriate(r_1,p_1) \leftarrow_l A_1(\mathcal{N}_W(appropriate(r_1,p_1)))$$

which, by Table 4.5 on page 94, is equivalent to

$$inappr^{A_1}_{r_1,p_1} : inappropriate(r_1,p_1) \leftarrow_l 0.5 \tag{4.7}$$

We can also compute $\rho_{A_1}(inappr_{r_1,p_1})$ as

$$\rho_{A_1}(inappr_{r_1,p_1}) = A_1(inappropriate(r_1,p_1) \leftarrow_l 1 - appropriate(r_1,p_1))$$

which, by Table 4.5 and Table 4.7, is equal to

$$\rho_{A_1}(inappr_{r_1,p_1}) = \mathcal{I}_W(0.5,0) = 0.5 \tag{4.8}$$

Now using (4.7) and (4.8) we know that

$$\Pi^{\star}_{P^{A_1},\rho_{A_1}}(inappropriate(r_1,p_1)) = \mathcal{I}_W(A_1(0.5),\rho_{A_1}(inappr_{r_1,p_1}))$$

$$= \mathcal{I}_W(0.5,0.5)$$

$$= 0$$

$$= A_1(inappropriate(r_1,p_1))$$

One can check that for all other atoms $l \in \mathcal{B}_{P_{paper}}$ we also obtain that $\Pi^{\star}_{P^{A_1},\rho_{A_1}}(l) = A_1(l)$ and thus that A_1 is an answer set of P_{paper}.

Now, from the $inappropriate$ scores in Table 4.7, we know that $\rho_{A_1}(inappr_{r_1,p_1}) = 0.5$ by (4.8). Likewise we can see from Table 4.5 and Table 4.7 that

$$A_1(inappr_{r_1,p_4}) = \mathcal{I}_W(\mathcal{N}_W(A_1(appropriate(r_1,p_4))),A_1(inappropriate(r_1,p_4)))$$

$$= \mathcal{I}_W(0.8,0.8) = 1$$

The values of $inappr_{r,p}$ for any $r \in Reviewers$ and $p \in Papers$ follow in the same fashion and thus we can compute

$$E_3(\rho_{A_1}) = \sum\{A_1(inappr_{r,p}) \mid r \in Reviewers, p \in Papers\} = 385/10$$

As the $enough$ rules should always be completely satisfied, we have that $enough(p)$ for a certain paper p should always be equal to $f_2(\sum\{assign(r,p) \mid r \in Reviewers\})$. Due to each paper having three reviewers in A_1 we then know that $A_1(enough(p))$ for any paper p will be equal to $f_2(3) = 3/4$. This means that for any $qualp_p$ rule we have that $A_1(qualp_p) = 3/4$. As there are 10 papers in total we can thus compute:

$$E_4(\rho_{A_1}) = \sum\{A_1(qualp_p) \mid p \in Papers\}$$

$$= \sum \{(3/4) \mid p \in \textit{Papers}\}$$

$$= 10 \cdot (3/4)$$

$$= 15/2$$

Now, in this answer set we have that, even though reviewer r_1 has 6 reviews, $A_1(\textit{overworked}(r)) = 0$ for each assigned reviewer r; thus for some reviewers we underestimate their degree of being overworked to ensure that papers have enough reviews. From the foregoing, we can compute

$$E_5(\rho_{A_1}) = \sum \{A_1(\textit{qualr}_r) \mid r \in \textit{Reviewers}\}$$

$$= \sum \{(f_1(\sum \{A_1(\textit{assign}(r,p)) \mid p \in \textit{Papers}\})) \mathscr{I}(,l)0 \mid r \in \textit{Reviewers}\}$$

$$= \sum \{1 - (f_1(\sum \{A_1(\textit{assign}(r,p)) \mid p \in \textit{Papers}\})) \mid r \in \textit{Reviewers}\}$$

$$= 19/7$$

Hence we obtain that

$$\mathscr{A}_{P_{paper}}(\rho_{A_1}) = E_1(\rho_{A_1}) \cdot E_2(\rho_{A_1}) \cdot (E_3(\rho_{A_1}) + 10 \cdot E_4(\rho_{A_1}) + 20 \cdot E_5(\rho_{A_1}))$$

$$= 2349/14$$

$$\approx 167.8$$

There is room for improvement, however, as this answer set clearly contains a high work burden for some reviewers, while creating a minimal workload for others. Due to the nature of our aggregator expression, we can spread the papers among reviewers, potentially giving papers to reviewers with a lower knowledge of the domain, to obtain a better answer set. Answer set A_2, for which the assignments are given in Table 4.6, relieves the burden of reviewers r_3 and r_5 by assigning more reviews to reviewer r_4. Computing the value of the aggregator expression, we first obtain from the *inappropriate* scores in Table 4.8 that $E_3(\rho_{A_2}) = \sum \{A_2(\textit{inappr}_{r,p}) \mid r \in \textit{Reviewers}, p \in \textit{Papers}\} = 371/10$; furthermore we can compute in a similar fashion as for A_1 that $E_4(\rho_{A_2}) = \sum \{A_2(\textit{qualp}_p) \mid p \in \textit{Papers}\} = 15/2$ as every paper again has three reviewers assigned. Now, by calculating the assignments per reviewer we obtain $E_5(\rho_{A_2}) = \sum \{A_2(\textit{qualr}_r) \mid r \in \textit{Reviewers}\} = 20/7$. The foregoing shows $\mathscr{A}_{P_{paper}}(\rho_{A_2}) = 11847/70 \approx 169.2$, hence answer set A_2 is more suitable than A_1, as we expected.

4.4 Relationship to Existing Approaches

The combination of answer set programming and logic programming with uncertainty and many-valued theories has received a great deal of attention over the past years.

Among others, there have been extensions of logic programming using probabilistic reasoning [Damásio and Pereira (2000); Fuhr (2000); Lukasiewicz (1998, 1999); Ng and Subrahmanian (1993, 1994); Straccia (2008)], possibilistic reasoning [Alsinet *et al.* (2002); Nicolas *et al.* (2005, 2006)], fuzzy reasoning [Cao (2000); Ishizuka and Kanai (1985); Lukasiewicz (2006); Lukasiewicz and Straccia (2007a,b); Madrid and Ojeda-Aciego (2008, 2009); Saad (2009a); Straccia (2008); Van Nieuwenborgh *et al.* (2007b); Vojtás (2001); Wagner (1998); Lukasiewicz and Straccia (2010)], and more general many-valued or uncertainty reasoning [Damásio *et al.* (2004); Damásio *et al.* (2007); Damásio and Pereira (2001a,b, 2004); Emden (1986); Fitting (1991); Kifer and Li (1988); Kifer and Subrahmanian (1992); Lakshmanan (1994); Lakshmanan and Sadri (1994a, 1997); Lakshmanan and Shiri (2001); Lakshmanan (1997); Loyer and Straccia (2002, 2003); Nerode *et al.* (1997); Shapiro (1983); Straccia (2005, 2006a); Straccia *et al.* (2009); Subrahmanian (1994); Loyer and Straccia (2009)]. Roughly, one can divide [Straccia (2006a)] these approaches in two classes, viz. *implication-based* (IB) and *annotation-based* (AB) frameworks. In the implication-based setting a rule is generally of the form

$$a \xleftarrow{w} f(b_1, \ldots, b_n; c_1, \ldots, c_m)$$

where a is an atom, f is a total, finitely computable $\mathscr{L}^{n+m} \to \mathscr{L}$ function that is increasing in its n first arguments and decreasing in its m last and $w \in \mathscr{L}$, with $\mathscr{L}$ the lattice used for truth values. For convenience, we will use α as a short-hand for $f(b_1, \ldots, b_n; c_1, \ldots, c_m)$. Intuitively, such a rule denotes that in any model of the program the truth degree of the implication $\mathscr{I}(\alpha, a)$ must be greater than or equal to the weight w. In the annotation-based approaches one considers *annotations*, which are either constants from the truth lattice $\mathscr{L}$, variables ranging over this truth lattice, or functions over elements of this truth lattice applied to annotations. A rule is then of the form

$$a : \mu \leftarrow b_1 : \mu_1, \ldots, b_n : \mu_n$$

where $a, a_1, \ldots, a_n$ are atoms and $\mu, \mu_1, \ldots, \mu_n$ are annotations. Intuitively, an annotated rule denotes that if the certainty of each b_i, $1 \leqslant i \leqslant n$, is at least μ_i, then the certainty of a is at least μ. The links between these two approaches are well-studied in e.g. [Damásio and Pereira (2004); Kifer and Subrahmanian (1992); Lakshmanan and Shiri (2001); Lakshmanan (1997)] and we will therefore not repeat these results. In this section, we give an overview of these related approaches and study the links between our framework and related proposals.

4.4.1 Fuzzy and Many-Valued Logic Programming Without Partial Rule Satisfaction

Many proposals for fuzzy and many-valued logic programming with rules that have to be completely fulfilled have been published. In this category one finds most annotation-based (AB) approaches, e.g. [Cao (2000); Kifer and Li (1988); Kifer and Subrahmanian (1992); Saad (2009a); Straccia (2006a); Subrahmanian (1994)] and some implication-based (IB) approaches where the weight of each rule is 1, e.g. [Damásio and Pereira (2001a,b, 2004); Lakshmanan and Sadri (1994a)]. The latter includes the FASP framework we discussed in Chapter 3. Some of these proposals only contain monotonic functions in rules (e.g. the AB approach from [Cao (2000); Kifer and Subrahmanian (1992)] and the IB approaches from [Damásio and Pereira (2001b, 2004); Lakshmanan and Sadri (1994a)]), while others feature negation (e.g. the AB approaches from [Kifer and Li (1988); Saad (2009a); Straccia (2006a); Subrahmanian (1994)]) or even arbitrary decreasing functions (e.g. the IB approach from [Damásio and Pereira (2001a)]). These proposals differ from ours as they do not incorporate the idea of partial rule satisfaction.

We can readily embed the IB approaches in our framework by supplying these programs with the infimum aggregator. When modeled like this, the 1-answer sets of the embedding will correspond exactly to the answer sets of programs from the aforementioned frameworks. Thanks to this embedding we also inherit the modeling power that is already present in some of these proposals. For example, from the embeddings shown in [Damásio and Pereira (2000, 2004)], and using the fact that we can embed [Damásio and Pereira (2001a)] in our approach, we inherit the capacity to model Generalized Annotated Logic Programs [Kifer and Subrahmanian (1992)], Probabilistic Deductive Databases [Lakshmanan and Sadri (1994b)], Possibilistic Logic Programming [Dubois et al. (1991)], Hybrid Probabilistic Logic Programs [Dekhtyar and Subrahmanian (1997)][2] and Fuzzy Logic Programming [Vojtás (2001)].

The AB approach from [Cao (2000)] is interesting in that annotations are actually fuzzy sets, which allows for an intuitive modeling language. Whether the semantics of this specific framework can be truthfully embedded in our approach is not immediately clear, but as the family of all fuzzy sets in a given universe forms a complete lattice, when equipped with the Zadeh intersection and union[3], the use of fuzzy sets, together with functions over

---

[2]Note that the translation process in [Damásio and Pereira (2000)] is exponential in the size of the program, but, as the authors point out, this is to be expected as reasoning in these programs in most cases is exponential.

[3]For two mappings A and B from X to $[0,1]$ the Zadeh union and intersection are the $X \to [0,1]$ mappings $\cup$ and $\cap$ respectively defined as $(A \cup B)(x) = \max(A(x), B(x))$ and $(A \cap B)(x) = \min(A(x), B(x))$.

fuzzy sets is certainly possible in the AFASP language.

Another interesting approach is the use of bilattices for giving the semantics of logic programs, as was initiated by Fitting in [Fitting (1991)]. It turns out that by using bilattices an elegant characterization of many-valued answer set programming can be shown [Loyer and Straccia (2006)] that clarifies the role of the closed world assumption in (many-valued) logic programming [Loyer and Straccia (2005)]. Furthermore, this characterization can be used for defining a top-down query procedure over many-valued logic programs [Straccia (2007, 2006b)].

4.4.2 *Weighted Rule Satisfaction Approaches*

Some IB approaches to fuzzy and many-valued logic programming feature partial rule fulfillment by adding "weights" to rules (e.g. [Damásio *et al.* (2004); Damásio *et al.* (2007); Emden (1986); Lakshmanan and Shiri (2001); Lakshmanan (1997); Loyer and Straccia (2002, 2003); Lukasiewicz (2006); Lukasiewicz and Straccia (2007a); Madrid and Ojeda-Aciego (2008, 2009, 2010a,b); Shapiro (1983); Mateis (2000, 1999)]). These weights are specified manually and they reflect the minimum degree of fulfillment required for a rule. Formally, such a rule takes on the form of

$$a \xleftarrow{w} \alpha$$

where a is an atom, α is a body expression, $\leftarrow$ is a residual implicator over $[0,1]$ and w is a value of $[0,1]$. We will use r_h and r_b to refer to the head, resp. the body of a rule r as usual, and r_w to refer to the weight w. In the case of [Emden (1986); Lukasiewicz (2006); Lukasiewicz and Straccia (2007a); Madrid and Ojeda-Aciego (2008, 2009); Shapiro (1983); Mateis (2000, 1999)], the bodies of rules are restricted to combinations of triangular norms, possibly with negation-as-failure literals in [Lukasiewicz (2006); Lukasiewicz and Straccia (2007a); Madrid and Ojeda-Aciego (2008, 2009, 2010a,b)], whereas in [Damásio *et al.* (2004); Damásio *et al.* (2007); Lakshmanan and Shiri (2001); Lakshmanan (1997); Loyer and Straccia (2002, 2003)] the bodies consist of monotonically increasing functions, where some approaches do not feature non-monotonic negation [Damásio *et al.* (2004); Damásio *et al.* (2007); Lakshmanan and Shiri (2001); Lakshmanan (1997)] and others feature negation under the well-founded semantics [Loyer and Straccia (2002, 2003)]. Furthermore, [Mateis (2000, 1999); Lukasiewicz and Straccia (2007a)] allow disjunctions in the head of rules and [Damásio *et al.* (2004)] allows a combination of multiple lattices to be used. This last feature is obtained in the AFASP setting by using the Cartesian product of all these lattices as the lattice for program rules and using the corresponding projections to extend the operators to this product lattice.

The semantics of a program consisting of weighted rules without negation-as-failure is defined in two ways in the literature. We will take [Lukasiewicz and Straccia (2007a)] and [Damásio *et al.* (2004)] as examples of these two methods, but the following discussion equally applies to all the approaches mentioned earlier, barring some minor syntactical issues. In the case of [Lukasiewicz and Straccia (2007a)], an interpretation M is called a **model** of a program P when for all r in P it holds that $M(r_h) \geqslant \mathscr{T}_r(M(r_b), r_w)$. **Answer sets** of these programs are then defined as minimal models. In [Damásio *et al.* (2004)], answer sets are defined as the least fixpoints of an **immediate consequence operator**, defined for a program P, interpretation I of P and atom $l \in \mathscr{B}_P$, as:

$$\Pi_P(I)(l) = \sup\{\mathscr{T}_r(I(r_b), r_w) \mid r \in P_l\}$$

It is known that these two semantics coincide, which can also be shown using the results on AFASP, as demonstrated below.

Note that due to Proposition 4.1, it holds that $\Pi_P = \Pi_{P,\rho_w}$, where $\rho_w(r) = r_w$. Hence, for simple AFASP programs, the semantics of [Damásio *et al.* (2004)] can be obtained by taking the least fixpoint w.r.t. the rule interpretation corresponding to the rule weights. Furthermore, from Proposition 4.8, we know that the least fixpoint of Π_{P,ρ_w} corresponds to the minimal ρ_w-rule model of P. An interpretation M is a ρ_w-rule model of P iff for each rule $r \in P$ it holds that $M(r_h \leftarrow r_b) \geqslant \rho_w(r)$ and hence, by the residuation principle, that $M(r_h) \geqslant \mathscr{T}_r(M(r_b), \rho_w(r))$. This means that ρ_w-rule models correspond to models in the sense of [Lukasiewicz and Straccia (2007a)]. Hence the semantics of [Lukasiewicz and Straccia (2007a)] and [Damásio *et al.* (2004)] coincide and can both be generated from a simple AFASP program.

Furthermore, due to the equivalence between Π_P and Π_{P,ρ_w}, we can use the termination conditions from [Damásio *et al.* (2004)] to determine structural conditions that ensure that the computation of the least fixpoint of $\Pi_{P,\rho}$ ends.

Note that, different to AFASP, programs with weight rules without negation-as-failure only have a single answer set corresponding to the minimal model satisfying the rules to the stated weights. This means that the weight of a rule should not simply be seen as the minimal degree of satisfaction, but that the semantics of these programs correspond to a cautious use of the rules and their weights.

At first, one might think that these semantics can easily be embedded in the AFASP framework by moving the weights into the aggregator expression and using them as lower bounds on the satisfaction of their corresponding rules. Formally, this means that we define for a program P in the sense of [Damásio *et al.* (2004); Lukasiewicz and Straccia (2007a)] and rule base $\{r_1, \ldots, r_n\}$ with corresponding weights $w_1, \ldots, w_n$, the program P' with rule base $\mathscr{R}_{P'} = \{r_i : r_h \leftarrow r_b \mid i \in 1 \ldots n\}$ and aggregator expression $\mathscr{A}_{P'}(\rho) = (\rho(r_1) \geqslant w_1) \wedge \ldots \wedge (\rho(r_n) \geqslant w_n)$. Note that in the former we regard $\geqslant$ as a boolean expressing and identify 0 with *False* and 1 with *True*. The semantics of programs P and P' do not coincide, however, as shown in the following example.

Example 4.15. Let P be a program in the sense of [Damásio *et al.* (2004); Lukasiewicz and Straccia (2007a)] with rule base $\mathscr{R}_P = \{r : a \xleftarrow{0.5}_m 1\}$. It is easy to see that the unique answer set of this program is $\{a^{0.5}\}$. The corresponding AFASP program P' with rule base $\mathscr{R}_{P'} = \{r : a \leftarrow_m 1\}$ and aggregator expression $\mathscr{A}_{P'}(\rho) = \rho(r) \geqslant 0.5$, however, has multiple k-answer sets for varying $k \in [0,1]$, such as the 1-answer set $\{a^1\}$. The original answer set of P is only an 0.5-answer set of P'.

A proper embedding of these semantics in the AFASP framework can be obtained as follows. Suppose P is a program with weighted rules, then the corresponding AFASP program P_{weight} is defined as

$$P_{weight} = \{r_h \leftarrow \mathscr{T}_r(r_b, r_w) \mid r \in P\}$$

The lattice to be used for evaluating the rules is then $([0,1], \leqslant)$, the aggregator lattice is $(\{0,1\}, \leqslant)$. The aggregator expression is given as

$$\mathscr{A}_{P_{weight}}(\rho) = \forall r \in P_{weight} \cdot (\rho(r) = 1)$$

Example 4.16. Consider program P from Example 4.15. Using the proper embedding discussed above we obtain an AFASP program P_{weight} with rule base $\mathscr{R}_{P_{weight}} = \{r : a \leftarrow_m \mathscr{T}_M(1, 0.5)\}$ and aggregator expression $\mathscr{A}_{P_{weight}} = (\rho(r) = 1)$. The 1-answer set of P_{weight} is now $\{a^{0.5}\}$, which corresponds to the answer set of P.

The following proposition shows that for simple AFASP programs, this is indeed a truthful embedding of these semantics:

Proposition 4.14. *Let P be a simple AFASP program in the sense of [Damásio et al. (2004)]. Then A is a 1-answer set of P_{weight} iff $A = \Pi_P^*$.*

Proof. First, remark that there is only a single rule interpretation ρ such that $\forall r \in P_{weight} \cdot \rho(r) = 1$ holds, viz. $\rho_\top$. As A is only a 1-answer set of P_{weight} iff $A = \Pi_{P,\rho}^*$ for some rule interpretation satisfying $\forall r \in P_{weight} \cdot \rho(r) = 1$ due to Corollary 4.2, it must hold that there is a unique 1-answer set A of P_{weight} where $A = \Pi_{P,\rho_\top}^*$. We can now show that $\Pi_P = \Pi_{P,\rho_\top}$, leading to the stated equivalence, as follows. Suppose I is some interpretation of P (and hence also of P_{weight}) and $l \in \mathscr{B}_P$ (and hence also $l \in \mathscr{B}_{P_{weight}}$), then:

$$
\begin{aligned}
\Pi_P(I)(l) = & \quad \langle \text{Def. } \Pi_P \rangle & \sup\{\mathscr{T}_r(I(r_b), r_w)I \mid r \in P_l\} \\
= & \quad \langle \text{Def. } P_{weight} \rangle & \sup\{I(r_b) \mid r \in (P_{weight})_l\} \\
= & \quad \langle \text{Def. } \rho_\top \rangle & \sup\{\mathscr{T}_r(I(r_b), \rho_\top(r))I \mid r \in (P_{weight})_l\} \\
= & \quad \langle \text{Def. } \Pi_{P_{weight}, \rho_\top} \rangle & \Pi_{P_{weight}, \rho_\top}(I)(l)
\end{aligned}
$$

From this, the stated readily follows.   □

For approaches featuring negation-as-failure under the answer set semantics in the body of rules, we will again take [Lukasiewicz and Straccia (2007a)] as a representative example. Although the approaches in [Madrid and Ojeda-Aciego (2008, 2009)] are slightly different in that the reduct operation moves the value of the negated literals in the weight of the rule instead of directly substituting it in the rule body, the net result is the same. Negation-as-failure in this approach is denoted as $not_{\mathcal{N}} l$, where l is an atom and $\mathcal{N}$ a negator over $[0, 1]$. If P is a program with negation-as-failure in the sense of [Lukasiewicz and Straccia (2007a)], then an interpretation A is called an **answer set** of P if A is the answer set of P^A, where P^A is a generalized Gelfond-Lifschitz transformation replacing all negation-as-failure literals $not_{\mathcal{N}} l$ by the value $\mathcal{N}(A(l))$. It is easy to see that this Gelfond-Lifschitz transformation is a special case of the reduct we introduced for FASP programs. From this, it easily follows that the embedding mentioned before still works in the presence of negation-as-failure. Hence we obtain the following proposition.

Proposition 4.15. *Let P be a program in the sense of [Lukasiewicz and Straccia (2007a)]. Then A is a 1-answer set of P_{weight} iff A is an answer set of P in the sense of [Lukasiewicz and Straccia (2007a)].*

Proof.   The proof follows easily from Proposition 4.14 and the fact that the Gelfond-Lifschitz reduct introduced in [Lukasiewicz and Straccia (2007a)] is a special case of our reduct.   □

Although these proposals feature partial rule satisfaction and are therefore better equipped to model real-life phenomena than previous proposals, the use of weights introduces the new problem of "weight-guessing". The AFASP framework eliminates the weight-guessing problem by using an aggregator expression, which encodes which combinations of partially satisfied rules are more desirable than others. In this light, one could think of AFASP programs as programs with *variables* as rule-weights instead of fixed weights, where the variables must be chosen according to the aggregator expression. In effect, due to Corollary 4.2 and the fact that rule interpretations are analogous to weights on rules, this means that semantically, a single AFASP program corresponds to a set of programs with weights. This shows that the aggregator expression has a substantial modeling advantage over attaching arbitrary weights.

Interestingly, in [Madrid and Ojeda-Aciego (2010a,b)], a measure is introduced that shows how the weights of the rules of a program without stable models should be increased or decreased to obtain a new program with stable models. This is related our approach, where rule weights are variable and can be changed to obtain approximate answer sets, if none exists. Our approach differs in the fact that we do not have predefined weights on rules and assume that the best solution is the solution satisfying all the rules best. Furthermore, due to the aggregator, we can compare approximate answer sets in our framework with a preference order that is chosen by the programmer.

4.4.3 *Van Nieuwenborgh* et al.

In [Van Nieuwenborgh *et al.* (2007b)], a language that is similar to AFASP is introduced. Our presented approach generalizes this framework by allowing a much richer vocabulary of expressions to use in rules and by allowing more sophisticated aggregator expressions. Specifically, we allow arbitrary monotonic functions in rule bodies, whereas [Van Nieuwenborgh *et al.* (2007b)] only allows t-norms and negators in bodies. Furthermore, we base our semantics on fixpoints, which more clearly shows the link between other FASP approaches, and also fixes a problem with the semantics of [Van Nieuwenborgh *et al.* (2007b)] when generalizing to arbitrary lattices as truth values, as demonstrated below. Moreover, it is not clear how the semantics of [Van Nieuwenborgh *et al.* (2007b)] can be extended to deal with arbitrary monotonic functions in rule bodies, where this is straightforward in our fixpoint approach.

Semantically, in [Van Nieuwenborgh *et al.* (2007b)], an answer set M has a degree k, which, as in the present approach, reflects the value of an *aggregator* function that combines the degree of satisfaction of the rules in the program. However, as opposed to the present approach, this aggregator must have a value in the same lattice as the one used for the rules. As shown throughout the examples in this chapter, our more general aggregator can be advantageous for modeling certain real-life problems. Furthermore, an answer set is defined in [Van Nieuwenborgh *et al.* (2007b)] as a model that is free from *unfounded sets*. Intuitively, the concept of unfounded set provides a direct formalization of "badly motivated" (as described in Section 4.2.2) conclusions.

Definition 4.11. A set X of atoms is called **unfounded** w.r.t. an interpretation I of a program P iff for all $a \in X$, every rule $r \in P_a$ satisfies either

(i) $X \cap r_b^+ \neq \emptyset$, or

(ii) $I_s(a, \rho_I(r)) < I(a)$, or

(iii) $I(r_b) = 0$

where for $r_b = \mathscr{T}(b_1, \ldots, b_n, \mathscr{N}_1(c_1), \ldots, \mathscr{N}_m(c_m))$, with $\mathscr{T}$ an arbitrary t-norm and $\mathscr{N}_i$ arbitrary negators, we define $r_b^+ = \{b_1, \ldots, b_n\}$.

Intuitively, condition (i) above describes a circular motivation while (ii) asserts that a is overvalued w.r.t. r. Condition (iii) is needed to ensure that the semantics are a proper generalization of the classical semantics. An interpretation I is called **unfounded-free** iff $supp(I) \cap X = \emptyset$ for any set X that is unfounded w.r.t. I.[4] Answer sets to a degree k are then defined in [Van Nieuwenborgh *et al.* (2007b)] as those k-models that are unfounded-free. A nice feature is that this single definition covers any program P, regardless of whether it is positive, or has constraint rules. One may wonder whether the concept of unfounded set can be generalized to AFASP programs. For example, a natural generalization would simply replace the circularity definition $X \cap r_b \neq \emptyset$ above by "some element of X occurs as an argument in which the body expression r_b is increasing". However, this approach fails, as illustrated by the program P from Example 4.10 where it can easily be verified that $\{a\}$ would be unfounded w.r.t. the interpretation $\{a^1\}$ since $r_1 : a \leftarrow_m 0.2$ satisfies (ii) above while $r_2 : a \leftarrow_m gt(a, 0)$ satisfies (i). Note that this failure is only due to the presence of $gt(a, 0)$ in rule bodies, which are not allowed in the framework presented in [Van Nieuwenborgh *et al.* (2007b)].

We now show the novel result that when a total ordering is used in the lattice, the semantics of [Van Nieuwenborgh *et al.* (2007b)] correspond to the semantics of our fixpoint definition (when obeying the syntactic restrictions noted above). First, note that the concept of k-models in [Van Nieuwenborgh *et al.* (2007b)] coincides with Definition 4.5 on page 57. Hence, we only need to show that an interpretation I of P is unfounded-free iff $I = \Pi_{P^I, \rho_I}$.

Lemma 4.3. *Let P be an AFASP program. For any interpretation I of P it holds that $I = \Pi_{P, \rho_I}(I)$ iff $I = \Pi_{\mathscr{R}_P^I, \rho_I}(I)$.*

Proof. Follows trivially by the construction of $\mathscr{R}_P^I$. □

---

[4]We recall that for an interpretation I of a program P the set $supp(I)$ contains all atoms $a \in \mathscr{B}_P$ for which $I(a) > 0$. See Definition 2.19 on page 26.

Lemma 4.4. *Let P be an AFASP program with only t-norms and negators in rule bodies. Then any unfounded-free interpretation I of P is a fixpoint of* Π_{P,ρ_I}.

Proof. Let I be an unfounded-free interpretation of P. We show that $I(a) = \sup\{I_s(r,\rho_I(r)) \mid r \in P_a\} = \Pi_{P,\rho_I}(I)(a)$ for any $a \in \mathcal{B}_P$, from which the stated readily follows. The proof is split into the case for $a \in supp(I)$ and $a \notin supp(I)$. For any $a \in supp(I)$ it must hold that $\{a\}$ is not unfounded w.r.t. I, meaning that $P_a \neq \emptyset$ and there is some $r \in P_a$ such that $I(a) \leqslant I_s(r,\rho_I(r))$. Due to Proposition 4.1 on page 59 this means

$$I(a) \leqslant \mathscr{T}_r(I(r_b), \rho_I(r)) \tag{4.9}$$

By definition of ρ_I we know that for any $r' \in P_a$ we have that $\mathscr{I}_{r'}(I(r'_b), I(a)) \geqslant \rho_I(r')$. Due to Proposition 2.9 on page 31 this means $I(a) \geqslant \mathscr{T}_{r'}(I(r'_b), \rho_I(r'))$. Combining this with (4.9) and Proposition 4.1 we obtain that $I_s(r,\rho_I(r)) = I(a) \geqslant I_s(r',\rho_I(r'))$ for any $r' \in P_a$. Hence $I_s(r,\rho_I(r)) = I(a)$ is the supremum of $\{I_s(r',\rho_I(r')) \mid r' \in P_a\}$.

The case for $a \notin supp(I)$ is as follows. First, remark that in the former case we already showed that for any $r \in P_a$ we have that $I(a) \geqslant \mathscr{T}_r(I(r_b), \rho_I(r))$. Since $I(a) = 0$ this means that $I_s(r,\rho_I(r)) = 0$ for any $r \in P_a$ due to Proposition 4.1. Hence $I(a) = \sup\{I_s(r,\rho_I(r)) \mid r \in P_a\}$. $\square$

Proposition 4.16. *Let P be an AFASP program with only t-norms and negators in rule bodies. An interpretation I of P is unfounded-free iff* $I = \Pi^{\star}_{\mathscr{R}^I_P,\rho_I}$.

Proof. In [Van Nieuwenborgh *et al.* (2007b)] it was shown that the least fixpoint of $\Pi_{\mathscr{R}^I_P,\rho_I}$ must necessarily be unfounded-free (Proposition 4). Hence we only need to show that if I is unfounded-free, it is the least fixpoint of $\Pi_{\mathscr{R}^I_P,\rho_I}$.

Suppose $I \neq \Pi^{\star}_{\mathscr{R}^I_P,\rho_I}$. Then, since any unfounded-free interpretation is a fixpoint of $\Pi_{\mathscr{R}^I_P,\rho_I}$ due to Lemmas 4.3 and 4.4, it holds that some set $I' \subset I$ exists such that $I' = \Pi^{\star}_{\mathscr{R}^I_P,\rho_I}$. Consider then $U = \{u \in \mathcal{B}_P \mid I'(u) < I(u)\}$. Surely $U \subseteq supp(I)$ and hence $U \cap supp(I) \neq \emptyset$. We now show that U is unfounded with respect to I, leading to a contradiction. First, we show that for any atom $u \in U$ and rule $r \in P_u$ it holds that

$$\left(r_b^+ \cap U = \emptyset\right) \Rightarrow I_s(r,\rho_I(r)) < I(u) \tag{4.10}$$

as follows

$$r_b^+ \cap U = \emptyset$$

$$\equiv \langle \text{Def. } \cap \rangle \quad \neg \exists l \in r_b^+ \cdot l \in U$$

$$\equiv \langle \text{Duality } \forall, \exists \rangle \quad \forall l \in r_b^+ \cdot l \notin U$$

$$\equiv \langle \text{Def. } U \rangle \quad \forall l \in r_b^+ \cdot I(l) = I'(l)$$

$$\Rightarrow \langle I(l) = I(l^I) \rangle \quad I(r_b^I) = I'(r_b^I)$$

$$\equiv \langle \text{Leibniz} \rangle \quad \mathcal{T}_r(I(r_b^I), \rho_I(r^I)) = \mathcal{T}_r(I'(r_b^I), \rho_I(r^I))$$

$$\equiv \langle \text{Prop. 4.1} \rangle \quad I_s(r^I, \rho_I(r^I)) = I'_s(r^I, \rho_I(r^I))$$

$$\Rightarrow \langle \text{Monotonicity sup} \rangle \quad I_s(r^I, \rho_I(r^I)) \leqslant \sup_{r' \in \mathcal{R}_{Pu}^I} I'_s(r', \rho_I(r'))$$

$$\equiv \langle I' = \Pi_{\mathcal{R}_P^I, \rho_I}(I') \rangle \quad I_s(r, \rho_I(r^I)) \leqslant I'(u)$$

$$\Rightarrow \langle u \in U, \text{Def. } U \rangle \quad I_s(r, \rho_I(r^I)) < I(u)$$

Thus, since it follows from the Definition of r^I that $I(r_b^I) = I(r_b)$ and $\rho_I(r^I) = \rho_I(r)$, we have shown that (4.10) holds. From this equation we obtain that

$$\left(r_b^+ \cap U \neq \emptyset \right) \vee \left(I_s(r, \rho_I(r)) \right) < I(u) \right)$$

Hence

$$\left(r_b^+ \cap U \neq \emptyset \right) \vee \left(I_s(r, \rho_I(r)) \right) < I(u) \right) \vee \left(I(r_b) = 0 \right)$$

Which means U is unfounded with respect to I, a contradiction. $\qquad \square$

When the ordering used is not total, however, this equivalence is no longer valid. For example, consider the lattice $(\mathbb{B} \times \mathbb{B}, \leqslant)$ such that $(1,1)$ is the top element of the lattice, $(0,0)$ is the bottom element and $(0,0) \leqslant (0,1) \leqslant (1,1)$ and $(0,0) \leqslant (1,0) \leqslant (1,1)$. Now consider an AFASP program P, with $\mathcal{A}_P(\rho) = \inf\{\rho(r) \mid r \in P\}$, over this lattice:

$$r_1 : a \leftarrow (1,0)$$

$$r_2 : a \leftarrow (0,1)$$

According to Proposition 2.10 on page 31, any interpretation I of P that satisfies rule r_1 to the degree $(1,1)$ must obey $I(a) \geqslant (1,0)$. Likewise any interpretation I that satisfies r_2 to the degree $(1,1)$ must obey $I(a) \geqslant (0,1)$. Hence the only 1-model of P is $I = \{a^{(1,1)}\}$. However, according to rule (ii) of Definition 4.11 $\{a\}$ is an unfounded set, which means that under the unfounded-based semantics I is not an answer set of P. On the other hand, $I = \Pi_{P^I, \rho_I}^\star$, and thus I is an answer set of P according to the fixpoint semantics. If we consider rules as constraints that need to be fulfilled, the fixpoint semantics correspond better to our intuition.

4.4.4   *Valued Constraint Satisfaction Problems*

A classical constraint satisfaction problem (CSP) consists of a set of variables $X = \{x_1, \ldots, x_n\}$, a set of finite domains $D = \{d_1, \ldots, d_n\}$ such that variable x_i ranges over domain d_i, and a set of constraints C of the form $c = (X_c, R_c)$ such that $X_c \subseteq X$ is a set of variables and R_c is a relation between the variables in X_c. In Valued Constraint Satisfaction Problems (VCSPs) [Schiex *et al.* (1995)], a CSP is augmented with a cost function φ, which associates a cost to every constraint. A solution to a VCSP is then an assignment of values to the variables in X such that the aggregated cost of all violated constraints is minimal. Typically, costs are represented as real numbers, and the maximum or sum is used to aggregate.

In the crisp case it has been noted that answer set programming can be used for solving constraint satisfaction problems [Marek and Truszczyński (1999); Niemelä (1999)]. The idea is to write an answer set program containing generate rules[5] that generate possible assignments of values to each of the variables, and constraints which remove those assignments that violate any constraints. In this way the resulting answer set program models a constraint satisfaction problem in the sense that answer sets of the program correspond to the solutions of the problem under consideration. It should come as no surprise that the AFASP framework can likewise be used for modeling VCSPs, as VCSPs can be seen as CSPs with an added aggregation operator. Basically, a VCSP corresponds to an AFASP program that only uses choice rules (which are the fuzzy equivalent of generate rules, i.e. rules assigning a random truth value to a certain atom) and constraints. Hard constraints correspond to rules that are required to be greater than 1 in the aggregator, whereas soft constraints are rules whose valuation in the aggregator can be lower than 1, such as rules aggregated using the infimum. An example of the use of this paradigm is the fuzzy graph coloring program introduced in Section 4.1, where we model the constraint satisfaction problem of coloring a graph with continuous colors, given some soft and hard constraints.

4.4.5   *Answer Set Optimization*

In [Brewka (2004); Brewka *et al.* (2003)], a framework for answer set optimization is proposed. The basic idea is that one can state preference rules which are combined to define an ordering over answer sets. For example, if we have a program that generates a

---

[5]These are rules involving cyclic negation such as the ASP program $\{a \leftarrow \mathrm{not}\,b.\ b \leftarrow \mathrm{not}\,a\}$. The answer sets of this program are $\{a\}$ and $\{b\}$, hence this program allows us to choose one of two options a and b in a solution of the modeled problem.

class room schedule, this framework allows to state that if teacher *John* is teaching *Math*, we prefer *John* to also teach *Physics* as follows:

$$teaches(John, Physics) : 0 > teaches(Mark, Physics) : 1 \leftarrow teaches(John, Math)$$

A rule is of the general form

$$C_1 : p_1 > \ldots > C_k : p_k \leftarrow a_1, \ldots, a_n, \text{not}\, b_1, \ldots, \text{not}\, b_m$$

where $C_i : p_i$ encodes that the penalty associated with the rule is p_i if i is the lowest index for which the atom set C_i is true. However, the penalty of the rule is only taken into account if the conditions on the left hand side, expressed as a conjunction of atoms, are true. Different rules can then be combined using strategies, which encode importance among these preference rules. Formally, [Brewka (2004)] defines a *Preference Description Language PDL* in which one can for example write that answer sets should be ordered using the Pareto ordering on rules r_1 and r_2 as $(pareto\, r_1, r_2)$. Many other complex (combinations of) orderings can be written in this language, such as $(lex\,(pareto\, r_1, r_2), r_3)$ which denotes that two answer sets first need to be compared using the Pareto ordering on rules r_1 and r_2; if they are Pareto-equal, then one must try to discriminate between them on the basis of rule r_3.

It is clear that the ideas of this approach and the one we proposed in this chapter are very similar. In [Janssen *et al.* (2009)] we showed how this framework could be generalized to AFASP, using an appropriate aggregator. For a practical implementation of AFASP it seems interesting to adopt the same strategy of having a fixed language for specifying the aggregator. For example, we could then write an aggregator defining a lexicographical ordering over the program rules r_1, r_2, r_3 as $(lex\, r_1, r_2, r_3)$. Furthermore, the idea of computing optimal answer sets by means of a generating program and optimality checking program could also be generalized to AFASP.

4.5 Summary

When using FASP to solve continuous optimization problems it is natural to consider approximate solutions, which correspond to answer sets that satisfy some of the rules partially. Current approaches require users to annotate rules with fixed weights, however, which is not flexible and leaves the programmer with the problem of guessing the right weights.

In this chapter we have introduced aggregated fuzzy answer set programming (AFASP), which uses aggregation functions to combine the degrees to which the rules are satisfied to a single value from a preordered set. Essentially, this approach attaches variable weights to rules, where the aggregator function determines the most desirable combinations of these weights. In contrast to languages with fixed weights this means that simple AFASP programs can have multiple answer sets.

Different to a previous proposal for fuzzy answer set programming with aggregators we base our semantics on fixpoints instead of unfounded sets, allow arbitrary monotonic functions instead of only t-norms in rule bodies and decouple the aggregator from the lattice underlying the program. We have shown that the unfounded-based semantics cannot easily be generalized to programs with arbitrary monotonic functions in rule bodies, whereas this is trivial with the fixpoint semantics. Furthermore, we proved that the fixpoint semantics coincide with the unfounded-based semantics when the lattice that is used in the program is total. This is an important result that will be used extensively in Chapter 6. For non-total lattices we have moreover shown that, in contrast to the fixpoint semantics, the unfounded-based semantics produce counter-intuitive results.

We also studied AFASP itself in great detail. Most importantly we demonstrated the relations that exist between our notion of approximate models and the fixpoints of our generalization of the immediate consequence operator of FASP. For example, in Proposition 4.7 we proved the relation between minimal approximate models and the fixpoints of the the AFASP immediate consequence operator and in Proposition 4.12 we proved that answer sets correspond to certain minimal approximate models. Furthermore we showed a number of interesting properties that are also relevant for FASP languages with fixed weights. For example, in Proposition 4.5 we proved that lower rule weights will lead to smaller answer sets.

Finally, we illustrated the use of AFASP on the reviewer assignment problem. The AFASP program that solves this problem was built in the usual generate-define-test pattern and used partial rule satisfaction to rank solutions according to the workload of each reviewer and the number of reviewers that each paper has.

From the results in this chapter we can conclude that the addition of partial rule satisfaction to FASP is very useful when modeling continuous optimization problems. However, as we have seen throughout the chapter, this also makes AFASP harder to reason about than FASP. In the next chapter we therefore investigate whether AFASP and other extensions of FASP can be simulated using a simpler core language.

$about(P,T)$	t_1	t_2	t_3	t_4	t_5	t_6	t_7
p_1	0.8	1	0.2	0.4	0.2	0	0
p_2	0	0.2	0.7	0.5	0.9	0.4	0.3
p_3	1	0.1	0.1	0.2	0.3	0.2	0
p_4	0.5	0	0	1	0.2	0.4	0.8
p_5	0.3	0.9	0.8	0.9	0.4	0.2	0.1
p_6	0.6	0.8	0.3	0.7	0.8	0.3	0
p_7	0	1	1	1	0	0.3	0.1
p_8	0.9	0.2	0.1	0.7	0	0.1	1
p_9	0.1	0.7	0.1	0.2	0.1	1	0.7
p_{10}	0.7	0.6	0.6	0.3	0.2	1	0.1

Table 4.1: $about(P,T)$ scores

$expert(R,T)$	t_1	t_2	t_3	t_4	t_5	t_6	t_7
r_1	0.8	0.5	0.2	0.5	0.9	1	0
r_2	0.2	0.9	1	0.4	0.2	0.1	0.1
r_3	0.5	0.2	0.8	0.7	0.4	0.6	0.2
r_4	0	0.3	0.2	0.4	0.5	0.9	0.9
r_5	1	0.7	0.8	0.6	0.9	0.7	0.7

Table 4.2: $expert(R,T)$ scores

$close(U,U')$	u_1	u_2	u_3	u_4	u_5	u_6	u_7	u_8	u_9	u_{10}
u'_1	0.5	0.3	0.4	0.8	0.1	1	0.4	0.3	0.9	0.4
u'_2	0.5	0.8	0.5	0.4	0.4	0.5	0.1	0	0.4	0.1
u'_3	0	0	0	1	0.3	0.6	0.3	0.9	0.2	0.1
u'_4	1	0.9	0.4	0.2	0.1	1	0.5	0.2	0.9	1
u'_5	0.8	0.1	0.1	0.4	0.2	0.3	1	0.3	0.1	0.2

Table 4.3: $close(U,U')$ scores

$conflict(R,P)$	p_1	p_2	p_3	p_4	p_5	p_6	p_7	p_8	p_9	p_{10}
r_1	0.5	0.3	0.4	0.8	0.1	1	0.4	0.3	0.9	0.4
r_2	0.5	0.8	0.5	0.4	0.4	0.5	0.1	0	0.4	0.1
r_3	0	0	0	1	0.3	0.6	0.3	0.9	0.2	0.1
r_4	1	0.9	0.4	0.2	0.1	1	0.5	0.2	0.9	1
r_5	0.8	0.1	0.1	0.4	0.2	0.3	1	0.3	0.1	0.2

Table 4.4: $conflict(R,P)$ scores

$appropriate(R,P)$	p_1	p_2	p_3	p_4	p_5	p_6	p_7	p_8	p_9	p_{10}
r_1	0.5	0.7	0.6	0.2	0.4	0	0.5	0.7	0.1	0.6
r_2	0.5	0.2	0.2	0.4	0.6	0.5	0.9	0.1	0.6	0.6
r_3	0.3	0.5	0.5	0	0.6	0.4	0.7	0.1	0.6	0.6
r_4	0	0.1	0.1	0.7	0.3	0	0.4	0.8	0.1	0
r_5	0.2	0.8	0.9	0.6	0.6	0.7	0	0.7	0.7	0.7

Table 4.5: $appropriate(R,P)$ scores

assignments	A_1	A_2
p_1	r_1, r_2, r_3	r_1, r_2, r_4
p_2	r_1, r_3, r_5	r_1, r_3, r_4
p_3	r_1, r_3, r_5	r_1, r_4, r_5
p_4	r_2, r_4, r_5	r_2, r_4, r_5
p_5	r_2, r_3, r_5	r_2, r_3, r_5
p_6	r_2, r_3, r_5	r_2, r_3, r_5
p_7	r_1, r_2, r_3	r_1, r_2, r_3
p_8	r_1, r_4, r_5	r_1, r_4, r_5
p_9	r_2, r_3, r_5	r_2, r_3, r_5
p_{10}	r_1, r_3, r_5	r_1, r_3, r_5

Table 4.6: Assignments for answer sets A_1 and A_2

$inappropriate(R,P)$	p_1	p_2	p_3	p_4	p_5	p_6	p_7	p_8	p_9	p_{10}
r_1	0	0	0	0.8	0.6	1	0	0	0.9	0
r_2	0	0.8	0.8	0	0	0	0	0.9	0	0.4
r_3	0	0	0	1	0	0	0	0.9	0	0
r_4	1	0.9	0.9	0	0.7	1	0.6	0	0.9	1
r_5	0.8	0	0	0	0	0	1	0	0	0

Table 4.7: $inappropriate(R,P)$ scores for A_1

$inappropriate(R,P)$	p_1	p_2	p_3	p_4	p_5	p_6	p_7	p_8	p_9	p_{10}
r_1	0	0	0	0.8	0.6	1	0	0	0.9	0
r_2	0	0.8	0.8	0	0	0	0	0.9	0	0.4
r_3	0.7	0	0.5	1	0	0	0	0.9	0	0
r_4	0	0	0	0	0.7	1	0.6	0	0.9	1
r_5	0.8	0.2	0	0	0	0	1	0	0	0

Table 4.8: $inappropriate(R,P)$ scores for A_2

Chapter 5

Core Fuzzy Answer Set Programming

5.1 Introduction

The study of extensions of classical ASP has received a great deal of attention over the past years, including the efforts of the European Working Group on Answer Set Programming (WASP) [Niemelä (2003)]. The main objectives of such a study are (1) researching the complexity and additional expressivity which certain extensions bring; (2) investigating whether extensions can be compiled to a core language that is easy to implement, or is already implemented. Certain interesting links have been brought to light in this research. For example, it has been shown that nested expressions can be translated to disjunctive logic programs [Pearce et al. (2002)] and that aggregates can be translated to normal logic programs [Pelov et al. (2003)]. Next to these general extensions of ASP, the translation of other frameworks to ASP has also been studied. For example DLV supports abduction with penalization [Perri et al. (2005)] through its front-end by compiling this framework to a logic program with weak constraints [Buccafurri et al. (2000)]. For preferences in ASP a common implementation method is to use a meta-formalism and first generate all answer sets for a program, and then filter the most preferred ones. Though the preference extensions have a higher complexity, this method ensures that programs with preferences can still be solved using off the shelf ASP solvers such as Smodels [Simons and Niemelä (2000)] and DLV [Faber and Pfeifer (2005)].

Over the years many different FASP formalisms have been proposed. Some of these only allow arbitrary monotonic functions (e.g. [Kifer and Subrahmanian (1992)]) in rule bodies, whereas others have negation-as-failure (e.g. [Madrid and Ojeda-Aciego (2008); Straccia (2006a)]) or decreasing functions (e.g. [Damásio and Pereira (2001a)] and the FASP framework that we described in Chapter 3). In contrast to ASP, the study of whether these formalisms can be compiled to a core language has not received much attention. One no-

table exception is [Damásio and Pereira (2001a)], which has been shown to be capable
of simulating Generalized Annotated Logic Programs [Kifer and Subrahmanian (1992)],
Probabilistic Deductive Databases [Lakshmanan and Sadri (1994b)], Possibilistic Logic
Programming [Dubois *et al.* (1991)], Hybrid Probabilistic Logic Programs [Damásio and
Pereira (2000)] and Fuzzy Logic Programming [Vojtás (2001)]. However, this study ad-
dresses neither constructs in existing FASP formalisms nor their extensions. Furthermore,
it compiles the aforementioned languages to a FASP formalism that is quite involved.

In this chapter we investigate the expressivity of different constructs and extensions of
existing FASP formalisms and show that many of them can be simulated in a language
that is considerably simpler. This creates a bridge between the desire to have a rich and
expressive FASP language on one hand and the wish to have a small core theory on the
other hand. The advantage of the former is that it removes the burden from programmers
to write the simulations by hand, making the language easier to use. The advantage of the
latter is that (i) this makes it easier to reason about the language (ii) it makes it easier to
investigate links to other theories and (iii) it facilitates the implementation of the backend
of a FASP solver.

In Section 5.2, we identify a core language for FASP that is sufficient to express FASP
constructs and extensions. The FASP constructs that can be simulated are the following:

(1) **Constraints**. One of the important constructs in ASP are constraint rules, which state
   that their *body* can never be true in a valid solution of the problem under consideration.
   In Section 5.3 we show that a well-known procedure for eliminating constraints in ASP
   can be generalized to the fuzzy case.

(2) **Monotonically decreasing functions**. When generalizing ASP to a many-valued setting, various types of functions may serve as generalizations of logical connectives,
   ranging from t-norms and t-conorms to averaging operators, as well as problem-
   specific hedges. In the FASP framework introduced in Chapter 3 we have therefore
   allowed arbitrary functions whose partial mappings are increasing or decreasing. It is
   easy to see that this class covers all commonly used operators from fuzzy logic. In
   Section 5.4, we show that any function with partial mappings that are decreasing can
   be simulated using increasing functions and negators.

Furthermore, we show that the following extensions of FASP can be simulated in our core
language:

(1) **Rule aggregation**. In the previous chapter we introduced an extension of FASP allow-

ing partial rule satisfaction, called AFASP. In Section 5.5 we show how AFASP can be simulated using only rules that are required to be completely satisfied.

(2) **S-implicators**. The AFASP framework introduced in the preceding chapter limits rules to correspond to residual implicators. However, there might still be some contexts in which an S-implicator is more natural than a residual implicator. This is further motivated in Section 5.6, where we show how to simulate rules based on S-implicators.

(3) **Strong negation**. In ASP, two types of negation are used intertwiningly, resp. called negation-as-failure and strong negation. In Section 5.7 we show that the simulation of classical negation in classical ASP can be generalized to the fuzzy case.

5.2   The FASP Core Language

We introduce a core language for the FASP language we described in Chapter 3, called **core fuzzy answer set programming** (**CFASP**), which will be shown to be sufficient to express many constructs and extensions of (A)FASP. CFASP is a subset of FASP with a more restricted syntax for rules: (i) constraints are removed from the language, hence each rule has an atom in its head; (ii) rule bodies only contain monotonically increasing functions and negators. The arguments of negators are also restricted to be atoms or values from a lattice, i.e. negators can not be applied to arbitrary expressions.

Definition 5.1. Consider a set of atoms A. An **extended literal** is either an atom $a \in A$, a value from a lattice $\mathscr{L}$, or a **naf-literal** of the form $\mathscr{N}(a)$, where $\mathscr{N}$ corresponds to a negator.

Definition 5.2. Given a set of atoms A, a CFASP **rule** on a complete lattice $\mathscr{L}$ is a FASP rule of the form

$$r : a \leftarrow f(b_1, \ldots, b_n) \tag{5.1}$$

where a is an atom, f is an increasing $\mathscr{L}^n \to \mathscr{L}$ function and b_i ($1 \leqslant i \leqslant n$) are extended literals.

CFASP programs are defined as sets of CFASP rules.

Definition 5.3. A **core FASP program** (**CFASP program**) is a FASP program consisting of CFASP rules.

Note that by their definition in Section 3.2 on page 36, **simple** CFASP programs do not contain naf-literals.

5.3 Constraints

As mentioned in Section 2.2, in ASP there are special rules called **constraints**. Constraints differ from regular rules by the omission of a head literal and are used to specify that in any valid solution, the body of the rule should not be satisfied. For example, in program P_{gc} from Example 2.7 on page 19 the constraint *constr* specifies that two adjacent nodes should be differently colored. This is an important aspect of answer set programming and a necessary feature to elegantly describe many problem domains. In FASP, constraints are generalized by allowing rules of the following form:

$$fconstr : l \leftarrow f(b_1, \ldots, b_n; c_1, \ldots, c_m)$$

where l is an element of some complete lattice $\mathscr{L}$ and f is a $\mathscr{L}^{n+m} \to \mathscr{L}$ function that is increasing in its n first and decreasing in its m last arguments. Such a constraint is satisfied by an interpretation I when $l \geqslant I(f(b_1, \ldots, b_n; c_1, \ldots, c_m))$, i.e. when the truth value of the body is lower than l.

In this section we show how constraints in FASP programs on $([0, 1], \leqslant)$ can be simulated in CFASP and furthermore explain how they can be used to lock the truth value of an atom in a certain interval. To do so we extend CFASP with constraints and show that any extended program can be translated to an equivalent CFASP program. The extension is defined as follows:

Definition 5.4. Consider a set of atoms A. A CFASP$^{\perp}$ rule on a complete lattice $\mathscr{L}$ is a FASP rule on $\mathscr{L}$ of the form

$$r : a \leftarrow f(b_1, \ldots, b_n)$$

where f is an increasing $\mathscr{L}^n \to \mathscr{L}$ function, a is either an atom or a value from $\mathscr{L}$ and b_i, for $1 \leqslant i \leqslant n$ is an extended literal.

Definition 5.5. A CFASP$^{\perp}$ program on a complete lattice $\mathscr{L}$ is a FASP program consisting only of CFASP$^{\perp}$ rules.

5.3.1 Implementing Constraints

The program $P_{empty} = \{c : p \leftarrow \text{not } p\}$[1] is well-known in answer set programming because it has no classical answer sets, as shown in Example 2.6 on page 19. In fact, any program containing rule c will have no answer sets [Baral (2003)]. This peculiarity actually turns

---

[1] For convenience, we have taken the liberty of extending ASP with rule labels.

out to be useful in eliminating answer sets under certain conditions. For example, consider the following classical program P_{nondet}:

$$r_1: a \leftarrow not\, b$$
$$r_2: b \leftarrow not\, a$$

which has answer sets $\{a\}$ and $\{b\}$, as shown in Example 2.5 on page 19. If we would like to eliminate the answer sets in which b holds, we can add b to the body of rule c and add the resulting rule to the program:

$$r_1: a \leftarrow not\, b$$
$$r_2: b \leftarrow not\, a$$
$$c_b: p \leftarrow not\, p, b$$

Suppose now that A is an interpretation of $P_{nondet} \cup \{c_b\}$ such that $b \in A$. If $p \notin A$, then A is not a model of $P_{nondet} \cup \{c_b\}$ and thus A is not an answer set. If $p \in A$, then rule c_b is removed in $(P_{nondet} \cup \{c_b\})^A$. However, from this we can easily see that A is not the least fixpoint of $\Pi_{(P_{nondet} \cup \{c_b\})^A}$, hence A is not an answer set. This means that $\{a\}$ is the only answer set of $P_{nondet} \cup \{c_b\}$ and the addition of rule c_b effectively eliminated answer set $\{b\}$. Hence, adding the c_b rule in P_{nondet} has the same effect as adding the ASP constraint $\leftarrow b$. In fact, this works in general: any constraint $\leftarrow b_1, \ldots, b_n, not\, c_1, \ldots, not\, c_m$ in an ASP program P can be replaced by the ASP rule $p \leftarrow not\, p, b_1, \ldots, b_n, not\, c_1, \ldots, not\, c_m$ without changing the semantics of the program (provided that $p \notin \mathscr{B}_P$) [Baral (2003)].

The FASP program $F_{empty} = \{c: p \leftarrow \mathscr{N}(p)\}$ corresponding to P_{empty} does have answer sets, however, meaning that its useful capacity to eliminate undesired answer sets has not directly been preserved in the fuzzy setting. Using the Łukasiewicz negation for $\mathscr{N}$, for instance, it is not hard to see that $\{p^{0.5}\}$ is the unique answer set. Therefore, an adaptation of program F_{empty} is needed to eliminate undesirable answer sets in the fuzzy case. To this end, consider the following program Z:

$$Z = \{r: p \leftarrow gt(\mathscr{N}_M(p), 0)\} \tag{5.2}$$

where rule r is defined on $([0,1], \leqslant)$. The function in the body is defined as $gt(x,y) = 1$ if $x > y$ and $gt(x,y) = 0$ otherwise. It is easy to see that this function is increasing in x, so rule r is a CFASP rule. One can easily see that the only models of Z are $M_l = \{p^l\}, l \in]0,1]$. None of these models are answer sets, however, since for $l > 0$ we get

$$Z^{M_l} = \{r^{M_l}: p \leftarrow gt(0,0)\}$$

hence $\Pi^*_{Z^{M_l}} = \{p^0\} \neq M_l$.

It turns out that, similar to ASP, our program Z can be used to simulate constraints in CFASP$^\perp$ programs. As an example, consider the CFASP$^\perp$ program P:

$$r_1: \quad a \leftarrow \mathcal{N}_W(b)$$
$$r_2: \quad b \leftarrow \mathcal{N}_W(a)$$
$$c: \quad 0.5 \leftarrow a$$

The only answer sets of this program are of the form $M_l = \{a^l, b^{1-l}\}$, with $l \in [0, 0.5]$, as rule c eliminates all solutions M where $M(a) > 0.5$. Now consider the CFASP program P':

$$r_1: \quad a \leftarrow \mathcal{N}_W(b)$$
$$r_2: \quad b \leftarrow \mathcal{N}_W(a)$$
$$r_c: \quad \perp \leftarrow \mathcal{T}_M(gt(\mathcal{N}_W(\perp), 0), gt(a, 0.5))$$

with $\perp$ a fresh atom. Note that P' is constraint-free and that for any $l \in [0, 0.5]$, $M'_l = M_l \cup \{\perp^0\}$ is an answer set of P'. Note that these are the only answer sets of P' as well. Indeed, suppose there is some fixpoint N of $\Pi_{P'}$ such that $N(a) > 0.5$. It then follows that $N(\perp)$ needs to satisfy

$$N(\perp) = \Pi_{P'}(N)(\perp)$$
$$= \sup\{N(r_b) \mid r \in P'_\perp\}$$
$$= N((r_c)_b)$$
$$= N(\mathcal{T}_M(gt(\mathcal{N}_W(\perp), 0), gt(a, 0.5)))$$
$$= N(gt(\mathcal{N}_W(\perp), 0))$$

The equality $N(\perp) = N(gt(\mathcal{N}_W(\perp), 0))$ has no solution, however, since we know that $N(gt(\mathcal{N}_W(\perp), 0))$ takes on a value in $\{0, 1\}$ but for $N(\perp) = 0$ we get $N(gt(\mathcal{N}_W(\perp), 0)) = 1$ and for $N(\perp) = 1$ we get $N(gt(\mathcal{N}_W(\perp), 0)) = 0$. In general, one can verify that P and P' have corresponding answer sets, i.e. if M is an answer set of P then $M \cup \{\perp^0\}$ is an answer set of P and, conversely, if M' is an answer set of P', then $M' \cap \mathcal{B}_P$ is an answer set of P.

We now show that the construction used in the preceding example can be applied to arbitrary CFASP$^\perp$ programs on the lattice $([0, 1], \leqslant)$. Formally, the general transformation is defined as follows:

Definition 5.6. Let P be a CFASP$^\perp$ program on the lattice $([0, 1], \leqslant)$ and let $\mathcal{C}_P$ be the set of constraint rules in P. The corresponding CFASP program P' of P then contains the following rules:

$$P' = \{r': a \leftarrow \alpha \mid (r: a \leftarrow \alpha) \in P \setminus \mathcal{C}_P\}$$
$$\cup \{r_c: \perp \leftarrow \mathcal{T}(gt(\mathcal{N}(\perp), 0), gt(\alpha, k)) \mid (c: k \leftarrow \alpha) \in \mathcal{C}_P\}$$

where $\mathcal{T}$ is an arbitrary t-norm, $\mathcal{N}$ is an arbitrary negator and $\perp \notin \mathcal{B}_P$.

The following propositions show that the answer sets of the CFASP$^\perp$ program P and its corresponding CFASP program P' coincide.

Proposition 5.1. *Let P be a CFASP$^\perp$ program and let P' be its corresponding CFASP program as defined by Definition 5.6. If M is an answer set of P, then $M' = M \cup \{\perp^0\}$ is an answer set of P'.*

Proof. Suppose that M is an answer set of P. To show that $M' = M \cup \{\perp^0\}$ is an answer set of P' we need to prove that 1. it is a model of P; 2. that it is the least fixpoint of $\Pi_{P'M'}$.

(1) Since M is a model of P it follows by construction of P' that for each $r \in P \setminus \mathscr{C}_P$ and corresponding $r' \in P'$ we have that $M'(r') = M(r) = 1$. For each constraint $(r : a \leftarrow \alpha) \in \mathscr{C}_P$ and corresponding rule $c_r \in P'$ we have that $M'(c_r) = 1$ iff $M'(\mathscr{T}(gt(\mathscr{N}(\perp), 0), gt(\alpha, k))) = 0$. That this is true follows easily from the fact that $M(r) = 1$ and thus $M(\alpha) \leqslant k$.

(2) We show that (a) M' is a fixpoint of $\Pi_{P'M'}$; (b) M' is the least fixpoint of $\Pi_{P'M'}$.

(a) For $a \in \mathscr{B}_P$ we easily obtain that $\Pi_{P'M'}(M')(a) = M'(a)$ using the definition of M' and P' and the fact that M is a fixpoint of Π_{PM}. Now, consider a rule $c_r : \perp \leftarrow \mathscr{T}(gt(\mathscr{N}(\perp), 0), gt(\alpha, k)) \in P_\perp$. Since M is a model of P we know that for the corresponding rule $(r : k \leftarrow \alpha) \in P$ we have that $M(\alpha) \leqslant k$ and thus $M'((c_r)_b) = 0$. By definition of $\Pi_{P'M'}$ this means $\Pi_{P'M'}(M')(\perp) = 0$. Hence, combining these two cases we obtain that M' is a fixpoint of $\Pi_{P'M'}$.

(b) Suppose $M' \neq \Pi^\star_{P'M'}$. Then there is some $M'' \subset M'$ such that $M'' = \Pi^\star_{P'M'}$. Consider then $M''' = M'' \cap \mathscr{B}_P$. From the definition of P', M' and M''' we can easily see that for each $(r : a \leftarrow \alpha) \in P \setminus \mathscr{C}_P$ and corresponding $(r' : a \leftarrow \alpha) \in P'$ we have that $M(\alpha) = M'(\alpha)$ and $M''(\alpha) = M'''(\alpha)$. Using the definition of Π_{PM} and the reduct together with the fact that M'' is assumed to be a fixpoint of $\Pi_{P'M'}$ we then obtain for any $a \in \mathscr{B}_P$ that:

$$\begin{aligned}
\Pi_{PM}(M''')(a) &= \sup\{M'''(\alpha) \mid (r : a \leftarrow \alpha) \in P^M\} \\
&= \sup\{M''(\alpha) \mid (r : a \leftarrow \alpha) \in P'^{M'}\} \\
&= M''(a) \\
&= M'''(a)
\end{aligned}$$

Hence, M''' is a fixpoint of Π_{PM} and $M''' \subset M$, which violates the assumption that M is an answer set of P. $\square$

Lemma 5.1. *Let P be a CFASP$^\perp$ program and let P' be its corresponding CFASP program as defined by Definition 5.6. If M' is an answer set of P' it holds that M'($\perp$) = 0.*

Proof.   Since M' is an answer set of P', it must be a fixpoint of $\Pi_{P'M'}$. By construction of P' we however know that if M' is a fixpoint of $\Pi_{P'M'}$ it follows that $M'(\perp) \in \{0, 1\}$. Suppose $M'(\perp) = 1$. Then $gt(\mathcal{N}(M'(\perp)), 0) = gt(0, 0) = 0$. Hence for every $r_c \in P'_\perp$ we obtain that $M'((r_c)_b) = 0$. By definition of $\Pi_{P'M'}$ it then follows that $\Pi_{P'M'}(M')(\perp) = 0 \neq M'(\perp)$, which is a contradiction. $\square$

Proposition 5.2. *Let P be a CFASP$^\perp$ program and let P' be its corresponding CFASP program as defined by Definition 5.6. If M' is an answer set of P', then M = M' $\cap$ $\mathscr{B}_P$ is an answer set of P.*

Proof.   Suppose M' is an answer set of P'. To show that $M = M' \cap \mathscr{B}_P$ is an answer set of P we need to prove that (i) it is a model of P; (ii) it is the least fixpoint of Π_{PM}.

(1) For any $(r : a \leftarrow \alpha) \in P \setminus \mathscr{C}_P$ we easily obtain by the fact that $M'(r') = 1$ for the corresponding $(r' : a \leftarrow \alpha) \in P'$ and the construction of M that $M(r) = 1$. For $(r : k \leftarrow \alpha) \in \mathscr{C}_P$ we know by construction of P' and the fact that M' is a fixpoint of $\Pi_{P'M'}$ that $M'(\perp) \geqslant \mathscr{T}(gt(\mathcal{N}(M'(\perp)), 0), gt(M'(\alpha), k))$. From Lemma 5.1 we however know that $M'(\perp) = 0$ and hence

$$0 \geqslant \mathscr{T}(gt(1, 0), gt(M'(\alpha), k)) = gt(M'(\alpha), k)$$

From the construction of M it then follows that $M(r) = 1$.

(2) We show that (i) M is a fixpoint of Π_{PM}; (ii) M is the least fixpoint of Π_{PM}.

    (a) For any $a \in \mathscr{B}_P$ we easily obtain by the definition of M and P' that:

$$\begin{aligned}
\Pi_{PM}(M)(a) &= \sup\{M(\alpha) \mid (r : a \leftarrow \alpha) \in P^M\} \\
&= \sup\{M'(\alpha) \mid (r' : a \leftarrow \alpha) \in P'^{M'}\} \\
&= \Pi_{P'M'}(M')(a) \\
&= M'(a) \\
&= M(a)
\end{aligned}$$

    Hence M is a fixpoint of Π_{PM}.

    (b) Suppose $M \neq \Pi_{PM}^\star$. Then there is some $M'' \subset M$ such that $M'' = \Pi_{PM}^\star$. Consider then $M''' = M'' \cup \{\perp^0\}$. For $a \in \mathscr{B}_P$ we easily obtain from the definition of P'

and the fact that M'' is a fixpoint of Π_{pM} that $\Pi^*_{p'M'}(M''')(a) = M'''(a)$. For $\perp$, by the fact that $M''' \subset M'$, we obtain the following:

$$\Pi_{p'M'}(M''')(\perp)$$
$$= \sup\{M'''(\mathscr{T}(gt(\mathscr{N}(M'(\perp)),0),gt(\alpha^{M'},k))) \mid (r{:}k \leftarrow \alpha) \in \mathscr{C}_P\}$$
$$= \sup\{M'''(\mathscr{T}(gt(\mathscr{N}(0),0),gt(\alpha^{M'},k))) \mid (r{:}k \leftarrow \alpha) \in \mathscr{C}_P\}$$
$$= \sup\{M'''(\mathscr{T}(1,gt(\alpha^{M'},k))) \mid (r{:}k \leftarrow \alpha) \in \mathscr{C}_P\}$$
$$= \sup\{M'''(gt(\alpha^{M'},k)) \mid (r{:}k \leftarrow \alpha) \in \mathscr{C}_P\}$$
$$\leqslant \sup\{M'(gt(\alpha^{M'},k)) \mid (r{:}k \leftarrow \alpha) \in \mathscr{C}_P\}$$
$$= \sup\{M'(\mathscr{T}(1,gt(\alpha^{M'},k))) \mid (r{:}k \leftarrow \alpha) \in \mathscr{C}_P\}$$
$$= \sup\{M'(\mathscr{T}(gt(\mathscr{N}(0),0),gt(\alpha^{M'},k))) \mid (r{:}k \leftarrow \alpha) \in \mathscr{C}_P\}$$
$$= \sup\{M'(\mathscr{T}(gt(\mathscr{N}(M'(\perp)),0),gt(\alpha^{M'},k))) \mid (r{:}k \leftarrow \alpha) \in \mathscr{C}_P\}$$
$$= \Pi_{p'M'}(M')(\perp)$$
$$= M'(\perp)$$
$$= 0$$

Hence, $\Pi_{p'M'}(M''')(\perp) = M'''(\perp)$ and thus M''' is a fixpoint of $\Pi_{p'M'}$, contradicting with our assumption that M' is an answer set of P'. $\square$

5.3.2 Locking the Truth Value

In some applications we might want to lock the truth value of an atom in a certain sub-interval of $[0,1]$. We can define an extension of CFASP$^\perp$, called CFASP$^{[\perp]}$, that supports this.

Definition 5.7. Consider a set of atoms A. A CFASP$^{[\perp]}$ rule is either a CFASP$^\perp$ rule on $([0,1],\leqslant)$ or a rule of the form

$$r{:}a \in [l,u] \leftarrow \tag{5.3}$$

where $a \in A$, $l \in \mathscr{L}$ and $u \in \mathscr{L}$. We call such a rule an **interval-locking rule**.

Definition 5.8. A CFASP$^{[\perp]}$ program P is a set of CFASP$^{[\perp]}$ rules. An interpretation I of P is said to **satisfy** an interval-locking rule of the form (5.4) above iff $I(a) \in [l,u]$.

Now, it turns out that we can translate any CFASP$^{[\perp]}$ program to an equivalent CFASP$^\perp$ program. First, note that a constraint introduces an upper bound on the value of a body function. We can use this to simulate interval-locking rules. Consider a CFASP$^{[\perp]}$ program P and an atom $a \in \mathscr{B}_P$ such that there is an interval-locking rule $r : a \in [0.3, 0.8] \leftarrow$ in P. If we wish to simulate r, we can add the following rules to P:

$$constr : 0.8 \leftarrow a$$

$$constr' : 0.7 \leftarrow \mathscr{N}_W(a)$$

It is easy to see that any model M of $(P \setminus \{r\}) \cup \{constr, constr'\}$ satisfies $0.8 \geqslant M(a)$ and $0.3 \leqslant M(a)$, hence $M(a) \in [0.3, 0.8]$. In general we can define the following transformation:

Definition 5.9. Let P be a CFASP$^{[\perp]}$ program over $([0,1], \leqslant)$ with $\mathscr{I}$ the set of interval-locking rules in P. Its corresponding CFASP$^{\perp}$ program P' is defined as the following set of rules

$$P' = (P \setminus \mathscr{I}) \cup \{low_a : (1-l) \leftarrow \mathscr{N}_W(a) \mid (r : a \in [l,u] \leftarrow) \in \mathscr{I}\}$$
$$\cup \{upp_a : u \leftarrow a \mid (r : a \in [l,u] \leftarrow) \in \mathscr{I}\}$$

The following proposition shows that the simulation of interval-locking rules works in general.

Proposition 5.3. *Let P be a CFASP$^{[\perp]}$ program over $([0,1], \leqslant)$. Then M is a model of P iff M is a model of its corresponding CFASP$^{\perp}$ program P' defined in Definition 5.9.*

Proof. We show this in two steps.

(1) Suppose M is a model of P. Then for each rule of the form $(r : a \in [l,u] \leftarrow) \in P$ we have that $M(a) \in [l,u]$. Hence $M(a) \geqslant l$ and thus $1 - M(a) \leqslant 1 - l$, meaning the corresponding rule $low_a \in P'$ is satisfied by M. Likewise we obtain that $M(a) \leqslant u$ and thus M satisfies the rule $upp_a \in P'$. Since the other rules in P' are equivalent to those in P we obtain that M is a model of P'.

(2) Suppose M' is a model of P'. Then by construction of P' for each rule of the form $(r : a \in [l,u] \leftarrow) \in P$ there are two corresponding rules upp_a and low_a in P'. Since M' is a model of P' both low_a and upp_a are satisfied, meaning $M'(a) \leqslant u$ and $M'(a) \geqslant l$. By definition of interval-locking rules this means M' satisfies the rule $(r : a \in [l,u] \leftarrow)$. Since the other rules in P are equivalent to those in P' we obtain that M' is a model of P. $\qquad\square$

Note that, since answer sets are models, it follows trivially that answer sets also obey the interval-locking rules.

5.4 Monotonically Decreasing Functions

The FASP framework introduced in Chapter 3 not only allows functions that are increasing in rule bodies, but also functions with partial mappings that are monotonically decreasing. Functions with decreasing partial mappings in fact generalize negation-as-failure to functions with more than one argument: if $f(x_1,\ldots,x_n)$ decreases in its ith argument, the function increases when x_i decreases. Since x_i decreases when the maximal value that we can derive for x_i decreases, this means that $f(x_1,\ldots,x_n)$ increases when the support for x_i decreases. This corresponds to the idea underlying negation-as-failure. However, it turns out that generalizing negation-as-failure to functions with decreasing partial mappings does not lead to a higher expressiveness. We show in this section that any program with monotonically decreasing functions can be translated to a program in which the only decreasing functions are negators that are applied to atoms, i.e. to CFASP programs. Similar to the previous section, we first define an extension of CFASP with decreasing functions and then show that any extended program can be translated to an equivalent CFASP program.

Definition 5.10. A CFASP^f rule on a complete lattice $\mathscr{L}$ is a FASP rule of the form

$$r : a \leftarrow f(b_1,\ldots,b_n;c_1,\ldots,c_m) \tag{5.4}$$

where a, b_i and c_j are atoms and f is a $\mathscr{L}^{n+m} \to \mathscr{L}$ function that is increasing in its n first and decreasing in its m last arguments. A CFASP^f program on a complete lattice $\mathscr{L}$ is a set of CFASP^f rules on $\mathscr{L}$.

Note that we only allow atoms, and not extended literals in CFASP^f programs. This is not a problem, however, as it is easy to see that literals of the form $\mathscr{N}(s)$ are $\mathscr{L} \to \mathscr{L}$ functions that have no increasing arguments. We now show that any CFASP^f program can be simulated using a CFASP program. Intuitively the procedure works as follows. Given a rule of the form (5.4) above, we replace the function f in its body with a new function f' defined by $f'(b_1,\ldots,b_n,not_{c_1},\ldots,not_{c_m};) = f(b_1,\ldots,b_n;\mathscr{N}(not_{c_1}),\ldots,\mathscr{N}(not_{c_m}))$, where not_c is a new atom supported by the rule $n_c : not_c \leftarrow \mathscr{N}(c)$, with $\mathscr{N}$ an involutive negator. In this way, we have replaced the decreasing function with two CFASP rules. Formally, this procedure is defined as follows:

Definition 5.11. Let P be a CFASP^f program over a lattice $\mathscr{L}$. Then its corresponding CFASP program P' contains the following rules:

$$P' = \{r' : a \leftarrow \alpha' \mid (r : a \leftarrow \alpha) \in P\}$$

$$\cup \{n_l : not_l \leftarrow \mathcal{N}_i(l) \mid l \in \mathscr{F}_P\}$$

where $\alpha = f(b_1, \ldots, b_n; c_1, \ldots, c_m)$, $\alpha' = f'(b_1, \ldots, b_n, not_{c_1}, \ldots, not_{c_m})$, $\mathcal{N}_i$ is an involutive negator on $\mathscr{L}$, $\mathscr{F}_P$ is the set of all atoms a for which a naf-literal $\mathcal{N}(a)$ occurs in the body of some rule in P, and f' is defined by $f'(b_1, \ldots, b_n, not_{c_1}, \ldots, not_{c_m}) = f(b_1, \ldots, b_n; \mathcal{N}_i(not_{c_1}), \ldots, \mathcal{N}_i(not_{c_m}))$. Also for each $l \in \mathscr{B}_P$ it must hold that $not_l \notin \mathscr{B}_P$, i.e. the not_l literal is a "fresh" literal.

As an example, consider a CFASP^f program P with the following rules:

$$r_1 : a \leftarrow_m \frac{1}{1 + b \cdot c}$$
$$r_2 : b \leftarrow_m 0.8$$
$$r_3 : c \leftarrow_m 0.5$$

An answer set of P is $M = \{a^{10/14}, b^{0.8}, c^{0.5}\}$. If we apply the transformation of Definition 5.11 on P we obtain P' with rules:

$$r_1' : \quad a \leftarrow_m f'(not_b, not_c)$$
$$r_2' : \quad b \leftarrow_m 0.8$$
$$r_3' : \quad c \leftarrow_m 0.5$$
$$n_b : not_b \leftarrow_m \mathcal{N}_W(b)$$
$$n_c : not_c \leftarrow_m \mathcal{N}_W(c)$$

where $f'(not_b, not_c) = \dfrac{1}{1 + (\mathcal{N}_W(not_b)) \cdot (\mathcal{N}_W(not_c))}$. We can then show that $M' = M \cup \{not_b^{\mathcal{N}_W(M(b))}, not_c^{\mathcal{N}_W(M(c))}\}$ is an answer set of P'. The reduct $P'^{M'}$ contains the following rules:

$$r_1'^{M'} : \quad a \leftarrow_m f'(not_b, not_c)$$
$$r_2'^{M'} : \quad b \leftarrow_m 0.8$$
$$r_3'^{M'} : \quad c \leftarrow_m 0.5$$
$$n_b^{M'} : not_b \leftarrow_m 0.2$$
$$n_c^{M'} : not_c \leftarrow_m 0.5$$

where f' is defined as above. From the reduct we can see that $\Pi^\star_{P'M'}(b) = 0.8$, $\Pi^\star_{P'M'}(c) = 0.5$, $\Pi^\star_{P'M'}(not_b) = 0.2$ and $\Pi^\star_{P'M'}(not_c) = 0.5$. This leads to $\Pi^\star_{P'M'}(a) = 10/14$ and thus M' is the least fixpoint of $\Pi_{P'M'}$, which is what we expected.

The following propositions show that this transformation preserves the answer set semantics.

Proposition 5.4. *Let P be a CFASP^f program and let P' be its corresponding CFASP program as defined by Definition 5.11. If M is an answer set of P, then $M' = M \cup \{not_l^{\mathcal{N}_i(M(l))} \mid l \in \mathscr{F}_P\}$ is an answer set of P'.*

Proof. We have to show that M' is the least fixpoint of $\Pi_{p'M'}$. First, note that for any $l \in \mathscr{F}_P$ by definition of P' and M'

$$\Pi_{p'M'}(M')(not_l) = \mathscr{N}(M'(l)) = \mathscr{N}(M(l)) = M'(not_l) \tag{5.5}$$

Now, for $a \in \mathscr{B}_P$ each rule $r\!:\!a \leftarrow f(b_1,\dots,b_n;c_1,\dots,c_m)$ in P is replaced by $r\!:\!a \leftarrow f'(b_1,\dots,b_n,not_{c_1},\dots,not_{c_m})$, with f' as in Definition 5.11. Hence since $M'(not_l) = \mathscr{N}_i(M(l))$ we obtain that

$$M(f(b_1,\dots,b_n;c_1,\dots,c_m)^M) = M'(f'(b_1,\dots,b_n,not_{c_1},\dots,not_{c_m})^{M'}) \tag{5.6}$$

and also

$$M(r) = M'(r') \tag{5.7}$$

since $\mathscr{N}_i$ is involutive, $M = M' \cap \mathscr{B}_P$ and the atoms occurring in $\mathscr{R}_P$ are all atoms of $\mathscr{B}_P$. As M is a fixpoint of Π_{PM}, it then follows from (5.5), (5.6), (5.7) and by definition of M' that M' must be a fixpoint of $\Pi_{p'M'}$ (one only has to work out the definition of $\Pi_{p'M'}$ together with the formerly mentioned equations to see this).

Suppose now there is some $M'' < M'$ that is also a fixpoint of $\Pi_{p'M'}$. By definition of P' it is easy to see that for each $l \in \mathscr{F}_P$ it then must hold that $M''(not_l) = \mathscr{N}_i(M'(l)) = \mathscr{N}_i(M(l))$. From this it follows that for each $r \in P$ we obtain $(M'' \cap \mathscr{B}_P)((r_b)^M) = M''(r'_b)$ by definition of P' and thus we obtain for each $a \in \mathscr{B}_P$:

$$\begin{aligned}
\Pi_{PM}(M'' \cap \mathscr{B}_P)(a) &= \sup\{M'' \cap \mathscr{B}_P(\alpha^M) \mid (r\!:\!a \leftarrow \alpha) \in P\} \\
&= \sup\{M''(\alpha') \mid r'\!:\!a \leftarrow \alpha' \in P'^{M'}\} \\
&= \Pi_{p'M'}(M'')(a) \\
&= M''(a)
\end{aligned}$$

Hence $M'' \cap \mathscr{B}_P$ is a fixpoint of Π_{PM}. However, since for each $l \in \mathscr{F}_P$ we have $M''(not_l) = M'(not_l)$ and as $M'' < M'$, it holds that $M'' \cap \mathscr{B}_P < M$. This however contradicts the fact that M is the least fixpoint of Π_{PM}, showing no such M'' can exist and thus M' is the least fixpoint of $\Pi_{p'M'}$. $\square$

Proposition 5.5. *Let P be a CFASP^f program and let P' be its corresponding CFASP program as defined by Definition 5.11. If M' is an answer set of P', then $M = M' \cap \mathscr{B}_P$ is an answer set of P.*

Proof. By definition of P' it is not hard to see that for each rule $r \in P$ we have

$$M((r_b)^M) = M'(r'_b) \tag{5.8}$$

We show that M is the least fixpoint of Π_{pM}. From (5.8) we can easily see that M must be a fixpoint of Π_{pM}. Now suppose some M'' (with $M'' < M$) is also a fixpoint of Π_{pM}. Then we can construct $M''' = M'' \cup \{not_l^{\mathcal{N}_i(M(l))} \mid l \in \mathcal{F}_P\}$. It is not hard to see that for each rule $r \in P$:

$$M''((r_b)^M) = M'''(r_b')$$

Hence, as M'' is a fixpoint of Π_{pM}, we obtain that M''' is also a fixpoint of $\Pi_{pM'}$, contradicting the fact that M' is an answer set of P'. $\qquad\square$

Note that when we combine the results introduced in this section with those from Section 5.3, we find that any FASP program can be translated to an equivalent CFASP program. In the following sections we show that for certain extensions of FASP, translations to CFASP can also be defined.

5.5 Aggregators

In Chapter 4 we introduced an extension of FASP that allowed rules to be partially fulfilled, called AFASP. At first sight, one might be tempted to think that an AFASP program P with an aggregator over $\mathcal{L}_P$ can be replaced by a CFASP^f program P' such that $P' = \mathcal{R}_P \cup \{r'_{aggr} : aggr \leftarrow f(\mathcal{I}_{r_1}((r_1)_b, (r_1)_h), \dots, \mathcal{I}_{r_n}((r_n)_b, (r_n)_h))\}$, where f corresponds to the function defined by the aggregator of P. The intended meaning is such that M is an m-answer set of P iff $M \cup \{aggr^m\}$ is an answer set of P'.

This trivial translation is not correct, however, as it does not correctly incorporate the notion of partial rule satisfaction. For example, consider the AFASP program P with rule base $\mathcal{R}_P = \{(r_1 : a \leftarrow 1), (r_2 : b \leftarrow 1)\}$ and with aggregator $\mathcal{A}_P(\rho) = \inf\{\rho(r) \mid r \in \mathcal{R}_P\}$. Using the transformation proposed above, we obtain the CFASP^f program $P' = \{(r_1' : a \leftarrow 1), (r_2' : b \leftarrow 1), (r'_{aggr} : aggr \leftarrow \inf(\mathcal{I}(1, a), \mathcal{I}(1, b)))\}$. For the 0.7-answer set $M = \{a^{0.7}, b^1\}$ of P the corresponding interpretation $M' = M \cup \{(r'_{aggr})^{0.7}\}$ is not an answer set of P', however, as P' only has one answer set, viz. $\{a^1, b^1, (r'_{aggr})^1\}$. This problem can be solved using the following alternate simulation:

Definition 5.12. Let P be an AFASP program with rule base $\mathcal{R}_P = \{r_1, \dots, r_n\}$ on the lattice $\mathcal{L}$. If there is an involutive negator $\mathcal{N}_i$ on $\mathcal{L}$ we can construct a CFASP^f program corresponding to P, denoted as P', that contains the following rules:

$$P' = \{r' : a \leftarrow \mathcal{T}_r(\alpha, r_i') \mid (r : a \leftarrow \alpha) \in \mathcal{R}_P, a \in \mathcal{B}_P\}$$
$$\cup \{r_a' : not_a \leftarrow \mathcal{N}_i(a) \mid a \in \mathcal{B}_P\}$$

$$\cup \{r'_\rho : r'_i \leftarrow \mathscr{I}_r(\alpha', \mathscr{N}_i(not_a)) \mid (r : a \leftarrow \alpha) \in \mathscr{R}_P, a \in \mathscr{B}_P\}$$

$$\cup \{r'_\rho : r'_i \leftarrow \mathscr{I}_r(\alpha', k) \mid (r : k \leftarrow \alpha) \in \mathscr{R}_P, k \in \mathscr{L}\}$$

$$\cup \{r'_{aggr} : aggr \leftarrow f(r'_{1i}, \ldots, r'_{ni})\}$$

Furthermore, none of the atoms not_a for $a \in \mathscr{B}_P$, r'_i for $r \in \mathscr{R}_P$ and $aggr$ occur in $\mathscr{B}_P$. Also, the function f corresponds to $\mathscr{A}_P$ in the sense that $\mathscr{A}_P(\rho) = f(\rho(r_1), \ldots, \rho(r_n))$ and for a given $\alpha = g(b_1, \ldots, b_n; c_1, \ldots, c_m)$ we have that $\alpha' = g'(b_1, \ldots, b_n, not_{c_1}, \ldots, not_{c_m})$, with g' defined as $g'(b_1, \ldots, b_n, not_{c_1}, \ldots, not_{c_m}) = g(b_1, \ldots, b_n; \mathscr{N}_i(not_{c_1}), \ldots, \mathscr{N}_i(not_{c_m}))$.

Note that due to the r'_ρ rules in Definition 5.12, we translate an AFASP program to a CFASP^f program, rather than a CFASP program. This is not a problem however, as we have shown in Section 5.4 that any CFASP^f program can be translated to a corresponding CFASP program. We summarized this in Figure 5.1 on page 131.

Now consider the program P from above again. If we use the translation defined in Definition 5.12 we obtain

$$P' = \{(r'_1 : a \leftarrow \mathscr{T}(1, r'_{1i})), (r'_2 : b \leftarrow \mathscr{T}(1, r'_{2i}))\}$$

$$\cup \{(r'_a : not_a \leftarrow \mathscr{N}_W(a)), (r'_b : not_b \leftarrow \mathscr{N}_W(b))\}$$

$$\cup \{(r'_{1\rho} : r'_{1i} \leftarrow \mathscr{I}(1, \mathscr{N}_W(not_a)))(r'_{2\rho} : r'_{2i} \leftarrow \mathscr{I}(1, \mathscr{N}_W(not_b)))\}$$

$$\cup \{(r'_{aggr} : aggr \leftarrow \inf(r'_{1i}, r'_{2i}))\}$$

One can easily verify that $M' = \{a^{0.7}, b^1, not_a^{0.3}, not_b^0, r'^{0.7}_{1i}, r'^1_{2i}, aggr^{0.7}\}$ is an answer set of P', hence the translation in Definition 5.12 preserves the AFASP semantics.

Example 5.1. Consider P with $\mathscr{A}_P(\rho) = \inf\{\rho(r) \mid r \in \mathscr{R}_P\}$ and $\mathscr{R}_P$:

$$r_1 : a \leftarrow_m \mathscr{N}_W(b)$$

$$r_2 : b \leftarrow_m 0.7$$

Applying Definition 5.12, we obtain the CFASP^f program P' with rules:

$$r'_1 : \qquad a \leftarrow_m \mathscr{T}_M(\mathscr{N}_W(b), r'_{1i})$$

$$r'_2 : \qquad b \leftarrow_m \mathscr{T}_M(0.7, r'_{2i})$$

$$r'_a : \quad not_a \leftarrow_m \mathscr{N}_W(a)$$

$$r'_b : \quad not_b \leftarrow_m \mathscr{N}_W(b)$$

$$r'_{1\rho} : \quad r'_{1i} \leftarrow_m \mathscr{I}_M(\mathscr{N}_W(\mathscr{N}_W(not_b)), \mathscr{N}_W(not_a))$$

$$r'_{2\rho} : \quad r'_{2i} \leftarrow_m \mathscr{I}_M(0.7, \mathscr{N}_W(not_b))$$

$$r'_{aggr} : aggr \leftarrow_m \inf(r'_{1i}, r'_{2i})$$

Consider now the 1-answer set $M = \{a^{0.3}, b^{0.7}\}$ of P. Definition 5.12 is constructed in such a way that $M' = \{a^{0.3}, b^{0.7}, r'^1_{1i}, r'^1_{2i}, not_a^{0.7}, not_b^{0.3}, r'^1_{aggr}\}$ is an answer set of P'.

The construction with the involutive negator and not_a for any $a \in \mathscr{B}_P$ is needed to correctly preserve the semantics. To see this, consider the following alternative CFASP^f translation P'' of program P in Example 5.1:

$$r_1': \qquad a \leftarrow_m \mathscr{T}_M(\mathscr{N}_W(b), r_{1i}')$$
$$r_2': \qquad b \leftarrow_m \mathscr{T}_M(0.7, r_{2i}')$$
$$r_{1\rho}': \qquad r_{1i}' \leftarrow_m \mathscr{T}_M(\mathscr{N}_W(b), a)$$
$$r_{2\rho}': \qquad r_{2i}' \leftarrow_m \mathscr{T}_M(0.7, b)$$
$$r_{aggr}': aggr \leftarrow_m \inf(r_{1i}', r_{2i}')$$

Now consider the 1-answer set $M = \{a^{0.3}, b^{0.7}\}$ of P_1. We wish the aggregator-free version of P to be constructed in such a way that $M' = M \cup \{r_i'^{M(r)} \mid r \in \mathscr{R}_P\} \cup \{aggr^{\mathscr{A}_P(\rho_M)}\}$ is an answer set of P''. Hence in the case of P'', we find that $M' = M \cup \{r_{1i}'^1, r_{2i}'^1\} \cup \{aggr^1\}$ should be an answer set of P''. However, there is an $M'' < M'$ such that M'' is a fixpoint of $\Pi_{p''M'}$, which contradicts the fact that M' is an answer set of P''. Indeed, for $M'' = \{a^{0.2}, b^{0.7}\} \cup \{r_{1i}'^{0.2}, r_{2i}'^1\} \cup \{aggr^{0.2}\}$ it can be seen that M'' is a model of P'' and a fixpoint of $\Pi_{p''M'}$ as follows. For a we obtain:

$$\Pi_{p''M'}(M'')(a) = \mathscr{T}_M(\mathscr{N}_W(M'(b)), M''(r_{1i}')) = \mathscr{T}_M(1 - 0.7, 0.2) = 0.2$$

Likewise we obtain that $\Pi_{p''M'}(M'')(b) = 0.7$. Now for r_{1i}' we obtain

$$\Pi_{p''M'}(M'')(r_{1i}') = M''((\mathscr{T}_M(\mathscr{N}_W(b), a))^{M'})$$
$$= M''(\mathscr{T}_M(\mathscr{N}_W(b), a))$$
$$= \mathscr{T}_M(\mathscr{N}_W(M''(b)), M''(a))$$
$$= \mathscr{T}_M(0.3, 0.2)$$
$$= 0.2$$

Likewise we obtain that $\Pi_{p''M'}(M'')(r_{2i}') = 1$. Last, for $aggr$ we obtain

$$\Pi_{p''M'}(M'')(aggr) = M''(\inf(r_{1i}', r_{2i}')) = \inf(0.2, 1) = 0.2$$

Hence M'' is a fixpoint of $\Pi_{p''M'}$, contradicting that M' is an answer set of P_1''.

The problem the preceding example illustrates is that we must be able to "fix" the value of the literals r_{1i}' and r_{2i}' when we are taking the reduct relative to M'. The only way to ensure this is by eliminating all literals from the body of the $r_{1\rho}'$ and $r_{2\rho}'$ rules by means of the reduct procedure. Hence we must replace each positively occurring literal in the bodies of $r_{1\rho}'$ and $r_{2\rho}'$ by a negatively occurring literal. This is done by replacing a positively occurring literal a with $\mathscr{N}_W(not_a)$, which preserves the same value, but will be replaced by the reduct operation.

The following propositions show that our translation preserves the semantics.

Proposition 5.6. *Let P be an AFASP program with $\mathscr{R}_P = \{r_1, \ldots, r_n\}$ and let P' be its corresponding CFASP^f program as defined in Definition 5.12. If M is an m-answer set of P, then $M' = M \cup \{aggr^{\mathscr{A}_P(\rho_M)}\} \cup \{not_a^{\mathscr{N}_i(M(a))} \mid a \in \mathscr{B}_P\} \cup \{r_i'^{M(r)} \mid r \in \mathscr{R}_P\}$ is an answer set of P'.*

Proof.   It should be clear from the definition of M' and P' that M' is a model of P'. Hence, we only need to show that M' is the least fixpoint of $\Pi_{p'M'}$. First we show that it is a fixpoint of $\Pi_{p'M'}$. We consider five cases:

(1) For $aggr \in \mathscr{B}_{p'}$ we obtain by definition of P' and M' that

$$\Pi_{p'M'}(M')(aggr) = M'(f(r'_{1_i}, \ldots, r'_{n_i})) = \mathscr{A}_P(\rho_M) = M'(aggr)$$

(2) For $a \in \mathscr{B}_P$ and corresponding $not_a \in \mathscr{B}_{p'}$ we obtain using the definition of M' that

$$\begin{aligned}
\Pi_{p'M'}(M')(not_a) &= M'((\mathscr{N}_i(a))^{M'}) \\
&= M'(\mathscr{N}_i(M'(a))) \\
&= M'(\mathscr{N}_i(M(a))) \\
&= M'(not_a)
\end{aligned}$$

(3) For $(r : a \leftarrow \alpha) \in \mathscr{R}_P$ with $a \in \mathscr{B}_P$ and corresponding $r'_i \in \mathscr{B}_{p'}$ we obtain using the definition of M' and the definition of P' that

$$\begin{aligned}
\Pi_{p'M'}(M')(r'_i) &= M'((\mathscr{I}_r(\alpha', \mathscr{N}_i(not_a)))^{M'}) \\
&= \mathscr{I}_r(M'(\alpha'), M'(\mathscr{N}_i(not_a))) \\
&= \mathscr{I}_r(M(\alpha), \mathscr{N}_i(\mathscr{N}_i(M(a)))) \\
&= \mathscr{I}_r(M(\alpha), M(a)) \\
&= M(r) \\
&= M'(r'_i)
\end{aligned}$$

(4) For $(k : a \leftarrow \alpha) \in \mathscr{R}_P$ with $k \in \mathscr{L}$ we obtain that $\Pi_{p'M'}(M')(r'_i) = M'(r'_i)$ similar to the previous case.

(5) For $a \in \mathscr{B}_P$ we obtain, using the definition of P', the fact that for any expression α and interpretation of α we have $I(\alpha') = I(\alpha)$, the definition of the reduct of a program and the fact that M is a fixpoint of Π_{pM, ρ_M} that

$$\Pi_{p'M'}(M')(a) = \sup\{\mathscr{T}_r(M'((\alpha')^{M'}), M'(r'_i)) \mid (r : a \leftarrow \alpha) \in P\}$$

$$= \sup\{\mathcal{T}_r(M(\alpha^M), \rho_M(r)) \mid (r{:}a \leftarrow \alpha) \in P\}$$
$$= \sup\{\mathcal{T}_r(M(\alpha^M), \rho_M(r^M)) \mid (r{:}a \leftarrow \alpha) \in P\}$$
$$= \sup\{\mathcal{T}_r(M(\alpha), \rho_M(r)) \mid (r{:}a \leftarrow \alpha) \in P^M\}$$
$$= \sup\{M_s(r, \rho_M(r)) \mid (r{:}a \leftarrow \alpha) \in P^M\}$$
$$= M(a)$$
$$= M'(a)$$

Hence we can conclude that M' is a fixpoint of $\Pi_{p'M'}$. Now suppose there is an interpretation $M'' < M'$ of P' such that M'' is also a fixpoint of $\Pi_{p'M'}$. For $a \in \mathcal{B}_P$ we then obtain by definition of P' that

$$\Pi_{p'M'}(M'')(not_a) = M''((\mathcal{N}_i(a))^{M'}) = M''(\mathcal{N}_i(M'(a))) = \mathcal{N}_i(M'(a))$$

Hence $M''(not_a) = M'(not_a)$ for each $a \in \mathcal{B}_P$. For $(r{:}a \leftarrow \alpha) \in \mathcal{R}_P$ with $a \in \mathcal{B}_P$ we obtain by definition of P', the fact that in α' there are no naf-literals and the fact that implicators are increasing in their first and decreasing in their second argument that

$$\Pi_{p'M'}(M'')(r_i') = M''((\mathcal{I}_r(\alpha', \mathcal{N}_i(not_a)))^{M'})$$
$$= M''(\mathcal{I}_r(M'(\alpha'), \mathcal{N}_i(M'(not_a))))$$
$$= M''(\mathcal{I}_r(M(\alpha), \mathcal{N}_i(\mathcal{N}_i(M(a)))))$$
$$= M''(\mathcal{I}_r(M(\alpha), M(a)))$$
$$= M(r)$$
$$= M'(r_i')$$

Similarly we obtain for any $(r{:}k \leftarrow \alpha) \in P$ with $k \in \mathcal{L}_P$ that $\Pi_{p'M'}(M'')(r_i') = M'(r_i')$. From this and the definition of P' it then also easily follows that $M''(aggr) = M'(aggr)$. Hence as $M'' < M'$, from the foregoing it follows that $M'' \cap \mathcal{B}_P < M$. Now for each $a \in \mathcal{B}_P$ we can show that

$$\Pi_{pM, \rho_M}(M'')(a) = \sup\{\mathcal{T}_r(M''(\alpha^M), \rho_M(r)) \mid (r{:}a \leftarrow \alpha) \in \mathcal{R}_P\}$$
$$= \sup\{\mathcal{T}_r(M''(\alpha^{M'}), \rho_M(r)) \mid (r{:}a \leftarrow \alpha) \in \mathcal{R}_P\}$$
$$= \sup\{\mathcal{T}_r(M''(\alpha^{M'}), M''(r_i')) \mid (r{:}a \leftarrow \alpha) \in \mathcal{R}_P\}$$
$$= \sup\{\mathcal{T}_{r'}(\mathcal{T}_r(M''(\alpha^{M'}), M''(r_i')), \rho_{M'}(r')) \mid (r{:}a \leftarrow \alpha) \in \mathcal{R}_P\}$$
$$= \sup\{M_s''(r', \rho_{M'}(r')) \mid (r{:}a \leftarrow \alpha) \in \mathcal{R}_P\}$$
$$= \Pi_{p'M'}(M'')(a)$$

$$= M''(a)$$

meaning $M'' \cap \mathscr{B}_P$ is a fixpoint of Π_{pM}, contradicting the fact that M is the least fixpoint of Π_{pM}. Hence such an M'' cannot exist and M' is the least fixpoint of $\Pi_{p'M'}$. $\square$

Proposition 5.7. *Let P be an AFASP program and let P' be its corresponding CFASP^f program as defined in Definition 5.12. If M' is an answer set of P', with $m = M'(aggr)$, then $M' \cap \mathscr{B}_P$ is an m-answer set of P.*

Proof. We have to show that for $M = M' \cap \mathscr{B}_P$ we have $\mathscr{A}_P(\rho_M) \geqslant m$ for any $m \leqslant M'(aggr)$ and that M is the least fixpoint of Π_{pM,ρ_M}. First we show that $\mathscr{A}_P(\rho_M) \geqslant m$ for any $m \leqslant M'(aggr)$. Suppose $m \in \mathscr{L}_P$ such that $m \leqslant M'(aggr)$. Since M' is a fixpoint of $\Pi_{p'M'}$ from the definition of P' we can easily see that for any $a \in \mathscr{B}_P$ we must have $M'(not_a) = \mathscr{N}_i(M'(a)) = \mathscr{N}_i(M(a))$ as there is only one rule with not_a in the head and likewise that for any $(r : a \leftarrow \alpha) \in \mathscr{R}_P$ with $a \in \mathscr{B}_P$ and corresponding $r'_i \in \mathscr{B}_{P'}$ we must have $M'(r'_i) = M'(\mathscr{I}_r(\alpha, \mathscr{N}_i(not_a))) = \rho_M(r)$. Similarly we obtain for any $(r : k \leftarrow \alpha) \in \mathscr{R}_P$ with $k \in \mathscr{L}_P$ and corresponding $r'_i \in \mathscr{B}_{P'}$ that $M'(r'_i) = \rho_M(r)$. Furthermore it must follow that $M'(\rho_{aggr}) = M'(f(r'_{1i}, \ldots, r'_{ni}))$ as again there is only one rule with ρ_{aggr} in the head and thus as $M'(f(r'_{1i}, \ldots, r'_{ni})) = \mathscr{A}_P(\rho_M)$ by construction of P' that $\mathscr{A}_P(\rho_M) \geqslant m$ as $M'(\rho_{aggr}) \geqslant m$.

Second we show that M is the least fixpoint of Π_{pM,ρ_M}. First we show that M is a fixpoint of Π_{pM,ρ_M}. Suppose $a \in \mathscr{B}_P$, then from the fact that M' is a fixpoint of $\Pi_{p'M'}$, the definition of M, the fact that for any expression α we have $M(\alpha^M) = M(\alpha)$ and the foregoing part of the proof we know that:

$$\begin{aligned}
M'(a) &= \Pi_{p'M'}(M')(a) \\
&= \sup\{M'((\mathscr{T}_r(\alpha, r'_i))^{M'}) \mid (r : a \leftarrow \alpha) \in \mathscr{R}_P\} \\
&= \sup\{\mathscr{T}_r(M'(\alpha^{M'}), M'(r'_i)) \mid (r : a \leftarrow \alpha) \in \mathscr{R}_P\} \\
&= \sup\{\mathscr{T}_r(M(\alpha^M), \rho_M(r)) \mid (r : a \leftarrow \alpha) \in \mathscr{R}_P\} \\
&= \sup\{\mathscr{T}_r(M(\alpha^M), \rho_M(r^M)) \mid (r : a \leftarrow \alpha) \in \mathscr{R}_P\} \\
&= \sup\{M_s(r, \rho_M(r)) \mid (r : a \leftarrow \alpha) \in (\mathscr{R}_P)^M\} \\
&= \Pi_{pM,\rho_M}(M)(a)
\end{aligned}$$

Hence M is a fixpoint of Π_{pM,ρ_M}. Now suppose there is some $M'' < M$ such that M'' is also a fixpoint of Π_{pM,ρ_M}. Consider then $M''' = M'' \cup \{aggr^{M'(aggr)}\} \cup \{not_a^{\mathscr{N}(M(a))} \mid a \in \mathscr{B}_P\} \cup \{r'^{\rho_M(r)}_i \mid (r : a \leftarrow \alpha) \in \mathscr{R}_P\}$. Obviously $M''' < M'$ by construction. We show that M''' is a fixpoint of $\Pi_{p'M'}$ contradicting the assumption that M' is an answer set of P'.

(1) For $a \in \mathscr{B}_P$ and the corresponding $not_a \in \mathscr{B}_{P'}$ we obtain

$$
\begin{aligned}
\Pi_{P'M'}(M''')(not_a) &= M'''((\mathscr{N}_i(a))^{M'}) \\
&= M'''(\mathscr{N}_i(M'(a))) \\
&= \mathscr{N}_i(M'(a)) \\
&= M'''(not_a)
\end{aligned}
$$

(2) For $(r{:}a \leftarrow \alpha) \in \mathscr{R}_P$ and the corresponding r_i' we obtain

$$
\begin{aligned}
\Pi_{P'M'}(M''')(r_i') &= M'''((\mathscr{I}_r(\alpha', \mathscr{N}_i(not_a)))^{M'}) \\
&= M'''(\mathscr{I}_r(M'(\alpha'), \mathscr{N}_i(\mathscr{N}_i((M'(a)))))) \\
&= \mathscr{I}_r(M'(\alpha'), M'(a)) \\
&= \mathscr{I}_r(M'(\alpha), M'(a)) \\
&= \mathscr{I}_r(M(\alpha), M(a)) \\
&= \rho_M(r) \\
&= M'''(r_i')
\end{aligned}
$$

(3) For $(r{:}k \leftarrow \alpha) \in \mathscr{R}_P$ and the corresponding r_i' we obtain similar to the above that $\Pi_{P'M'}(M''')(r_i') = M'''(r_i')$.

(4) For $aggr$ we obtain

$$
\begin{aligned}
\Pi_{P'M'}(M''')(aggr) &= M'''(f(r_{1i}', \ldots, r_{ni}')) \\
&= f(\rho_M(r_1), \ldots, \rho_M(r_n)) \\
&= \mathscr{A}_P(\rho_M) \\
&= M'(aggr) \\
&= M'''(aggr)
\end{aligned}
$$

(5) Suppose $a \in \mathscr{B}_P$. Since M'' is a fixpoint of Π_{PM,ρ_M} and $M'' = M''' \cap \mathscr{B}_P$ it follows that $M''' \cap \mathscr{B}_P$ is a fixpoint of Π_{PM,ρ_M}. From this we obtain:

$$
\begin{aligned}
\Pi_{P'M'}(M''')(a) &= \sup\{M'''((\mathscr{T}_r(\alpha, r_i'))^{M'}) \mid (r{:}a \leftarrow \alpha) \in \mathscr{R}_P\} \\
&= \sup\{\mathscr{T}_r(M'''(\alpha^{M'}), M'''(r_i')) \mid (r{:}a \leftarrow \alpha) \in \mathscr{R}_P\} \\
&= \sup\{\mathscr{T}_r(M'''(\alpha^M), \rho_M(r)) \mid (r{:}a \leftarrow \alpha) \in \mathscr{R}_P\} \\
&= \sup\{M_s'''(r^M, \rho_M(r)) \mid (r{:}a \leftarrow \alpha) \in \mathscr{R}_P\} \\
&= \Pi_{PM,\rho_M}(M''')(a) \\
&= M'''(a)
\end{aligned}
$$

Hence M''' is a fixpoint of $\Pi_{P'M'}$. This is however impossible as M' is an answer set of P' and thus the least fixpoint of $\Pi_{P'M'}$. Thus no such M'' can exist and M is the least fixpoint of Π_{PM}.   □

5.6 S-implicators

Occasionally, when using aggregators, the ability to use other types of implicators in rules could be useful. If the Kleene-Dienes implicator were used, for example, then $r : a \leftarrow f(b_1, \ldots, b_n)$ would only evaluate to 1 if either the body evaluates to 0, or the head evaluates to 1. This means that as soon as $I(f(b_1, \ldots, b_n)) > 0$, the rule is triggered and the head is taken to be completely true.

Example 5.2. Consider the following program P_{bbq}, encoding that we want to have a barbecue, unless the weather is bad:

$$r_1 : bad\_weather \leftarrow_{kd} rain$$
$$r_2 : bad\_weather \leftarrow_l \mathcal{N}(sunshine)$$
$$r_3 : \qquad bbq \leftarrow_l \mathcal{N}(bad\_weather)$$

where *rain* is the degree to which it is raining and *sunshine* is the expected amount of sunshine. Because the Kleene–Dienes implicator is used in the first rule, a barbecue is out of the question even if it rains only a little bit (e.g. drizzle). If it is not raining, our motivation for having a barbecue depends linearly on the amount of sunshine, hence a Łukasiewicz implicator is used.

However, as the rules in AFASP are restricted to residual implicators, we are not directly able to write the program above. In this section we explain how the semantics of AFASP can be extended to support S-implicators and moreover show that any AFASP program with S-implicators can be simulated by a normal AFASP program. Similar to the previous sections, we first define an extension of AFASP with S-implicator rules, called AFASP^S and then show that any program in AFASP^S can be reduced to an equivalent AFASP program.

Definition 5.13. An AFASP^S rule is a FASP rule that is associated with either a residual implicator or an S-implicator constructed from a t-norm and an involutive negator. An AFASP^S program is a tuple $\langle \mathcal{R}, \mathcal{A} \rangle$ where $\mathcal{R}$ is a FASP program with AFASP^S rules and $\mathcal{A}$ is an aggregator function over $\mathcal{R}$.

For an AFASP^S program P we define the Herbrand Base, the set P_a for a given atom a, the rule base $\mathcal{R}_P$, the aggregator $\mathcal{A}_P$, the immediate consequence operator, the reduct and interpretations similar to AFASP. For a given AFASP^S rule $r : a \leftarrow \alpha$ we denote the attached implicator with $\mathscr{I}_r$. If $\mathscr{I}_r$ is a residual implicator, the t-norm of which $\mathscr{I}_r$ is the residual implicator is denoted as $\mathscr{T}_r$ as before. Likewise, if $\mathscr{I}_r$ is an S-implicator, we denote the t-norm and negator used to construct $\mathscr{I}_r$ as $\mathscr{T}_r$, respectively $\mathscr{N}_r$. To extend the semantics of AFASP programs with S-implicator rules, we first extend the *support* for AFASP rules[2] to rules that are associated with an S-implicator, i.e. for any AFASP^S program P, $w \in \mathscr{L}_P$ and rule $r \in P$ that is associated with an S-implicator we define $I_s(r,w) = \inf\{k \in \mathscr{L}_P \mid \mathscr{I}_r(I(\alpha),k) \geqslant w\}$. The following lemma and proposition shows how this support can be computed in an easy manner.

Lemma 5.2. *Let $\mathscr{L}$ be a lattice, $\mathscr{N}_i$ an involutive negator on $\mathscr{L}$ and $\mathscr{T}$ a t-norm on $\mathscr{L}$. Then for any $x, y, w \in \mathscr{L}$ it holds that[3]:*

$$\mathscr{I}_{\mathscr{T},\mathscr{N}_i}(x,y) \geqslant w \equiv y \geqslant \mathscr{N}_i(\mathscr{I}_{\mathscr{T}}(x,\mathscr{N}_i(w))) \geqslant 1$$

Proof. Using the definition of $\mathscr{I}_{\mathscr{T},\mathscr{N}_i}$ and the residuation principle we obtain:

$$\mathscr{I}_{\mathscr{T},\mathscr{N}_i}(x,y) \geqslant w \equiv \mathscr{N}_i(\mathscr{T}(x,\mathscr{N}_i(y))) \geqslant w$$
$$\equiv \mathscr{T}(x,\mathscr{N}_i(y)) \leqslant \mathscr{N}_i(w)$$
$$\equiv \mathscr{N}_i(y) \leqslant \mathscr{I}_{\mathscr{T}}(x,\mathscr{N}_i(w))$$
$$\equiv y \geqslant \mathscr{N}_i(\mathscr{I}_{\mathscr{T}}(x,\mathscr{N}_i(w)))$$

$\square$

Proposition 5.8. *Let $\mathscr{L}$ be a lattice and consider an AFASP^S rule $r : a \leftarrow \alpha$ over $\mathscr{L}$ to which an S-implicator $\mathscr{I}_{\mathscr{T},\mathscr{N}_i}$ is attached, where $\mathscr{N}_i$ is an involutive negator on $\mathscr{L}$. For any $w \in \mathscr{L}$ and interpretation I of an AFASP^S program P over $\mathscr{L}$ that contains r it holds that:*

$$I_s(r,w) = \mathscr{N}_r(\mathscr{I}_{\mathscr{T}_r}(I(\alpha),\mathscr{N}_r(w)))$$

where we recall that $\mathscr{I}_{\mathscr{T}_r}$ is the residual implicator of $\mathscr{T}_r$.

Proof. Using the definition of $I_s(r,w)$ and Lemma 5.2 we obtain:

$$I_s(r,w) = \inf\{k \in \mathscr{L} \mid \mathscr{I}_{\mathscr{T},\mathscr{N}_i}(I(\alpha),k) \geqslant w\}$$
$$= \inf\{k \in \mathscr{L} \mid y \geqslant \mathscr{N}_i(\mathscr{I}_{\mathscr{T}}(I(\alpha),\mathscr{N}_i(w)))\}$$
$$= \mathscr{N}_i(\mathscr{I}_{\mathscr{T}}(I(\alpha),\mathscr{N}_i(w)))$$

$\square$

---

[2]See Definition 4.6 on page 59.
[3]Recall that $\mathscr{I}_{\mathscr{T},\mathscr{N}_i}$ is the S-implicator constructed using the t-norm $\mathscr{T}$ and the negator $\mathscr{N}_i$, as defined in Definition 2.26 on page 29.

Using the characterization of the support above, the semantics of an AFASP^S program are defined as in Chapter 4.

Now we show that, under certain conditions on the underlying lattice, we can transform an AFASP^S program to an equivalent AFASP program.

Definition 5.14. Let P be an AFASP^S program with rule base $\mathscr{R}_P = \mathscr{R}_P^r \cup \mathscr{R}_P^s$ such that $\mathscr{R}_P^r$ is the set of rules associated with residual implicators and $\mathscr{R}_P^s$ is the set of rules associated with S-implicators. Furthermore assume that $\mathscr{L}_P$ is such that there is a residual implicator $\mathscr{I}_i$ that induces an involutive negator $\mathscr{N}_i$. Then the rule base of the AFASP program P' corresponding to P is defined as:

$$\mathscr{R}_{P'} = \mathscr{R}_P^r$$
$$\cup \{r': a \leftarrow \mathscr{N}_r(\mathscr{I}_{\mathscr{T}_r}(\alpha, not_{w_{r'}})) \mid (r: a \leftarrow_s \alpha) \in \mathscr{R}_P^s, a \in \mathscr{B}_P\}$$
$$\cup \{r'_w: w_{r'} \leftarrow \mathscr{I}_r(\alpha', \mathscr{N}_i(not_a)) \mid (r: a \leftarrow_s \alpha) \in \mathscr{R}_P^s, a \in \mathscr{B}_P\}$$
$$\cup \{r'_w: w_{r'} \leftarrow \mathscr{I}_r(\alpha', k) \mid (r: k \leftarrow_s \alpha) \in \mathscr{R}_P^s, k \in \mathscr{L}_P\}$$
$$\cup \{r'_{not_a}: not_a \leftarrow \mathscr{N}_i(a) \mid a \in \mathscr{B}_P\}$$
$$\cup \{r'_{nw_{r'}}: not_{w_{r'}} \leftarrow \mathscr{N}_r(w_{r'}) \mid (r: a \leftarrow_s \alpha) \in \mathscr{R}_P^s, a \in \mathscr{B}_P\}$$
$$\cup \{r'_c: 0 \leftarrow_i \mathscr{N}_i(w_{r'}) \mid (r: a \leftarrow_s \alpha) \in \mathscr{R}_P^s\}$$

where the literals $w_{r'}$, not_a and $not_{w_{r'}}$ are fresh literals not contained in $\mathscr{B}_P$ and a rule of the form $r: a \leftarrow_i \alpha$ is associated with the implicator $\mathscr{I}_i$. Furthermore for $\alpha = f(b_1, \ldots, b_n; c_1, \ldots, c_m)$ we define $\alpha' = f'(b_1, \ldots, b_n, not_{c_1}, \ldots, not_{c_m})$, with $f'(b_1, \ldots, b_n, not_{c_1}, \ldots, not_{c_m}) = f(b_1, \ldots, b_n; \mathscr{N}_i(not_{c_1}), \ldots, \mathscr{N}_i(not_{c_m}))$. The aggregator of P' is defined as:

$$\mathscr{A}_{P'}(\rho) = \begin{cases} (\mathscr{A}_P)(\rho') & \text{if } \mathscr{T}_M(\rho(r'), \rho(r'_w), \rho(r'_{not_a}), \rho(r'_{nw_{r'}})) \geqslant 1 \\ 0 & \text{otherwise} \end{cases}$$

where $\rho'(r) = \rho(r'_c)$ for any $r \in \mathscr{R}_P^s$ and $\rho'(r) = \rho(r)$ for any $r \in \mathscr{R}_P \setminus \mathscr{R}_P^s$.

Recall that if the subscript is missing from the $\leftarrow$ symbol in an AFASP rule, the implicator that is associated with this rule can be arbitrarily chosen. Hence in the above definition rules r', r'_w, r'_{not_a} and $r'_{nw_{r'}}$ are associated with an arbitrary (residual) implicator. The constraint on the lattice $\mathscr{L}$ states that there must exist at least one negator $\mathscr{N}_i$ on $\mathscr{L}$ such that for all $x \in \mathscr{L}$ we have that $\mathscr{N}_i(x) = \mathscr{I}_i(x, 0)$ and $\mathscr{I}_i(\mathscr{I}_i(x, 0), 0) = x$. This constraint is needed to properly inject the value of the interpretation of the rule in the aggregator. It is clear that in $[0, 1]$ the Łukasiewicz implication satisfies this criterion. In general every MV-algebra[4] satisfies

---

[4] An MV-algebra is an algebraic structure with a binary operation, a unary operation and the constant 0, satisfying certain axioms. They are models of Łukasiewicz logic. See [Hájek (1998)] for more information.

this by definition [Hájek (1998)]. Also note that the program defined above still contains S-implicators (viz. the $\mathscr{I}_r$ functions in the bodies). However, they appear as functions in the rule bodies, and not as the implication associated to a rule. Hence, we have reduced the semantics of a program with mixed S-implication and residual implication rules to a program solely consisting of the latter. Furthermore note that for any interpretation I of P and corresponding interpretation I' of P' we have $\rho_I(r_c') = I(w_{r'})$. In this way the aggregator expression obtains the same value for any interpretation of P' as it does for P. Last, the construction with not_a is necessary to be able to fix the value of not_a w.r.t. a certain reduct as in Section 5.5.

As an example, consider the AFASP^S program P_{bbq} from Example 5.2. The corresponding AFASP program contains the following rule base:

$$
\begin{aligned}
r_2: \qquad\qquad bad\_weather &\leftarrow_l \mathscr{N}_W(sunshine) \\
r_3: \qquad\qquad bbq &\leftarrow_l \mathscr{N}_W(bad\_weather) \\
r_1': \qquad\qquad bad\_weather &\leftarrow_l \mathscr{N}_W(\mathscr{I}_M(rain, not_{w_{r_1'}})) \\
r_{1w}': \qquad\qquad w_{r_1'} &\leftarrow_l \mathscr{I}_{\mathscr{T}_M, \mathscr{N}_W}(rain, \mathscr{N}_W(not_{bad\_weather})) \\
r_{1_{not_{bad\_weather}}}': not_{bad\_weather} &\leftarrow_l (\mathscr{N}_W(bad\_weather)) \\
r_{1nw_{r_1'}}': \qquad\qquad not_{w_{r_1'}} &\leftarrow_l \mathscr{N}_W(w_{r_1'}) \\
r_{1c}': \qquad\qquad 0 &\leftarrow_l \mathscr{N}_W(w_{r_1'})
\end{aligned}
$$

Suppose we add some facts that tell us that it is raining to a degree of 0.2 and it is sunny to a degree of 0.7. The 1-answer set we obtain for the program from Example 5.2 is $A = \{rain^{0.2}, sunny^{0.7}, bad\_weather^1, bbq^0\}$. One can verify that the 1-answer set of the S-implicator free version is $A' = A \cup \{w_{r_1'}^1\} \cup \{not_{bad\_weather}^0\} \cup \{not_{w_{r_1'}}^0\}$.

The following propositions show that the answer sets of the AFASP^s program coincide with those of the corresponding AFASP program. Hence AFASP^s programs can be translated to equivalent CFASP programs using the results from Section 5.5. We summarized this in Figure 5.1 on page 131.

Proposition 5.9. *Let P be an AFASP^s program and let P' be the corresponding AFASP program in Definition 5.14. If M is an m-answer set ($m \in \mathscr{P}_P$ and $m > 0$) of P, it holds that*
$$M' = M \cup \{w_{r'}^{\rho_M(r)} \mid r \in \mathscr{R}_P^s\} \cup \{not_a^{\mathscr{N}_i(M'(a))} \mid a \in \mathscr{B}_P\} \cup \{not_{w_{r'}}^{\mathscr{N}_r(\rho_M(r))} \mid r \in \mathscr{R}_P^s, r_h \in \mathscr{B}_P\}$$
is an m-answer set of P', where $\mathscr{N}_i$ and $\mathscr{N}_r$ are as in Definition 5.14.

Proof.   See Section 5.A on page 125.   □

Proposition 5.10. *Let P be an AFASP^s program and let P' be the corresponding AFASP program as defined in Definition 5.14. If M' is an m-answer set ($m \in \mathscr{P}_{P'}$ and $m > 0$) of P,* *it holds that $M = M' \cap \mathscr{B}_P$ is an m-answer set of P.*

Proof.   See Section 5.A on page 125.   □

5.7   Strong Negation

As mentioned in Section 2.2.2, in ASP, there is a second form of negation besides negation-as-failure, called *classical negation* (also known as *strong negation*). This form of negation is used when explicit derivation of negative information is needed. The resulting semantic difference can be very important. For example, if we wish to state that it is safe to cross the train tracks when no train is coming we write the following program when using negation-as-failure (from [Baral (2003)]):

$$cross \leftarrow \text{not } train$$

This however means that when the information about a train coming is absent, we cross the tracks, which is not the safest thing to do. With strong negation, the problem is written as:

$$cross \leftarrow \neg train$$

where $\neg train$ is a special literal that can appear in the head of rules. As the value of $\neg train$ is derived using the rules of the program and not derived by the absence of information about *train*, we only cross the tracks when we can explicitly derive that no train is coming. Of course, when both a and $\neg a$ appear in the head of rules there is the possibility of inconsistency. The usual semantics for ASP determine that whenever the standard definition would lead to an answer set of a program P in which both a and $\neg a$ occur, by definition, the only answer set of P is given by $Lit(P) = \mathscr{B}_P \cup \{\neg a \mid a \in \mathscr{B}_P\}$ (see [Baral (2003)]). A program in which this occurs is inconsistent and, as in classical propositional logic, anything can be derived from an inconsistent program.

In [Van Nieuwenborgh *et al.* (2007b)] a fuzzy version of classical negation is introduced. The inconsistency problem in this fuzzy case is solved by attaching to each interpretation I of a program P and literal $a \in \mathscr{B}_P$ a score of consistency $I_c(a) = \mathscr{N}_c(\mathscr{T}_c(I(a), I(\neg a)))$, where $\mathscr{N}_c$ is a negator and $\mathscr{T}_c$ a t-norm. The interpretation I is then called x-**consistent**, with $x \in \mathscr{L}_P$, iff $\mathscr{A}_c(I_c) \geqslant x$, where $\mathscr{A}_c$ is the consistency aggregator that maps I_c to a global consistency score for I. This consistency aggregator, which differs from the regular aggregator, is required to be increasing when the consistencies for literals increase.

It is well-known that ASP programs with strong negation can be translated to equivalent programs without strong negation by substituting a new literal a' and adding the constraint

$c: \leftarrow a, a'$ for each $\neg a \in Lit(P)$. The resulting program has no consistent answer sets iff program P has the unique answer set $Lit(P)$.

We can generalize the procedure for eliminating strong negation in classical ASP to fuzzy programs and embed strong negation in AFASP. In particular, to implement the strong negation approach of [Van Nieuwenborgh *et al.* (2007b)] into AFASP, we proceed as follows:

Definition 5.15. Let P be an AFASP program with strong negation and let $\mathcal{N}_c$, $\mathcal{T}_c$ and $\mathscr{A}_c$ be the negator, t-norm and aggregator expression determining the consistency score of P w.r.t. some interpretation. Furthermore assume that we can define an implicator $\mathscr{I}_i$ in $\mathscr{L}_P$ that induces an involutive negator $\mathscr{N}_i$. Then P', the strong-negation free version of P is defined as follows:

(1) $\mathscr{B}_{P'} = (\mathscr{B}_P \setminus \{\neg a \mid a \in \mathscr{B}_P\}) \cup \{a' \mid \neg a \in \mathscr{B}_P\}$

(2) $\mathscr{R}_{P'} = \{r{:}a \leftarrow \alpha' \mid (r{:}a \leftarrow \alpha) \in \mathscr{R}_P\} \cup \{c_a{:}0 \leftarrow_i \mathscr{N}_i(\mathscr{N}_c(\mathscr{T}_c(a,a'))) \mid a \in \mathscr{B}_P\}$

(3) $\mathscr{A}_{P'}(\rho) = (\mathscr{A}_c(\{a^{\rho(c_a)} \mid a \in \mathscr{B}_P\}), \mathscr{A}_P(\rho))$

where for a rule $(r{:}a \leftarrow \alpha) \in \mathscr{R}_P$ we define α' as the expression obtained by replacing each $\neg a$ by the corresponding a'. Furthermore a rule of the form $r{:}a \leftarrow_i \alpha$ is associated with the $\mathscr{I}_i$ implicator. Last, for each $a \in \mathscr{B}_P$ it must hold that $a' \notin \mathscr{B}_P$, i.e. a' is a "fresh" literal.

Technically, we first replace all classically negated literals with a fresh variable. Then we "inject" the value of $I_c(a)$ for a literal a into the aggregator of the new program using the c_a rule. Since $\mathscr{I}_i$ and $\mathscr{N}_i$ are chosen such that $\mathscr{I}_i(x,0) = \mathscr{N}_i(x)$ and $\mathscr{N}_i(\mathscr{N}_i(x)) = x$ we obtain that the evaluation of rule c_a will always be equal to $\mathscr{N}_c(\mathscr{T}_c(a,a'))$, thus ensuring that the aggregator has access to this value. The reason for this injection method is the fact that the aggregator only takes rule interpretations into account, not regular interpretations, and therefore cannot refer to the value of a single literal. Last, we create the new aggregator as a tuple of the consistency degree and the old aggregator, allowing us to order answer sets using both measures. Note that for an AFASP program P this aggregator obtains a value in $\mathscr{L}_P^2$, which is a complete lattice.

Example 5.3. Consider an AFASP program P with rule base $\mathscr{R}_P$:

$$r_1{:}\quad a \leftarrow_m \neg b$$
$$r_2{:}\ \neg b \leftarrow_m 0.2$$
$$r_3{:}\ \neg a \leftarrow_m 0.4$$

The rule aggregator is defined as $\mathscr{A}_P(\rho) = \min(1, \rho(r_1) + \rho(r_2) + \rho(r_3))$ and the consistency aggregator as $\mathscr{A}_c(I_c) = \inf\{I_c(a) \mid a \in \mathscr{B}_P\}$. For all literals the consistency negator $\mathscr{N}_c$ is $\mathscr{N}_W$ and the consistency t-norm $\mathscr{T}_c$ is $\mathscr{T}_M$. According to Definition 5.15, the strong-negation free version of P is a program P' with rule base $\mathscr{R}_{P'}$:

$$r_1: \ a \leftarrow_m b'$$
$$r_2: \ b' \leftarrow_m 0.2$$
$$r_3: \ a' \leftarrow_m 0.4$$
$$c_a: \ 0 \leftarrow_l \ \mathscr{N}_W(\mathscr{N}_W(\mathscr{T}_M(a,a')))$$
$$c_b: \ 0 \leftarrow_l \ \mathscr{N}_W(\mathscr{N}_W(\mathscr{T}_M(b,b')))$$

The aggregator of P' is $\mathscr{A}_{P'}(\rho) = (\mathscr{A}_c(\{a^{\rho(c_a)}, b^{\rho(c_b)}\}), \mathscr{A}_P(\rho))$. Now, consider an interpretation $I = \{a^{0.2}, (\neg b)^{0.2}, (\neg a)^{0.4}\}$ of P and the corresponding interpretation $I' = \{a^{0.2}, b'^{0.2}, a'^{0.4}\}$ of P'. Computing I_c we obtain that $I_c(a) = 1 - \mathscr{T}_M(I(a), I(\neg a)) = 1 - \mathscr{T}_M(0.2, 0.4) = 0.8$ and likewise $I_c(b) = 1 - \mathscr{T}_M(I(b), I(\neg b)) = 1 - \mathscr{T}_M(0, 0.2) = 1$. Computing $\rho_{I'}$ we easily obtain $\rho_{I'}(r_1) = \rho_{I'}(r_2) = \rho_{I'}(r_3) = 1$; for c_a and c_b we obtain $\rho_{I'}(c_a) = \mathscr{N}_W(\mathscr{I}_W(\mathscr{N}_W(\mathscr{T}_M(a,a')), 0)) = 1 - (\mathscr{I}_W(I_c(a), 0)) = 1 - (1 - I_c(a)) = I_c(a)$ and likewise for c_b we get $\rho_{I'}(c_b) = I_c(b)$. The evaluation of $\mathscr{A}_{P'}$ with $\rho_{I'}$ then gives $\mathscr{A}_{P'}(\rho_{I'}) = (\mathscr{A}_c(\{a^{I_c(a)}, b^{I_c(b)}\}), \mathscr{A}_P(\rho_{I'})) = (\mathscr{A}_c(I_c), \mathscr{A}_P(\rho_{I'}))$. Hence, the aggregator indeed maps an interpretation to a tuple containing the consistency degree and the rule aggregation score.

The following proposition links our definition to the strong negation approach of [Van Nieuwenborgh *et al.* (2007b)].

Proposition 5.11. *Let P be an AFASP program with strong negation and let P' be its strong-negation free version. Then an interpretation I' of P' is an (x,y)-answer set of P iff the corresponding answer set I of P is x-consistent in the sense of [Van Nieuwenborgh et al. (2007b)].*

Proof. Immediate from the construction of P' and $\mathscr{A}_{P'}$. $\qquad\qquad\square$

5.8 Summary

To investigate the expressivity of certain FASP constructs we introduced a core language for FASP, called CFASP, that only contains non-constraint rules with monotonically increasing functions and negators in rule bodies. We then studied whether these constructs can be simulated in CFASP.

First, we extended CFASP with constraints, resulting in the language CFASP$^\perp$. We investigated whether CFASP$^\perp$ can be translated to CFASP, i.e. whether CFASP is capable of simulating constraints. We showed that by using specific FASP programs without answer sets, we are able to simulate constraints. This is similar to an existing constraint-elimination procedure for ASP and in fact our method generalizes this procedure to the fuzzy case. Furthermore we showed that constraints can also be used for locking the value of certain atoms in a specific interval.

Second, we extended CFASP with monotonically decreasing functions, resulting in the language CFASP^f. We showed that by using an involutive negator we can simulate the decreasing behavior of these functions using only monotonic functions and extended literals. Hence, we proved that any CFASP^f program can be translated to an equivalent CFASP program.

Third, we investigated whether AFASP programs with an aggregator that ranges over the same lattice as the program rules can be simulated in CFASP. At first sight this seems straightforward since for each rule r_i $(1 \leqslant i \leqslant n)$ in an AFASP program P we can add rules of the form $s_{r_i}: r_i \leftarrow \mathscr{I}_{r_i}((r_i)_b, (r_i)_h)$ to its CFASP^f translation P' and then add a rule $aggr: k \leftarrow f_{\mathscr{A}}(r_1, \ldots, r_n)$ that computes the aggregated value. We showed that this naive translation does not correctly preserve the semantics and that care needs to be taken when monotonically decreasing functions, such as $\mathscr{I}_{r_i}$, occur. We defined a translation that includes the necessary bookkeeping rules for arguments of decreasing functions and proved that it correctly translates an AFASP program to a CFASP^f program, which can be translated to a CFASP program.

Fourth, we extended AFASP with rules that are associated with S-implicators instead of residual implicators, resulting in the language AFASP^S. To define the semantics of this language we extended the support concept of AFASP to AFASP^S and showed that the support of rules associated with specific S-implicators can be computed using only a residual implicator and negator. We then used this result to show that AFASP^S can be simulated in AFASP using a simulation that is similar to the AFASP to CFASP^f translation.

Last, we investigated whether a previously proposed extension of AFASP with classical negation can be simulated in AFASP. This extension has a separate negation aggregator that combines the scores of the conjunction of the classically negated literal $\neg l$ and its corresponding atom l. We showed that we can inject the value of literals in the rule aggregator function of AFASP by using an involutive negator and constraints. This allows us to simulate the negation aggregator using the rule aggregator function of AFASP.

Our results are important to create a bridge between FASP users who want a rich and di-verse modeling language and FASP theoreticians and implementers who want a small core language that is easy to reason about and implement. We summarized our translations in Figure 5.1 on page 131. In the next chapter we show how a subclass of CFASP can be implemented using fuzzy SAT solving techniques. Due to the results in this chapter we know that our implementation method can also be used to solve programs with constraints, monotonically decreasing functions, aggregators, S-implicators and classical negation by including an appropriate solver front-end that translates these constructs to the correspond-ing CFASP program.

5.A   Proofs

To show Proposition 5.9, we introduce a few technical lemmas.

Lemma 5.3. *Let P be an AFASP^S program and let P' be its corresponding AFASP program as defined in Definition 5.14. Then if M is a fixpoint of Π_{PM,ρ_M} of P, it holds for the interpretation $M' = M \cup \{w_{r'}^{\rho_M(r)} \mid r \in \mathscr{R}_P^s\} \cup \{not_a^{\mathcal{N}_i(M(a))} \mid a \in \mathscr{B}_P\} \cup \{not_{w_{r'}}^{\mathcal{N}_r(\rho_M(r))} \mid r \in \mathscr{R}_P^s\}$ of P' that*

(1) $\forall r \in \mathscr{R}_P^r \cdot \rho_{M'}(r) = \rho_M(r)$
(2) $\forall r \in \mathscr{R}_P^s \cdot \rho_{M'}(r') = 1$
(3) $\forall r \in \mathscr{R}_P^s \setminus \mathscr{C}_P \cdot \rho_{M'}(r_w') = 1$
(4) $\forall r \in \mathscr{R}_P^s \cap \mathscr{C}_P \cdot \rho_{M'}(r_w') = 1$
(5) $\forall r \in \mathscr{R}_P^s \cdot \rho_{M'}(r_{not_a}') = 1$
(6) $\forall r \in \mathscr{R}_P^s \cdot \rho_{M'}(r_{nw_{r'}}') = 1$
(7) $\forall r \in \mathscr{R}_P^s \cdot \rho_{M'}(r_c') = \rho_M(r)$

where r', r_w', r_{not_a}', and r_c' are defined as in Definition 5.14 and $\mathscr{C}_P$ is the set of constraints in P.

Proof.   We consider these cases separately:

(1) Trivial from the definition of P' and M'.
(2) When $r: a \leftarrow_s \alpha \in \mathscr{R}_P^s$, from Proposition 5.8 we have for the corresponding $r' \in \mathscr{R}_{P'}$ by definition of M' that

$$\rho_{M'}(r') = \mathscr{I}_{r'}(\mathcal{N}_r(\mathscr{I}_{\mathcal{T}_r}(M'(\alpha), not_{w_{r'}})), M'(a))$$
$$= \mathscr{I}_{r'}(\mathcal{N}_r(\mathscr{I}_{\mathcal{T}_r}(M'(\alpha), \rho_M(r))), M(a))$$

$$= \mathcal{I}_{r'}(\mathcal{N}_r(\mathcal{I}_{\mathcal{T}_r}(M(\alpha), \rho_M(r))), M(a))$$

$$= \mathcal{I}_{r'}(M_s(r, \rho_M(r)), M(a))$$

$$= 1$$

The last step follows from Proposition 2.10 and from the fact that M is a fixpoint of Π_{pM, ρ_M}.

(3) When $(r : a \leftarrow_s \alpha) \in \mathcal{R}_P^s$ and $a \in \mathcal{B}_P$, using the definition of M' we have for the corresponding $r'_w \in \mathcal{R}_{P'}$ that

$$\rho_{M'}(r'_w) = \mathcal{I}_{r'_w}(\mathcal{I}_r(M'(\alpha), \mathcal{N}_i(M'(not_a))), M'(w_{r'}))$$

$$= \mathcal{I}_{r'_w}(\mathcal{I}_r(M(\alpha), \mathcal{N}_i(\mathcal{N}_i(M(a)))), \rho_M(r))$$

$$= \mathcal{I}_{r'_w}(\mathcal{I}_r(M(\alpha), M(a)), \rho_M(r))$$

$$= 1$$

(4) When $(r : k \leftarrow_s \alpha) \in \mathcal{R}_P^s$ and $k \in \mathcal{L}_P$, we obtain that $\rho_{M'}(r'_w) = 1$ similar to the above case.

(5) When $r \in \mathcal{R}_P^s$ with $r_h = a$, we have for the corresponding $r'_{not_a} \in \mathcal{R}_{P'}$ that

$$\rho_{M'}(r'_{not_a}) = \mathcal{I}_{r'_{not_a}}(\mathcal{N}_i(M'(a)), M'(not_a))$$

$$= \mathcal{I}_{r'_{not_a}}(\mathcal{N}_i(M(a)), \mathcal{N}_i(M(a)))$$

$$= 1$$

(6) When $(r : a \leftarrow_s \alpha) \in \mathcal{R}_P^s$ we obtain for the corresponding $r'_{nw_{r'}} \in \mathcal{R}_{P'}$ that

$$\rho_{M'}(r'_{nw_{r'}}) = \mathcal{I}_{r'_{nw_{r'}}}(\mathcal{N}_i(\rho_M(r)), \mathcal{N}_i(\rho_M(r))) = 1$$

(7) When $r \in \mathcal{R}_P^s$ we obtain for the corresponding $r'_c \in \mathcal{R}_{P'}$ that

$$\rho_{M'}(r'_c) = \mathcal{I}_i(\mathcal{N}_i(M'(w_{r'})), 0) = \mathcal{N}_i((\mathcal{N}_i(M'(w_{r'})))) = \rho_M(r) \qquad \square$$

Lemma 5.4. *Let P be an $AFASP^S$ program with M a fixpoint of Π_{pM, ρ_M} and let $M' = M \cup \{w_{r'}^{\rho_M(r)} \mid r \in \mathcal{R}_P^s\} \cup \{not_a^{\mathcal{N}_i(M(a))} \mid a \in \mathcal{B}_P\} \cup \{not_{w_{r'}}^{\mathcal{N}_r(\rho_M(r))} \mid r \in \mathcal{R}_P^s\}$ be an interpretation of its corresponding AFASP program P', as defined by Definition 5.14. Then any interpretation I of P and I' of P' such that $I(a) = I'(a)$ for all $a \in \mathcal{B}_P$ satisfies*

$$\Pi_{P'M', \rho_{M'}}(I') = \Pi_{pM, \rho_M}(I) \cup \{w_{r'}^{\rho_M(r)} \mid r \in \mathcal{R}_P^s\}$$

$$\cup \{not_a^{\mathcal{N}_i(M(a))} \mid a \in \mathcal{B}_P\}$$

$$\cup \{not_{w_{r'}}^{\mathcal{N}_r(\rho_M(r))} \mid r \in \mathcal{R}_P^s\}$$

with $\mathcal{N}_i$ and $\mathcal{N}_r$ as in Definition 5.14.

Proof. Note that by Definition 5.14 one can immediately see that $\mathscr{B}_{P'}$ consists of four partitions, i.e. $\mathscr{B}_{P'} = \mathscr{B}_P \cup \{w_{r'} \mid r \in \mathscr{R}^s_P \setminus \mathscr{C}_P\} \cup \{w_{r'} \mid r \in \mathscr{R}^s_P \cap \mathscr{C}_P\} \cup \{not_a \mid a \in \mathscr{B}_P\} \cup \{not_{w_{r'}} \mid r \in \mathscr{R}^s_P\}$, where $\mathscr{C}_P$ is the set of constraints in P. We consider the elements of these partitions separately.

(1) Suppose $(r : a \leftarrow_s \alpha) \in \mathscr{R}^s_P$ with $a \in \mathscr{B}_P$ and consider the corresponding $w_{r'} \in \mathscr{B}_{P'}$, then by definition of $\Pi_{P'^{M'},\rho_{M'}}$ and Proposition 4.1 we have

$$\Pi_{P'^{M'},\rho_{M'}}(I')(w_{r'}) = \sup\{\mathscr{T}_{r'}(I'(r'_b),\rho_{M'}(r')) \mid r' \in P'^{M'}_{w_{r'}}\}$$

By Definition 5.14 we know that $P'^{M'}_{w_{r'}} = \{(r'_w)^{M'}\}$. From Lemma 5.3 we know $\rho_{M'}(r'_w) = 1$, which, together with Definition 5.14, leads to

$$\Pi_{P'^{M'},\rho_{M'}}(I')(w_{r'}) = I'((\mathscr{I}_r(\alpha,\mathscr{N}_i(not_a)))^{M'})$$

Now by definition of the reduct and M', combined with the fact that $\mathscr{N}_i$ is involutive, this leads to

$$\Pi_{P'^{M'},\rho_{M'}}(I')(w_{r'}) = I'(\mathscr{I}_r(M'(\alpha),M'(a))) = \rho_{M'}(r)$$

Now by the definition of ρ_M we obtain

$$\Pi_{P'^{M'},\rho_{M'}}(I')(w_{r'}) = \rho_{M'}(r) = \rho_M(r)$$

(2) Suppose $(r : k \leftarrow_s \alpha) \in \mathscr{R}^s_P$ with $k \in \mathscr{L}_P$ and consider the corresponding $w_{r'} \in \mathscr{B}_{P'}$. This case follows similar to the above case.

(3) Suppose $r : a \leftarrow_s \alpha \in \mathscr{R}^s_P$ and consider the corresponding $not_a \in \mathscr{B}_{P'}$. As $P'^{M'}_{not_a} = \{(r'_{not_a})^{M'}\}$, we obtain by the definition of $\Pi_{P'^{M'},\rho_{M'}}$ and Proposition 4.1 that

$$\Pi_{P'^{M'},\rho_{M'}}(I')(not_a) = \mathscr{T}_{r'_{not_a}}(I'((r'^{M'}_{not_a})b),\rho_{M'}(r'_{not_a}))$$

By Lemma 5.3 we know that $\rho_{M'}(r'_{not_a}) = 1$, hence by definition of r'_{not_a} we get

$$\Pi_{P'^{M'},\rho_{M'}}(I')(not_a) = I'((\mathscr{N}_i(a))^{M'})$$

By the definition of the reduct and the fact that $M(a) = M'(a)$ for $a \in \mathscr{B}_P$ this means

$$\Pi_{P'^{M'},\rho_{M'}}(I')(not_a) = \mathscr{N}_i(M(a)) = M'(not_a)$$

(4) Suppose $r : a \leftarrow_s \alpha \in \mathscr{R}^s_P$ and consider the corresponding $not_{w_{r'}} \in \mathscr{B}_{P'}$. This case is entirely analogous to the case for not_a.

(5) Finally, for $a \in \mathscr{B}_P$ we consider two cases:

(a) Suppose $(r:a \leftarrow \alpha) \in \mathscr{R}_P^r$, then it is easy to see by definition of P', Proposition 4.1 and Lemma 5.3 that

$$I_s(r^M, \rho_M(r)) = I_s'(r^{M'}, \rho_{M'}(r)) \tag{5.9}$$

(b) Suppose $r:a \leftarrow_s \alpha \in \mathscr{R}_P^s$ with corresponding $r' : a \leftarrow \mathscr{N}_r(\mathscr{I}_{\mathscr{T}_r}(\alpha, not_{w_{r'}}))$ in $\mathscr{R}_{P'}$. By definition of reduct, we obtain

$$r'^{M'} : a \leftarrow \mathscr{N}_r(\mathscr{I}_{\mathscr{T}_r}(\alpha^{M'}, M'(not_{w_{r'}})))$$

Hence by definition of M' we obtain

$$r'^{M'} : a \leftarrow \mathscr{N}_r(\mathscr{I}_{\mathscr{T}_r}(\alpha^{M'}, \mathscr{N}_r(\rho_M(r))))$$

Combining this with Proposition 4.1, Proposition 5.8, Lemma 5.3 and the fact that for $a \in \mathscr{B}_P \cap \mathscr{B}_{P'}$ it holds that $I(a) = I'(a)$, we obtain:

$$\begin{aligned}
I_s'(r'^{M'}, \rho_{M'}(r')) &= \mathscr{T}_{r'}(\rho_{M'}(r'), I'(\mathscr{N}_r(\mathscr{I}_{\mathscr{T}_r}(\alpha^{M'}, \mathscr{N}_r(\rho_M(r)))))) \\
&= \mathscr{N}_r(\mathscr{I}_{\mathscr{T}_r}(I'(\alpha^{M'}), \mathscr{N}_r(\rho_M(r)))) \\
&= \mathscr{N}_r(\mathscr{I}_{\mathscr{T}_r}(I'(\alpha^{M'}), \mathscr{N}_r(\rho_M(r^M)))) \\
&= I_s(r^M, \rho_M(r^M))
\end{aligned}$$

Combining Equation 5a and item 5b we easily obtain that

$$\Pi_{\rho_M, \rho_M}(I) = \Pi_{P'^{M'}, \rho_{M'}}(I') \cap \mathscr{B}_P$$

Hence, by combining these cases the stated follows. $\qquad\square$

Proof. [Proof of Proposition 5.9] First, by Lemma 5.3 and Definition 5.14 it is easy to see that $\mathscr{A}_{P'}(\rho_{M'}) \geqslant m$.

Second, we show that M' is an answer set of P', i.e. that it is the least fixpoint of $\Pi_{P'^{M'}, \rho_{M'}}$. From Lemma 5.4 we can readily see that M' is a fixpoint of $\Pi_{P'^{M'}, \rho_{M'}}$. Suppose now there is an $M'' < M'$ such that M'' is also a fixpoint of $\Pi_{P'^{M'}, \rho_{M'}}$. We show by contradiction that such an M'' cannot exist. First, note that due to Lemma 5.4 and the fact that both M' and M'' are fixpoints of $\Pi_{P'^{M'}, \rho_{M'}}$ it must hold that for all $l \in \mathscr{B}_{P'} \setminus \mathscr{B}_P$ we have $M''(l) = M'(l)$. Hence by Lemma 5.4 this means $M'' \cap \mathscr{B}_P < M' \cap \mathscr{B}_P$ and thus $M'' \cap \mathscr{B}_P < M$. However, by Lemma 5.4 and the fact that M'' is a fixpoint of $\Pi_{P'^{M'}, \rho_{M'}}$ we have that $M'' \cap \mathscr{B}_P$ must be a fixpoint of Π_{P^M, ρ_M}, contradicting the fact that M is the least fixpoint Π_{P^M, ρ_M} due to M being an answer set of P. $\qquad\square$

To show Proposition 5.10, we introduce the following Lemma.

Lemma 5.5. *Suppose P is an AFASP^s program and let P' be its corresponding AFASP program as defined in Definition 5.14. Then for any m-answer set M' of P', with $0 < m$, $m \in \mathscr{L}_P$ and $M = M' \cap \mathscr{B}_P$, it holds for all $r : a \leftarrow_s \alpha \in \mathscr{R}_P^s$ that*

(1) $M'(not_a) = \mathscr{N}_i(M'(a))$

(2) $M'(not_{w_{r'}}) = \mathscr{N}_r(M'(w_{r'}))$

(3) $M'(w_{r'}) = \rho_M(r)$

Proof. Since M' is a fixpoint of $\Pi_{P^{\prime M'}, \rho_{M'}}$ these cases follow easily from the definition of $\Pi_{P^{\prime M'}, \rho_{M'}}$, Proposition 4.1, the definition of P' and the fact that $P^{\prime M'}_{not_a} = \{(r'_{not_a})^{M'}\}$, $P^{\prime M'}_{not_{w_{r'}}} = \{(r'_{nw_{r'}})^{M'}\}$ and $P^{\prime M'}_{w_{r'}} = \{(r'_w)^{M'}\}$.   □

Proof. [Proof of Proposition 5.10] First we show that $\mathscr{A}_P(\rho_M) \geqslant m$. For a rule $r \in \mathscr{R}_P^r$, by definition of P' it holds trivially that $\rho_M(r) = \rho_{M'}(r)$. Further, for each rule $r \in \mathscr{R}_P^s$ there is a corresponding rule $r'_c : 0 \leftarrow_i \mathscr{N}_i(w_{r'})$ in P'. From Lemma 5.5 we know that $M'(w_{r'}) = \rho_M(r)$ and thus, as $\mathscr{N}_i(x) = \mathscr{I}_i(x,0)$ and $\mathscr{N}_i(\mathscr{N}_i(x)) = x$ that $\rho_{M'}(r'_c) = \rho_M(r)$. Hence, as $\mathscr{A}_{P'}(\rho_{M'}) \geqslant m$ and $m > 0$, this means $\mathscr{A}_P(\rho_M) \geqslant m$ by definition of $\mathscr{A}_{P'}$.

Second we show that M is the least fixpoint of Π_{P^M, ρ_M}. First we show that it is a fixpoint. From the definition of Π_{P^M, ρ_M} and Proposition 4.1 we obtain for $a \in \mathscr{B}_P$ that

$$\Pi_{P^M, \rho_M}(M)(a) = \sup\{M_s(r^M, \rho_M) \mid (r : a \leftarrow \alpha) \in \mathscr{R}_P\}$$

We consider two cases: $(r : a \leftarrow \alpha) \in \mathscr{R}_P^r$ and $(r : a \leftarrow \alpha) \in \mathscr{R}_P^s$.

(1) If $(r : a \leftarrow \alpha) \in \mathscr{R}_P^r$, then in P' we have an equivalent rule and thus combining this with the former remark that $\rho_M(r) = \rho_{M'}(r)$ for such rules we obtain

$$M_s(r^M, \rho_M(r)) = M'_s(r^M, \rho_{M'}(r))$$

(2) If $(r : a \leftarrow_s \alpha) \in \mathscr{R}_P^s$, then there is a rule $r' : a \leftarrow \mathscr{N}_r(\mathscr{I}_{\mathscr{T}_r}(\alpha, not_{w_{r'}}))$ in $\mathscr{R}_{P'}$. We can show that $M_s(r^M, \rho_M(r)) = M'_s(r'^{M'}, \rho_{M'}(r))$ for this rule using Proposition 4.1, the fact that $\rho_{M'}(r') \geqslant 1$ since $\mathscr{A}_{P'}(\rho_{M'}) > 0$, the fact that $I(\beta') = I(\beta)$ for any interpretation I, Lemma 5.5, Proposition 5.8 and the definition of the reduct:

$$M'_s(r'^{M'}, \rho_{M'}(r)) = \mathscr{T}_{r'}((M'(\mathscr{N}_r(\mathscr{I}_{\mathscr{T}_r}(\alpha, not_{w_{r'}})^{M'}))), \rho_{M'}(r'))$$
$$= \mathscr{T}_{r'}(M'(\mathscr{N}_r(\mathscr{I}_{\mathscr{T}_r}(\alpha, not_{w_{r'}}))), 1)$$
$$= \mathscr{N}_r(\mathscr{I}_{\mathscr{T}_r}(M'(\alpha), \mathscr{N}_r(M'(w_{r'}))))$$
$$= \mathscr{N}_r(\mathscr{I}_{\mathscr{T}_r}(M'(\alpha), \mathscr{N}_r(\rho_M(r))))$$

$$= \mathscr{N}_r(\mathscr{I}_{\mathscr{T}_r}(M(\alpha), \mathscr{N}_r(\rho_M(r))))$$

$$= \mathscr{N}_r(\mathscr{I}_{\mathscr{T}_r}(M(\alpha^M), \mathscr{N}_r(\rho_M(r))))$$

$$= M_s(r^M, \rho_M(r))$$

From item 1 and item 2 we thus obtain for $a \in \mathscr{B}_P$ that

$$\Pi_{PM,\rho_M}(M)(a) = \sup\{M_s(r^M, \rho_M(r)) \mid r \in P_a\}$$

$$= \sup\{M'_s(r^{M'}, \rho_{M'}(r)) \mid r \in P'_a\}$$

$$= \Pi_{P'M',\rho_{M'}}(M')(a)$$

$$= M'(a)$$

$$= M(a)$$

Hence, M is a fixpoint of Π_{PM,ρ_M}. Now, suppose that M is not the least fixpoint of Π_{PM,ρ_M}, then some $M'' = \Pi^\star_{PM,\rho_M} < M$ must exist. Consider then

$$M''' = M'' \cup \{w_{r'}^{\rho_M(r)} \mid r \in \mathscr{R}_P^s\} \cup \{not_a^{\mathscr{N}_i(M(a))} \mid a \in \mathscr{B}_P\}$$

$$\cup \{not_{w_{r'}}^{\mathscr{N}_r(\rho_M(r))} \mid r \in \mathscr{R}_P^s\}$$

It is clear from the construction of M''' that $M''' < M'$. Now, using Lemma 5.5 we know from the construction of M'' and M''' that

$$\Pi_{P'M',\rho_{M'}}(M''') = M'''$$

Hence, M''' is a fixpoint of $\Pi_{P'M',\rho_{M'}}$, which contradicts the fact that M' is the least fixpoint of $\Pi_{P'M',\rho_{M'}}$. $\qquad\square$

5.B   Diagram

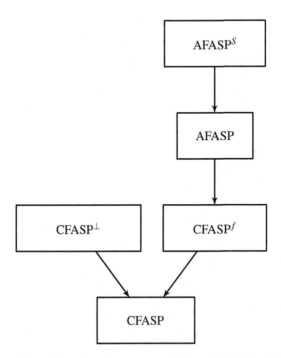

Fig. 5.1: Diagram of the relationships between the different CFASP and AFASP languages.

Chapter 6

Reducing FASP to Fuzzy SAT

6.1 Introduction

In recent years, efficient solvers for classical ASP have been developed. Some of these are based on the DPLL algorithm [Davis and Putnam (1960)] such as Smodels [Simons and Niemelä (2000)] and DLV [Faber and Pfeifer (2005)], others use ideas from SAT solving such as clasp [Gebser *et al.* (2009)], while still others directly use SAT solvers to find answer sets, e.g. ASSAT [Lin and Zhao (2004)], cmodels [Giunchiglia *et al.* (2004)], and pbmodels [Liu and Truszczyński (2005)]. The SAT based approaches have been shown to be fast, and have the advantage that they can use the high number of efficient SAT solvers that have been released in recent years. The DPLL based solvers have the advantage that they allow a flexible modeling language, since they are not restricted to what can directly and efficiently be translated to SAT, and that they can be optimized for specific types of programs.

Probabilistic ASP can be reduced to classical SAT [Saad (2009b)], allowing implementations using regular SAT solvers. Likewise, possibilistic ASP can be reduced to classical ASP [Nicolas *et al.* (2006)], which means ASP solvers can be used for solving possibilistic ASP programs.

In the case of FASP programs with a finite number of truth values, it has been shown in [Van Nieuwenborgh *et al.* (2007a)] that FASP can be solved using regular ASP solvers. However, to date, no FASP solvers or solving methods have been developed for programs with infinitely many truth values. Our goal in this chapter is to take a first step towards creating such efficient solvers by showing how the idea of translating ASP programs to SAT instances can be generalized to FASP. In this way we can create FASP solvers that use existing techniques for solving fuzzy satisfiability problems, such as mixed-integer programming and other forms of mathematical programming (see for example [Hähnle (1994);

Bobillo and Straccia (2007)]) or, in the case of certain fuzzy satisfiability problems with Łukasiewicz connectives, constraint solvers (see for example [Schockaert *et al.* (2009)]). Specifically, we focus on the ASSAT approach introduced in [Lin and Zhao (2004)]. While translating ASP to SAT is straightforward when ASP programs do not contain cyclic dependencies, called loops, careful attention is needed to correctly cover the important case of programs with loops. The solution presented by ASSAT is based on constructing particular propositional formulas for any loop in the program. In this chapter, we pursue a similar strategy where **fuzzy loop formulas** are used to correctly deal with loops. Our main contributions can be summarized as follows:

(1) We define the completion of the subclass of CFASP$^\perp$ programs on $([0,1], \leqslant)$ with only t-norms and negators in their bodies and show that the answer sets of programs without loops are exactly the models of its completion.
(2) By generalizing the loop formulas from [Lin and Zhao (2004)], we then show how the answer sets of arbitrary CFASP$^\perp$ programs in this subclass can be found. We furthermore show how the ASSAT procedure, which attempts to overcome the problem that the number of loops may be exponential, can be generalized to the fuzzy case.

The structure of the chapter is as follows. We begin by defining the completion of CFASP$^\perp$ programs on $([0,1], \leqslant)$ in Section 6.2 and by discussing the problems that occur with programs containing loops. Section 6.3 then shows how these problems can be solved by adding loop formulas to the completion. We illustrate our approach on the problem of placing a set of ATM machines on the roads connecting a set of cities such that each city has an ATM machine nearby in Section 6.4. Finally, we discuss the issues that arise when generalizing our approach to arbitrary (A)FASP programs in Section 6.5.

6.2   Completion of FASP Programs

In this section we show how a subclass of FASP programs can be translated to fuzzy theories such that the models of these theories correspond to answer sets of the program and vice versa. The class of FASP programs we consider is the subclass of CFASP$^\perp$ on the lattice $([0,1], \leqslant)$ containing programs with only t-norms as monotonic functions. Hence, in the remainder of this chapter the term *FASP program* refers to a program in this subclass. Note that in Section 4.4.3 on page 86 we have shown that for this subclass the fixpoint semantics and unfounded-based semantics coincide. Since the development of our fuzzy

SAT translation can more easily be done using the unfounded-based semantics, whereas our generalization of the ASSAT procedure in Section 6.3 is based on the fixpoint semantics, this is the main reason for only considering this specific subclass of FASP.

Definition 6.1. Let P be a FASP program. The **completion** of P, denoted as $comp(P)$, is defined as the following set of fuzzy formulas:

$$\{a \approx (\max\{r_b \mid r \in P_a\}) \mid a \in \mathscr{B}_P\} \cup \{\mathscr{I}(r_b, r_h) \mid r \in P, r_h \in [0,1]\}$$

where $\mathscr{I}$ is an arbitrary residual implicator and $\approx$ is the biresiduum of $\mathscr{I}$ and an arbitrary t-norm $\mathscr{T}$, i.e. for all $x, y \in [0,1]$ we have that $x \approx y = \mathscr{T}(\mathscr{I}(x,y), \mathscr{I}(y,x))$.

The completion of a program consists of two parts, viz. a part for the literals $\{a \approx (\max\{r_b \mid r \in P_a\}) \mid a \in \mathscr{B}_P\}$, and a part for constraints $\{\mathscr{I}_r(r_b, r_h) \mid r \in P, r_h \in [0,1]\}$. The constraints part simply ensures that all constraints are satisfied. The literal part ensures two things. By definition of the biresiduum and the fact that $\mathscr{I}(x,y) = 1$ iff $x \leqslant y$ for any residual implicator[1] $\mathscr{I}$ and $x, y \in [0,1]$, we have that $x \approx y = 1$ iff $x \leqslant y$ and $y \leqslant x$. Hence, the literal part of the completion establishes first that rules are satisfied and second that the value of the literal is not higher than what is supported by the rule bodies.

Example 6.1. Consider the following FASP program $P_{ex6.1}$:

$$r_1 : a \leftarrow \mathscr{T}_M(b,c)$$
$$r_2 : b \leftarrow 0.8$$
$$r_3 : c \leftarrow \mathscr{T}_M(a, \mathscr{N}_W(b))$$
$$r_4 : 0 \leftarrow \mathscr{T}_W(a,b)$$

The completion of the above program is the following set of fuzzy propositions

$$a \approx \mathscr{T}_M(b,c)$$
$$b \approx 0.8$$
$$c \approx \mathscr{T}_M(a, \mathscr{N}_W(b))$$
$$\mathscr{I}_W(\mathscr{T}_W(a,b), 0)$$

Note that when applying Definition 6.1 for a literal l that does not appear in the head of any rule, we get $a \approx \max \emptyset$, where we define $\max \emptyset = 0$.

We can now show that any answer set of a program P is a model of its completion $comp(P)$.

Proposition 6.1. *Let P be a FASP program and let $comp(P)$ be its completion. Then any answer set of P is a model of $comp(P)$.*

---
[1] See Proposition 2.10 on page 31.

Proof. Suppose A is an answer set of P. Since A is a model of P it follows from Lemma 4.4 on page 88 that A is a fixpoint of Π_{P,ρ_I}. Hence for each $a \in \mathcal{B}_P$ we have that $A(a) = \sup\{\mathcal{T}_r(A(r_b), 1) \mid r \in P_a\} = \sup\{A(r_b) \mid r \in P_a\}$. By construction of $comp(P)$, it then easily follows that $A \models comp(P)$.   □

Example 6.2. Consider program $P_{ex6.1}$ from Example 6.1 and its interpretation $I_1 = \{a^0, b^{0.8}, c^0\}$. It is easy to see that I_1 is an answer set of $P_{ex6.1}$ and a model of $comp(P_{ex6.1})$.

The reverse of Proposition 6.1 is not true in general, which is unsurprising because it is already invalid for classical answer set programming. The problem occurs for programs with "loops", as shown in the following example.

Example 6.3. Consider program $P_{ex6.1}$ from Example 6.1 and its interpretation $I_2 = \{a^{0.2}, b^{0.8}, c^{0.2}\}$. We can easily see that I_2 is a model of $comp(P_{ex6.1})$, but it is not an answer set of $P_{ex6.1}$.

One might wonder whether taking the minimal models of the completion would solve the above problem. The following example shows that the answer is negative.

Example 6.4. Consider the following program P_{min}

$$r_1 : a \leftarrow a$$
$$r_2 : p \leftarrow \mathcal{T}_W(\mathcal{N}_W(p), \mathcal{N}_W(a))$$

The completion $comp(P_{min})$ is

$$a \approx a$$
$$p \approx \mathcal{T}_W(\mathcal{N}_W(p), \mathcal{N}_W(a))$$

Consider now the interpretation $I = \{a^{0.2}, p^{0.4}\}$. Since $I(a) = I(a)$ and $\mathcal{T}_W(\mathcal{N}_W(I(p)), \mathcal{N}_W(I(a))) = \max(0, 1 - I(p) + 1 - I(a) - 1) = 0.4$ we can see that I is a model of $comp(P_{min})$. We show that it is a minimal model as follows. Suppose some $I' \subset I$ exists. Then we can consider three cases: (i) $I'(a) < I(a)$ and $I'(p) = I(p)$; (ii) $I'(a) = I(a)$ and $I'(p) < I(p)$; (iii) $I'(a) < I(a)$ or $I'(p) < I(p)$. In all three cases we obtain that $\mathcal{T}_W(\mathcal{N}_W(I'(p)), \mathcal{N}_W(I'(a))) > 0.4 > I'(p)$, since $\mathcal{N}_W(I'(a)) = 1 - I'(a) > 0.8$ or $\mathcal{N}_W(I'(p)) > 0.6$. Hence I' is not a model of $comp(P_{min})$ and I is thus a minimal model of $comp(P_{min})$. However, I' is not an answer set of P_{min} since $\Pi^{\star}_{P^I_{min}} = \{a^0, p^{0.4}\}$.

However, similar to the crisp case, when a program has no loops in its positive dependency graph, the models of the completion and the answer sets coincide. First we define exactly what a loop of a FASP program is, and then we show that this property still holds for FASP.

Definition 6.2. Let P be a FASP program. The **positive dependency graph** of P is a directed graph $G_P = \langle \mathscr{B}_P, D \rangle$ where $(a, b) \in D$ iff $\exists r \in P_a \cdot b \in r_b^+$, where r_b^+ is defined as in Definition 4.11 on page 87. For ease of notation we also denote this relation with $(a, b) \in G_P$ for atoms a and b in the Herbrand base of P. We call a non-empty set $L \subseteq \mathscr{B}_P$ a **loop** of P iff for all literals a and b in L there is a path (with length > 0) from a to b in G_P such that all vertices of this path are elements of L.

Note that in the remainder of this chapter the term *dependency graph* is used for the *positive* dependency graph.

Example 6.5. Consider program P_{min} from Example 6.4. The dependency graph of P_{min} is pictured in Figure 6.1. We can see that $\{a\}$ is a loop. If this loop was not in the program, its completion would become

$$a \approx 0$$
$$p \approx \mathscr{T}_W(\mathscr{N}_W(p), \mathscr{N}_W(a))$$

This fuzzy theory has the single model $M = \{p^{0.5}\}$. One can easily verify that M coincides with the answer set of $P_{min} \setminus \{r_1\}$, i.e. the answer set of the program without the loop $\{a\}$.

Example 6.6. Consider program $P_{ex6.1}$ from Example 6.1. The dependency graph of $P_{ex6.1}$ is pictured in Figure 6.2. We can clearly see that there is a loop between nodes a and c. Due to this loop, the values of a and c are not sufficiently constrained in the completion.

From the preceding examples one might think that removing the loops from the program would be sufficient to make the models of the completion and the answer sets coincide. However, this is not the case, as the semantics of the program then changes.

Example 6.7. Consider program P_{change} consisting of the following rules

$$r_1 : a \leftarrow 0.3$$
$$r_2 : a \leftarrow b$$
$$r_3 : b \leftarrow a$$

Its single answer set is $\{a^{0.3}, b^{0.3}\}$. If we remove rule r_2 or r_3, the answer set of the resulting program is $\{a^{0.3}\}$.

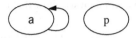

Fig. 6.1: Dependency graph of program P_{min} from Example 6.4

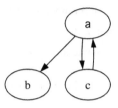

Fig. 6.2: Dependency graph of program $P_{ex6.1}$ from Example 6.1

We can now show that for programs without loops the answer sets coincide with the models of their completion. We first introduce two lemmas. Note that in the proofs of these lemmas and other propositions and lemmas we will use the unfounded-based semantics for FASP that are described in Definition 4.11 on page 87.

Lemma 6.1. *Let $G = \langle V, E \rangle$ be a directed graph with a finite set of vertices and $X \subseteq V$ with $X \neq \emptyset$. If every node in X has at least one outgoing edge to another node in X, there must be a loop in X.*

Proof. From the assumptions it holds that each $x \in X$ has an outgoing edge to another node in X. This means that there is an infinite sequence of nodes $x_1, x_2, \ldots$ such that $(x_i, x_{i+1}) \in E$ for $i \geqslant 1$. Since X is finite, it follows that some vertex occurs twice in this sequence, and hence that there is a loop in X. $\qquad\square$

Lemma 6.2. *Let P be a FASP program, I an interpretation of P and $U \subseteq \mathscr{B}_P$. Then if $I \models comp(P)$ and U is unfounded w.r.t. I it holds that for each u in $U \cap supp(I)$ there is some r in P_u for which $r_b^+ \cap U \cap supp(I) \neq \emptyset$ holds[2].*

Proof. Assume that $u \in U \cap supp(I)$, in other words $u \in U$ and $I(u) > 0$. As U is unfounded w.r.t. I, for each $r \in P_u$ it holds that either

(1) $r_b^+ \cap U \neq \emptyset$; or
(2) $I(r_b) < I(u)$; or
(3) $I(r_b) = 0$

---

[2]We recall that for an interpretation I of a program P the set $supp(I)$ contains all atoms $a \in \mathscr{B}_P$ for which $I(a) > 0$. See Definition 2.19 on page 26.

We can now show that there is at least one rule $r \in P_u$ that violates the second and third of these conditions, meaning it must satisfy the first.

From $I \models comp(P)$ we know by construction of $comp(P)$ that for each $u \in U$, $I(u) = \sup\{I(r_b) \mid r \in P_u\}$. Hence for each $u \in U$ there is a rule $r \in P_u$ such that $I(u) = I(r_b)$, thus the second condition is violated. Since $I(u) > 0$, it then also follows that the third condition is violated.

In other words there must be some $r \in P_u$ such that $I(r_b) = I(u)$ and $I(r_b) \neq 0$. Since U is unfounded w.r.t. I, this means that $r_b^+ \cap U \neq \emptyset$. Since $I(r_b) \neq 0$ implies that $r_b^+ \subseteq supp(I)$ due to the fact that $\mathscr{T}(0,x) = 0$ for any t-norm $\mathscr{T}$, we can conclude that there is some $r \in P_u$ such that $r_b^+ \cap U \cap supp(I) \neq \emptyset$.   □

Using these lemmas we can now show that the answer sets of any program without loops in its dependency graph coincide with the models of its completion. This resembles Fages' theorem on tight programs in classical ASP [Fages (1994)].

Proposition 6.2. *Let P be a FASP program. If P has no loops in its positive dependency graph it holds that an interpretation I of P is an answer set of P iff $I \models comp(P)$.*

Proof.   We already know from Proposition 6.1 that any answer set of P is necessarily a model of $comp(P)$, hence we only need to show that every model of $comp(P)$ is an answer set of P under the conditions of this proposition. As $I \models comp(P)$, it holds that I is a model of P. We show by contradiction that I is unfounded-free. Assume that there is a set $U \subseteq \mathscr{B}_P$ such that U is unfounded w.r.t. I and $U \cap supp(I) \neq \emptyset$. From Lemma 6.2 we know that for each $u \in U \cap supp(I)$ it holds that there is some rule $r \in P_u$ such that $r_b^+ \cap U \cap supp(I) \neq \emptyset$. Using the definition of G_P, this means that for each such u there is some $u' \in U \cap supp(I)$ such that $G_P(u,u')$. This however means that there is a loop in G_P by Lemma 6.1, contradicting the assumption.   □

Hence, finding the answer sets of a program with no loops in its positive dependency graph can be done by finding models of its completion.

6.3   Loop Formulas

As mentioned in the previous section, sometimes the models of the completion are not answer sets. For boolean answer set programming two solutions have been proposed for this problem. The first solution [Ben-Eliyahu and Dechter (1994)] consists of assigning indices to atoms and requiring for any atom a in a loop L that if the derivation of a depends on some $a' \in L$, this a' must have a lower index than a. Interestingly, this requirement can be encoded in SAT, leading to a translation of an ASP program P to a SAT problem S such that the models of S coincide with the answer sets of P. The second solution consists of adding *loop formulas* to the completion, which ensure that models of the completion that are not answer sets cannot occur [Lin and Zhao (2004)]. Since in the case of FASP a generalization of the former would need an infinite number of indices, one for each combination of atom and truth value, we focus on a generalization of the latter.

To define loop formulas, we start from a partition of the rules whose heads are in some particular loop L. Based upon this partition, for every loop L we define a formula in fuzzy logic, such that any model of the completion satisfying these formulas is an answer set.

For any program P and loop L we consider the following partition of the rules in P whose head belongs to the set L (due to [Lin and Zhao (2004)])

$$R_P^+(L) = \{r : a \leftarrow \alpha \mid ((r : a \leftarrow \alpha) \in P) \land (a \in L) \land (r_b^+ \cap L \neq \emptyset)\} \tag{6.1}$$

$$R_P^-(L) = \{r : a \leftarrow \alpha \mid ((r : a \leftarrow \alpha) \in P) \land (a \in L) \land (r_b^+ \cap L = \emptyset)\} \tag{6.2}$$

Note that this partition only takes the positive occurrences of atoms in the loop into account. Intuitively, the set $R_P^+(L)$ contains the rules that are "in" the loop L, i.e. the rules that are jointly responsible for the creation of the loop in the positive dependency graph, whereas the rules in $R_P^-(L)$ are the rules that are outside of this loop. We will refer to them as "loop rules", resp. "non-loop rules."

Example 6.8. Consider program P from Example 6.1. It is clear that for the loop $L = \{a, c\}$ the set of loop rules is $R_P^+(L) = \{r_1, r_3\}$ and the set of non-loop rules is $R_P^-(L) = \emptyset$.

Example 6.9. Consider program P from Example 6.1 with interpretations $I_1 = \{a^0, b^{0.8}, c^0\}$ and $I_2 = \{a^{0.2}, b^{0.8}, c^{0.2}\}$ once again. It is clear that in I_1 no loop rules were used to derive the values of a and c, whereas in I_2 only loop rules are used.

Hence there is a problem when the value of literals in a loop are only derived from rules in the loop. To solve this problem, we should require that at least one non-loop rule motivates the value of these loop literals. As illustrated in the next example, one non-loop rule is sufficient as the value provided by this rule can propagate through the loop by applying loop rules.

Example 6.10. Consider program P_{change} from Example 6.7 again. Clearly this program has a loop $L = \{a, b\}$ with $R_P^+(L) = \{r_2, r_3\}$ and $R_P^-(L) = \{r_1\}$. Consider then interpretations $I_1 = \{a^{0.3}, b^{0.3}\}$ and $I_2 = \{a^1, b^1\}$. We can easily see that I_1 is an answer set of P, whereas I_2 is not, although they are both models of $comp(P)$. The problem is that in I_2 the values of a and b are higher than what can be derived from the non-loop rule r_1, whereas in I_1 their values are exactly what can be derived from applying rule r_1. The latter is allowed, as values are properly supported from outside the loop, while the former is not, as in this case the loop is "self-motivating".

To remove the non-answer set models of the completion, we add loop formulas to the completion, defined as follows.

Definition 6.3 (Loop Formula). *Let P be a FASP program and* $L = \{l_1, \ldots, l_m\}$ *a loop of P. Suppose that* $R_P^-(L) = \{r_1, \ldots, r_n\}$. *Then the loop formula induced by loop L, denoted by* $\mathbb{LF}(L, P)$, *is the following fuzzy logic formula:*

$$\mathcal{I}(\max(l_1, \ldots, l_m), \max((r_1)_b, \ldots, (r_n)_b)) \tag{6.3}$$

where $\mathcal{I}$ *is an arbitrary residual implicator. If* $R_P^-(L) = \emptyset$, *the loop formula becomes*

$$\mathcal{I}(\max(l_1, \ldots, l_m), 0)$$

The loop formula proposed for boolean answer set programs in [Lin and Zhao (2004)] is of the form

$$\neg(\bigwedge(r_1)_b \vee \ldots \vee \bigwedge(r_n)_b) \Rightarrow (\neg l_1 \wedge \ldots \wedge \neg l_m) \tag{6.4}$$

It can easily be seen that (6.3) is a straightforward generalization of (6.4) as the latter is equivalent to

$$(l_1 \vee \ldots \vee l_m) \Rightarrow (\bigwedge(r_1)_b \vee \ldots \vee \bigwedge(r_n)_b)$$

Note that this equivalence is preserved in Łukasiewicz logic, but not in Gödel or product logic. Furthermore, since $I \models \mathcal{I}(\max(l_1, \ldots, l_m), 0)$ only when $\max(I(l_1), \ldots, I(l_m)) \leqslant 0$, it is easy to see that in the case where $R_P^-(L) = \emptyset$, the truth value of all atoms in the loop L is 0.

Example 6.11. Consider program $P_{ex6.1}$ from Example 6.1 on page 135 and its interpretations $I_1 = \{a^0, b^{0.8}, c^0\}$ and $I_2 = \{a^{0.2}, b^{0.8}, c^{0.2}\}$. The loop formula for its loop $L = \{a, c\}$ is the fuzzy formula $\mathcal{I}_M(\max(a, c), 0)$, since $R_P^-(L) = \emptyset$. It is easy to see that I_2 – which is not an answer set – does not satisfy this formula, while interpretation I_1 – which is an answer set – does.

Example 6.12. Consider program P_{change} from Example 6.7. The loop formula for its loop $L = \{a, b\}$ is the propositional formula $\mathcal{I}_M(\max(a, b), 0.3)$, since $R_P^-(L) = \{r_1\}$. Again we see that interpretation I_1 from Example 6.10 satisfies this loop formula, whereas interpretation I_2 from the same example does not.

We now show that by adding loop formulas to the completion of a program, we get a fuzzy propositional theory that is both sound and complete with respect to the answer set semantics. First we show that this procedure is complete.

Proposition 6.3. *Let P be a FASP program, let $\mathscr{L}$ be the set of all loops of P, and define*
$\mathbb{LF}(P) = \{\mathbb{LF}(L,P) \mid L \in \mathscr{L}\}$. *For any answer set I of P, it holds that $I \models \mathbb{LF}(P) \cup comp(P)$.*

Proof. Suppose I is an answer set of P and $I \not\models \mathbb{LF}(P) \cup comp(P)$. Since any answer set is a model of $comp(P)$ according to Proposition 6.1 on page 135, this means that $I \not\models \mathbb{LF}(P)$. Hence, the loop formula of some loop L in P is not fulfilled; this means:

$$\sup_{u \in L} I(u) > \sup_{r \in R_P^-(L)} I(r_b)$$

Consider then the set $U = \{u \in L \mid I(u) > \sup_{r \in R_P^-(L)} I(r_b)\}$. We show that U is unfounded w.r.t. I, i.e. we show that for each $u \in U$ and rule $r \in P_u$, at least one of the conditions of Definition 4.11 on page 87 applies.

Since $P_u = R_{P_u}^+(L) \cup R_{P_u}^-(L)$, each rule $r \in P_u$ must either be in $R_{P_u}^+(L)$ or in $R_{P_u}^-(L)$. We consider the following cases:

1. If $r \in R_{P_u}^-(L)$ then by construction of U it holds that $I(r_b) < I(u)$.

2. If $r \in R_{P_u}^+(L)$ and $I(r_b) \leqslant \sup_{r' \in R_{P_u}^-(L)} I(r'_b)$, by construction of U we have that $I(r_b) < I(u)$.

3. Suppose $r \in R_{P_u}^+(L)$ and $I(r_b) > \sup_{r' \in R_{P_u}^-(L)} I(r'_b)$. Since $\mathscr{T}(x,y) \leqslant \min(x,y)$ for each t-norm $\mathscr{T}$, we know that $I(r_b) \leqslant I(l)$ for each $l \in r_b^+$. Hence for each $l \in r_b^+$ we have $I(l) > \sup_{r' \in R_{P_u}^-(L)} I(r'_b)$. This means that, since $r \in R_P^+(L)$ and thus $r_b^+ \cap L \neq \emptyset$, we know from the definition of U that $r_b^+ \cap U \neq \emptyset$.

Now remark that $U \cap supp(I) \neq \emptyset$ as $U \subseteq supp(I)$ due to $I(u) > 0$ for each $u \in U$. From the above we can thus conclude that U is unfounded w.r.t. I, and since $U \cap supp(I) \neq \emptyset$, that I is not unfounded-free: a contradiction. $\qquad\square$

Second we show that adding the loop formulas to the completion of a program is a sound procedure.

Lemma 6.3. *Let $G = \langle V, E \rangle$ be a directed graph and $X \subseteq V$, with V finite, such that each node of X has at least one outgoing edge to another node in X. Then there is a set $L \subseteq X$ such that L is a maximal loop in X and for each $l \in L$ we have that there is no $x \in X \setminus L$ for which $(l,x) \in E$.*

Proof. From Lemma 6.1 on page 138 we already know that there must be a loop in X. Hence, there must also be a maximal loop in X. First, remark that maximal loops must of course be disjoint as otherwise their union would form a bigger loop. Consider then the set X, which is a collection of disjoint maximal loops L and remaining nodes S (single nodes that are not in any loop). There is an induced graph G' of G with nodes $S \cup L$ (i.e. each maximal loop is a single node in the induced graph) and edges E induced as usual (i.e. $(L_1, L_2) \in E$ if for some node l_1 in L_1 there is a node l_2 in L_2 such that $(l_1, l_2) \in E$ and likewise for the nodes in S). Clearly, G' is acyclic as otherwise the nodes in G' on the cycle would create a bigger loop in X. Hence, G' has leafs without outgoing edges. However, a leaf cannot be in S since that would imply a node in X without an outgoing edge. Thus we can conclude that all leafs in G' are maximal loops in X. $\qquad\qquad\qquad\square$

Proposition 6.4. *Let P be a FASP program and let $\mathbb{LF}(P)$ be the set of all loop formulas of P. Then for any interpretation I of P it holds that if $I \models \mathbb{LF}(P) \cup comp(P)$, then I must be an answer set of P.*

Proof. Suppose $I \models \mathbb{LF}(P) \cup comp(P)$ and I is not an answer set of P. Since any model of $comp(P)$ must be a model of P, this must mean that I is not unfounded-free, i.e. that there exists a set $U \subseteq \mathscr{B}_P$ such that U is unfounded w.r.t. I. From Lemma 6.2 on page 138 we know that for each $u \in U \cap supp(I)$ there must be some $r \in P_u$ such that $r_b^+ \cap U \cap supp(I) \neq \emptyset$. Hence, by definition of G_P this means that for each $u \in U \cap supp(I)$ there is some $u' \in U \cap supp(I)$ such that $(u, u') \in G_P$. Using Lemma 6.3 this means that there is a set $L \subseteq U \cap supp(I)$ such that L is a loop in P and for each $l \in L$ there is no $u \in (U \cap supp(I)) \setminus L$ such that $(l, u) \in G_P$. In other words, for each $l \in L$ and rule $r \in P_l$ we have that

$$\left(U \cap supp(I) \cap r_b^+ \neq \emptyset \right) \Rightarrow \left(L \cap r_b^+ \neq \emptyset \right) \tag{6.5}$$

Now, consider $l \in L$. Since $L \subseteq U \cap supp(I)$, we know that $I(l) > 0$. Hence, if $I(r_b) = I(l)$ for some rule $r \in P_l$, we know that $I(r_b) > 0$. As U is unfounded w.r.t. I, it follows from Definition 4.11 that $L \cap r_b^+ \neq \emptyset$.

Using contraposition, this means that for each $l \in L$ and $r \in P_l$ we have that

$$\left(L \cap r_b^+ = \emptyset \right) \Rightarrow \left(I(r_b) \neq I(l) \right) \tag{6.6}$$

By the definition of $comp(P)$, however, we know that for each model of $comp(P)$ and for each $a \in \mathscr{B}_P$ and $r \in P_a$ we have $I(a) \geqslant I(r_b)$. Hence for each $l \in L$ and $r \in P_l$ from (6.6) we have that

$$\left(L \cap r_b^+ = \emptyset \right) \Rightarrow \left(I(r_b) < I(l) \right) \tag{6.7}$$

Now, for each $l \in L$ and $r \in R_P^-(L) \cap P_l$ by definition of $R_P^-(L)$ it holds that $L \cap r_b^+ = \emptyset$, meaning $I(r_b) < I(l)$. Thus, $\sup\{I(r_b) \mid r \in R_P^-(L)\} < \sup\{I(l) \mid l \in L\}$, meaning $I \not\models \mathbb{LF}(L, P)$, a contradiction. $\square$

A straightforward procedure for finding answer sets would now be to extend the completion of a program with all possible loop formulas and let a fuzzy SAT solver generate models of the resulting fuzzy propositional theory. The models of this theory are the answer sets of the program, as ensured by Propositions 6.3 and 6.4. As there may be an exponential number of loops, however, this translation is not polynomial in general. A similar situation arises for classical ASP. The solution proposed in [Lin and Zhao (2004)] overcomes this limitation by iteratively adding loop formulas. In particular, a SAT solver is first used to find a model of the completion of a classical ASP program. Then it is checked in polynomial time whether this model is an answer set. If this is not the case, a loop formula, which is not satisfied by the model that was found, is added to the completion. The whole process is then repeated until an answer set is found. We will show that a similar procedure can be used to find answer sets of a FASP program.

Starting from the fixpoint characterization of answer sets of FASP programs, we show in Proposition 6.5 that for any given model of the completion of a program that is not an answer set, we can construct a loop that is violated. Before stating this proposition we define the specific fuzzy set intersection on which it is based.

Definition 6.4. Consider a FASP program P and two interpretations I and J of P. The **intersection** of I and J is the interpretation $I \ominus J$ defined for any $a \in \mathscr{B}_P$ as $(I \ominus J)(a) = \max(0, I(a) - J(a))$.

Proposition 6.5. Let P be a FASP program. If an interpretation I of P is a model of $comp(P)$ and $I \neq \Pi_{pI}^\star$, then some $L \subseteq supp(I \ominus \Pi_{pI}^\star)$ must exist such that $I \not\models \mathbb{LF}(P, L)$.

Proof. Suppose I is an interpretation of P and $I \models comp(P)$, then from the definition of $comp(P)$ and Lemma 4.3 on page 87, we can easily see that I is a fixpoint of Π_{pI}. Since $I \neq \Pi_{pI}^\star$, some $I' \subset I$ must exist such that $I' = \Pi_{pI}^\star$.

Consider then the set $U = \{u \in \mathscr{B}_P \mid I(u) > I'(u)\}$. It holds that $U = supp(I \ominus I')$ since $I' \subset I$ and thus $U = supp(I \ominus \Pi_{pI}^\star)$ by definition of I'. From the proof of Proposition 4.16 on page 88 we then also know that for this set U the following property holds

$$\forall u \in U \cdot \forall r \in P_u \cdot \left(r_b^+ \cap U = \emptyset \right) \Rightarrow \left(I(r_b) < I(u) \right) \tag{6.8}$$

We can then show that there is a loop in U whose loop formula is violated. Since $I = \Pi_{pI}(I)$

we know from Lemma 4.3 that $I = \Pi_P(I)$. From the definition of Π_P this means

$$\forall l \in \mathscr{B}_P \cdot I(l) = \sup\{I(r_b) \mid r \in P_l\}$$

Since the supremum is attained because P is finite we obtain

$$\forall l \in \mathscr{B}_P \cdot \exists r \in P_l \cdot I(l) = I(r_b)$$

As $U \subseteq \mathscr{B}_P$ this means

$$\forall u \in U \cdot \exists r \in P_u \cdot I(l) = I(r_b)$$

Using (6.8) it then holds that

$$\forall u \in U \cdot \exists r \in P_u \cdot r_b^+ \cap U \neq \emptyset$$

From the definition of G_P we thus get

$$\forall u \in U \cdot \exists u' \in U \cdot (u, u') \in G_P$$

Using Lemma 6.3 it follows that there is a set $L \subseteq U$ that is a loop in P such that for each $l \in L$ there is no $l' \in U \setminus L$ such that $(l, l') \in E$. In other words, for each $l \in L$ there is no $l' \in U \setminus L$ such that there is a rule $r \in P_l$ for which $l' \in r_b^+$. Hence for each $l \in L$ and rule $r \in P_l$ such that $U \cap r_b^+ \neq \emptyset$, it follows that $L \cap r_b^+ \neq \emptyset$. From (6.8) and using contraposition this means there is some $L \subseteq U$ that is a loop in P and for each $l \in L$ and $r \in P_l$ if $L \cap r_b^+ = \emptyset$ it must hold that $I(r_b) < I(l)$. Now, for each $l \in L$ and $r \in R_P^-(L) \cap P_l$ by definition it holds that $L \cap supp(I) = \emptyset$, meaning $I(r_b) < I(l)$. Thus, $\sup\{I(r_b) \mid r \in R_P^-(L)\} < \sup\{I(l) \mid l \in L\}$, meaning $I \not\models \mathbb{LF}(L, P)$. $\qquad\square$

Now, we can extend the ASSAT-procedure from [Lin and Zhao (2004)] to fuzzy answer set programs P. The main idea of this method is to use fuzzy SAT solving techniques to find models of the fuzzy propositional theory which consists of the completion of P, together with the loop formulas of particular maximal loops of P. If a model is found which is not an answer set, then we determine a loop that is violated by the model and add its loop formula to the fuzzy propositional theory, after which the fuzzy SAT solver is invoked again. The algorithm thus becomes:

(1) Initialize $Loops = \emptyset$

(2) Generate a model M of $comp(I) \cup \mathbb{LF}(P, Loops)$, where $\mathbb{LF}(P, Loops)$ is the set of loop formulas of all loops in $Loops$.

(3) If $M = \Pi_{pM}^\star$, return M as it is an answer set. Else, find the loops occurring in $supp(I \ominus \Pi_{pM}^\star)$, add their loop formulas to $Loops$ and return to step 2.

The reason that we can expect this process to be efficient is articulated by Proposition 6.5. Indeed, when searching for violated loops, we can restrict our attention to subsets of $supp(I \ominus \Pi_{pl}^{\star})$. Although the worst-case complexity of this algorithm is still exponential, in most practical applications, we can expect $supp(I \ominus \Pi_{pl}^{\star})$ to be small, as well as the number of iterations of the process that is needed before an answer set is found. In [Lin and Zhao (2004)] experimental evidence for this claim is provided in the case of classical ASP. Last, note that the fuzzy SAT solving technique depends on the t-norms used in the program. If only the Łukasiewicz t-norm is used, we can use (bounded) mixed integer programming (bMIP) [Hähnle (1994)] or constraint solvers [Schockaert *et al.* (2009)]. Since Fuzzy Description Logic Solvers are based on the same techniques as fuzzy SAT solvers, we also know that for the product t-norm we need to resort to bounded mixed integer quadratically constrained programming (bMICQP) [Bobillo and Straccia (2007)].

6.4 Example: the ATM location selection problem

In this section we illustrate our algorithm on a FASP program modeling a real-life problem. Suppose we are tasked with placing k ATM machines $ATM = \{a_1, \ldots, a_k\}$ on roads connecting n towns $Towns = \{t_1, \ldots, t_n\}$ such that the distance between each town and some ATM machine is minimized, i.e. we aim to find a configuration in which each town has an ATM that is as close as practically possible. To obtain this we optimize the sum of closeness degrees for each town and ATM. Note that this problem closely resembles the well-known k-center selection problem (see e.g. [Ausiello *et al.* (1999)]). The difference is that in the k-center problem the ATMs need to be placed in towns, where we allow them to be placed on the roads connecting towns. We can model this problem as an undirected weighted graph $G = \langle V, E \rangle$ where $V = Towns$ is the set of vertices and the edge set E connects two towns if they are directly connected by a road. Given a distance function $d : Towns \times Towns \to \mathbb{R}$ that models the distance between two towns[3], the weight of the edge $(a, b) \in E$ is given by the normalized distance $d(a, b)/d_{sum}$, where $d_{sum} = \sum\{d(t_1, t_2) \mid t_1, t_2 \in Towns\}$.

Since our FASP programs can only have t-norms in rule bodies, we also need to find a way to sum up the distances between towns and ATM machines. By using the *nearness degree*, or closeness degree, which for a normalized distance d is defined as $1 - d$, we can perform summations of distances in our program. To see this, consider the following derivation:

$$\mathscr{T}_W(1 - dist_1, 1 - dist_2) = \max(1 - dist_1 + 1 - dist_2 - 1, 0)$$

---

[3]For cities that are not connected the function d models the distance of the shortest path between them.

$$= \max(1 - (dist_1 + dist_2), 0)$$
$$= 1 - \min(dist_1 + dist_2, 1)$$

Hence, by applying the Łukasiewicz t-norm on the nearness degrees, we are summing the distances. The program P_{ATM} solving the ATM selection problem is given as follows:

$gloc$: $\quad loc(A, T1, T2) \leftarrow \mathcal{T}_W(conn(T1, T2), \beta)$

$gnear$: $\quad locNear(A, T1) \leftarrow \mathcal{N}_W(locNear'(A, T1))$

$gnear'$: $locNear'(A, T1) \leftarrow \mathcal{T}_W(loc(A, T1, T2), \mathcal{N}_W(near(T1, T2)),$
$$\qquad\qquad\qquad locNear(A, T2)), T1 \neq T2$$

$nearr$: $\quad near(T1, T2) \leftarrow \mathcal{T}_W(conn(T1, T3), near(T1, T3), near(T3, T2))$

$locr$: $\quad loc(A, T1, T2) \leftarrow loc(A, T2, T1)$

$atmr$: $ATMNear(A, T) \leftarrow \mathcal{T}_W(loc(A, T1, T2), locNear(A, T1), near(T, T1))$

$tDist$: $\quad totNear \leftarrow \mathcal{T}_W(\{ATMNear(a, t) \mid a \in ATM, t \in Towns\})$

where

$$\beta = \mathcal{T}_W(\{\mathcal{N}_M(loc(A, T1', T2')) \mid \{T_1', T_2'\} \neq \{T_1, T_2\}\})$$

Note that, after grounding, a rule such as $locr$ actually corresponds to a set of variable-free rules $\{locr_{a,t_1,t_2} \mid a \in ATM, t_1, t_2 \in Towns\}$. We will keep referring to the specific grounded instance of a rule by the subscript.

Program P_{ATM} consists of a *generate* and *define* part, which for a specific configuration is augmented with an *input* part consisting of facts. The *generate* part consists of the three rules $gloc$, $gnear$, and $gnear'$, which generate a specific configuration of ATMs. The $gloc$ rule chooses an edge on which the ATM machine A is placed by guessing a location for an ATM that has not yet been assigned a location, as ensured by the β part of this rule. The $gnear$ and $gnear'$ rules generate a location on this edge where A is placed. Rules $gnear$ and $gnear'$ originate from the constraint $d(a, t_1) = d(t_1, t_2) - d(a, t_2)$, where $d(x, y)$ is the distance between x and y, if ATM a is placed on the edge between t_1 and t_2. Defining $n(x, y)$ as the nearness degree between x and y and noting that $n(a, t_1) = 1 - d(a, t_1) = 1 - (d(t_1, t_2) - d(a, t_2))$, we can rewrite this constraint in terms of t-norms and nearness degrees:

$$n(a, t_1) = 1 - (d(t_1, t_2) - d(a, t_2))$$
$$= 1 - (d(t_1, t_2) + (1 - d(a, t_2)) - 1)$$
$$= 1 - \mathcal{T}_W(d(t_1, t_2), 1 - d(a, t_2))$$
$$= 1 - \mathcal{T}_W(1 - n(t_1, t_2), n(a, t_2))$$

$$= \mathscr{N}_W(\mathscr{T}_W(1 - n(t_1, t_2), n(a, t_2)))$$

Hence, the bodies of rules *gnear* and *gnear'* ensure that this constraint is satisfied. The reason we need two rules and cannot directly write a rule with body $\mathscr{N}_W(\mathscr{T}_W(loc(A, T1, T2), \mathscr{N}_W(near(T1, T2)), locNear(A, T2))$ is that the syntax does not allow negation in front of arbitrary expressions.

Rule *nearr* recursively defines the degree of closeness between two towns based on the known distances for connected towns. Additionally, since the bodies of rules with the same head are combined using the maximum, the nearness degree obtained by *nearr* is always one minus the distance of the shortest path. The *locr* rule makes sure that if an ATM is located on the edge between town $T1$ and $T2$, it is also recognized as being on the edge between $T2$ and $T1$, as we are working with an undirected graph. The *atmr* rule defines the location between a particular ATM machine and a town. Note that due to rule *locr* this rule also covers the case when $near(T, T2)$ is higher than $near(T, T1)$. The *tDist* rule aggregates the total distances such that different answer sets of this program can be compared and ordered. In this way we could for example search for the answer set that has a maximal total degree of nearness, i.e. in which the distance from the towns to the ATMs is lowest.

Consider the specific configuration $G_P = \langle V, E \rangle$ of towns $Towns = \{t_1, t_2, t_3\}$ depicted in Figure 6.3 and suppose $ATM = \{a_1, a_2\}$. In Figure 6.4 we depicted a subset of the dependency graph of the grounded version of $P'_{ATM} = P_{ATM} \cup F$, where F is the input part of the problem, given by the following rules

$$F = \{conn(t, t') \leftarrow 1 \mid t, t' \in Towns, (t, t') \in E\}$$
$$\cup \{near(t, t') \leftarrow k \mid t, t' \in Towns, (t, t') \in E, k = 1 - (d(t, t')/d_{sum})\}$$

For the configuration depicted in Figure 6.3 the input part F is

$$F = \{conn(t_1, t_1) \leftarrow 1, conn(t_1, t_2) \leftarrow 1, conn(t_1, t_3) \leftarrow 1\}$$
$$\cup \{conn(t_2, t_1) \leftarrow 1, conn(t_2, t_2) \leftarrow 1, conn(t_2, t_3) \leftarrow 1\}$$
$$\cup \{conn(t_3, t_1) \leftarrow 1, conn(t_3, t_2) \leftarrow 1, conn(t_3, t_3) \leftarrow 1\}$$
$$\cup \{near(t_1, t_1) \leftarrow 1, near(t_1, t_2) \leftarrow 0.8, near(t_1, t_3) \leftarrow 0.7\}$$
$$\cup \{near(t_2, t_1) \leftarrow 0.8, near(t_2, t_2) \leftarrow 1, near(t_2, t_3) \leftarrow 0.5\}$$
$$\cup \{near(t_3, t_1) \leftarrow 0.7, near(t_3, t_2) \leftarrow 0.5, near(t_3, t_3) \leftarrow 1\}$$

Note that *conn* and *near* need to be reflexive since an ATM a can be placed directly in a town t. It is clear that P'_{ATM} contains a number of loops. The completion of P'_{ATM} is the following fuzzy propositional theory:

$$conn(t_1,t_1) \approx 1, \quad conn(t_1,t_2) \approx 1, \quad conn(t_1,t_3) \approx 1$$

$$conn(t_2,t_1) \approx 1, \quad conn(t_2,t_2) \approx 1, \quad conn(t_2,t_3) \approx 1$$

$$conn(t_3,t_1) \approx 1, \quad conn(t_3,t_2) \approx 1, \quad conn(t_3,t_3) \approx 1$$

$$near(t_1,t_1) \approx 1, \quad near(t_1,t_2) \approx 0.8, \quad near(t_1,t_3) \approx 0.7$$

$$near(t_2,t_1) \approx 0.8, \quad near(t_2,t_2) \approx 1, \quad near(t_2,t_3) \approx 0.5$$

$$near(t_3,t_1) \approx 0.7, \quad near(t_3,t_2) \approx 0.5, \quad near(t_3,t_3) \approx 1$$

$$loc(a_1,t_1,t_1) \approx \max(\mathcal{T}_W(conn(t_1,t_1),\beta_{1,1,1}),loc(a_1,t_1,t_1))$$

$$loc(a_1,t_1,t_2) \approx \max(\mathcal{T}_W(conn(t_1,t_2),\beta_{1,1,2}),loc(a_1,t_2,t_1))$$

$$loc(a_1,t_1,t_3) \approx \max(\mathcal{T}_W(conn(t_1,t_3,\beta_{1,1,3}),loc(a_1,t_3,t_1))$$

$$\ldots$$

$$loc(a_2,t_3,t_1) \approx \max(\mathcal{T}_W(conn(t_3,t_1),\beta_{2,3,1}),loc(a_2,t_1,t_3))$$

$$loc(a_2,t_3,t_2) \approx \max(\mathcal{T}_W(conn(t_3,t_2),\beta_{2,3,2}),loc(a_2,t_2,t_3))$$

$$loc(a_2,t_3,t_3) \approx \max(\mathcal{T}_W(conn(t_3,t_3),\beta_{2,3,3}),loc(a_2,t_3,t_3))$$

$$locNear(a_1,t_1) \approx \mathcal{N}_W(locNear'(a_1,t_1))$$

$$\ldots$$

$$locNear(a_2,t_3) \approx \mathcal{N}_W(locNear'(a_2,t_3))$$

$$locNear'(a_1,t_1) \approx \max(\mathcal{T}_W(loc(a_1,t_1,t_2),locNear(a_1,t_2),\mathcal{N}_W(near(t_1,t_2))),$$
$$\mathcal{T}_W(loc(a_1,t_1,t_3),locNear(a_1,t_3),\mathcal{N}_W(near(t_1,t_3))))$$

$$\ldots$$

$$locNear'(a_2,t_3) \approx \max(\mathcal{T}_W(loc(a_2,t_3,t_1),locNear(a_2,t_1),\mathcal{N}_W(near(t_3,t_1))),$$
$$\mathcal{T}_W(loc(a_2,t_3,t_2),locNear(a_2,t_2),\mathcal{N}_W(near(t_3,t_2))))$$

$$near(t_1,t_1) \approx \max(\mathcal{T}_W(conn(t_1,t_1),near(t_1,t_1),near(t_1,t_1)),$$
$$\mathcal{T}_W(conn(t_1,t_2),near(t_1,t_2),near(t_2,t_1)),$$
$$\mathcal{T}_W(conn(t_1,t_3),near(t_1,t_3),near(t_3,t_1)),1)$$

$$near(t_1,t_2) \approx \max(\mathcal{T}_W(conn(t_1,t_1),near(t_1,t_1),near(t_1,t_2)),$$
$$\mathcal{T}_W(conn(t_1,t_2),near(t_1,t_2),near(t_2,t_2)),$$
$$\mathcal{T}_W(conn(t_1,t_3),near(t_1,t_3),near(t_3,t_2)),0.8)$$

$$\ldots$$

$$near(t_3,t_3) \approx \max(\mathscr{I}_W(conn(t_3,t_3),near(t_3,t_3),near(t_3,t_3)),$$
$$\mathscr{I}_W(conn(t_3,t_2),near(t_3,t_2),near(t_2,t_3)),$$
$$\mathscr{I}_W(conn(t_3,t_1),near(t_3,t_1),near(t_1,t_3)),1)$$
$$ATMNear(a_1,t_1) \approx \max(\mathscr{I}_W(loc(a_1,t_1,t_1),locNear(a_1,t_1),near(t_1,t_1)),$$
$$\mathscr{I}_W(loc(a_1,t_1,t_2),locNear(a_1,t_1),near(t_1,t_1)),$$
$$\dots$$
$$\mathscr{I}_W(loc(a_1,t_3,t_2),locNear(a_1,t_3),near(t_1,t_3))$$
$$\mathscr{I}_W(loc(a_1,t_3,t_3),locNear(a_1,t_3),near(t_1,t_3)))$$

$$\dots$$

$$ATMNear(a_2,t_3) \approx \max(\mathscr{I}_W(loc(a_2,t_1,t_1),locNear(a_2,t_1),near(t_3,t_1)),$$
$$\mathscr{I}_W(loc(a_2,t_1,t_2),locNear(a_2,t_1),near(t_3,t_1)),$$
$$\dots$$
$$\mathscr{I}_W(loc(a_2,t_3,t_2),locNear(a_2,t_3),near(t_3,t_3))$$
$$\mathscr{I}_W(loc(a_2,t_3,t_3),locNear(a_2,t_3),near(t_3,t_3)))$$
$$totNear \approx \mathscr{I}_W\{ATMNear(a,t) \mid a \in ATM, t \in Towns\}$$

where

$$\beta_{i,j,k} = \mathscr{I}_W(\{\mathcal{N}_M(loc(a_i,t'_j,t'_k)) \mid \{t'_j,t'_k\} \neq \{t_j,t_k\}\})$$

Note that e.g. the 1 in the right-hand side of the fuzzy proposition with $near(t_1,t_1)$ on the right-hand side stems from the inputs F we added to P_{ATM}. From the completion $comp(P'_{ATM})$ we can see that an interpretation M satisfying $M(near(t1,t2)) = 1$ can be a model of $comp(P'_{ATM})$, which is clearly unwanted as this would overestimate the nearness degrees between towns (i.e. underestimate the distances). For example, consider

$$M = \{loc(a_1,t_1,t_2)^1, loc(a_1,t_2,t_1)^1, loc(a_2,t_1,t_3)^1, loc(a_2,t_3,t_1)^1,$$
$$locNear(a_1,t_1)^1, locNear(a_1,t_2)^1, locNear(a_2,t_1)^{0.75}, locNear(a_2,t_3)^{0.75},$$
$$locNear'(a_2,t_1)^{0.25}, locNear'(a_2,t_3)^{0.25}, near(t_1,t_1)^1, near(t_1,t_2)^1,$$
$$near(t_2,t_1)^1, near(t_1,t_3)^{0.7}, near(t_3,t_1)^{0.7}, near(t_2,t_3)^{0.5}, near(t_3,t_2)^{0.5},$$
$$near(t_2,t_2)^1, near(t_3,t_3)^1, ATMNear(a_1,t_1)^1, ATMNear(a_1,t_2)^1,$$
$$ATMNear(a_1,t_3)^{0.7}, ATMNear(a_2,t_1)^{0.75}, ATMNear(a_2,t_2)^{0.75},$$

$ATMNear(a_2,t_3)^{0.75}\}$

Note that atoms a for which $M(a) = 0$ are not included in the set notation, which is e.g. the case for *totNear*. One can easily verify that M is a model of $comp(P'_{ATM})$. To check whether M is an answer set we compute $\Pi^\star_{(P'_{ATM})^M}$ by repeatedly applying $\Pi_{(P'_{ATM})^M}$, starting from the empty set, until we obtain a fixpoint, and check whether $M = \Pi^\star_{(P'_{ATM})^M}$. Performing this procedure, we obtain

$$
\begin{aligned}
\Pi^\star_{(P'_{ATM})^M} =\{ & loc(a_1,t_1,t_2)^1, loc(a_1,t_2,t_1)^1, loc(a_2,t_1,t_3)^1, loc(a_2,t_3,t_1)^1, \\
& locNear(a_1,t_1)^1, locNear(a_1,t_2)^1, locNear(a_2,t_1)^{0.75}, locNear(a_2,t_3)^{0.75}, \\
& locNear'(a_2,t_1)^{0.25}, locNear'(a_2,t_3)^{0.25}, near(t_1,t_1)^1, near(t_1,t_2)^{0.8}, \\
& near(t_2,t_1)^{0.8}, near(t_1,t_3)^{0.5}, near(t_3,t_1)^{0.5}, near(t_2,t_3)^{0.7}, near(t_3,t_2)^{0.7}, \\
& near(t_2,t_2)^1, near(t_3,t_3)^1, ATMNear(a_1,t_1)^1, ATMNear(a_1,t_2)^1, \\
& ATMNear(a_1,t_3)^{0.7}, ATMNear(a_2,t_1)^{0.75}, ATMNear(a_2,t_2)^{0.75}, \\
& ATMNear(a_2,t_3)^{0.75}\}
\end{aligned}
$$

We can see that $\Pi^\star_{(P'_{ATM})^M}(near(t_1,t_2)) = 0.8 \neq M(near(t_1,t_2))$, hence M is not an answer set of P'_{ATM}. From Proposition 6.5 we then know that there must be a loop in $supp(M \ominus \Pi^\star_{(P'_{ATM})^M}) = \{near(t_1,t_2), near(t_2,t_1)\}$ whose loop formula is violated. Looking at the dependency graph, we can see that $L = supp(M \ominus \Pi^\star_{(P'_{ATM})^M}) = \{near(t_1,t_2), near(t_2,t_1)\}$ contains three loops: $L_1 = L$, $L_2 = \{near(t_1,t_2)\}$ and $L_3 = \{near(t_2,t_1)\}$. Their loop formulas are

$$
\begin{aligned}
\mathbb{LF}(L_1, P'_{ATM}) = \mathscr{I}\Big(& \max\Big(near(t_1,t_2), near(t_2,t_1)\Big), \max\Big(\mathscr{T}_W(conn(t_1,t_3), \\
& near(t_1,t_3), near(t_3,t_2)), 0.8, \mathscr{T}_W(conn(t_2,t_3), near(t_2,t_3), near(t_3,t_1))\Big)\Big)
\end{aligned}
$$

$$
\begin{aligned}
\mathbb{LF}(L_2, P'_{ATM}) = \\
\mathscr{I}\Big(& \max\Big(near(t_1,t_2)\Big), \max\Big(\mathscr{T}_W(conn(t_1,t_3), near(t_1,t_3), near(t_3,t_2)), 0.8\Big)\Big)
\end{aligned}
$$

$$
\begin{aligned}
\mathbb{LF}(L_3, P'_{ATM}) = \\
\mathscr{I}\Big(& \max\Big(near(t_2,t_1)\Big), \max\Big(\mathscr{T}_W(conn(t_2,t_3), near(t_2,t_3), near(t_3,t_1)), 0.8\Big)\Big)
\end{aligned}
$$

Clearly, these loop formulas are violated by M, hence following the algorithm introduced in Section 6.3, we create a new fuzzy propositional theory $comp(P'_{ATM}) \cup$

$\{\mathbb{LF}(L_1,P'_{ATM}),\mathbb{LF}(L_2,P'_{ATM}),\mathbb{LF}(L_3,P'_{ATM})\}$, and try to find a model of this new theory. Consider then the following model of this new theory:

$$
\begin{aligned}
M =\{&loc(a_1,t_1,t_2)^1,loc(a_1,t_2,t_1)^1,loc(a_2,t_1,t_3)^1,loc(a_2,t_3,t_1)^1,\\
&locNear(a_1,t_1)^{0.15},locNear(a_1,t_2)^{0.05},locNear'(a_1,t_1)^{0.85},locNear'(a_1,t_2)^{0.95}\\
&locNear(a_2,t_1)^{0.75},locNear(a_2,t_3)^{0.75},locNear'(a_2,t_1)^{0.25},locNear'(a_2,t_3)^{0.25}\\
&near(t_1,t_1)^1,near(t_1,t_2)^{0.8},near(t_2,t_1)^{0.8},near(t_1,t_3)^{0.7},near(t_3,t_1)^{0.7},\\
&near(t_2,t_3)^{0.5},near(t_3,t_2)^{0.5},near(t_2,t_2)^1,near(t_3,t_3)^1,\\
&ATMNear(a_1,t_1)^{0.85},ATMNear(a_1,t_2)^{0.95},ATMNear(a_1,t_3)^{0.55},\\
&ATMNear(a_2,t_1)^{0.75},ATMNear(a_2,t_2)^{0.55},ATMNear(a_2,t_3)^{0.75}\}
\end{aligned}
$$

One can readily verify that this model is an answer set of P'_{ATM}, hence the algorithm stops and returns M.

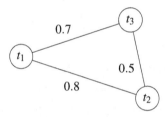

Fig. 6.3: Town configuration for P_{ATM}. The weights on the edges denote the nearness degrees between towns t_1, t_2 and t_3

We could have solved this problem using Mixed Integer Programming (MIP)[4]. However, the exact encoding of this problem would be less clear and straightforward to write. The reason for this is that in the MIP translation the loop formulas would need to be explicitly represented in the program, while in FASP this is handled implicitly. Hence, only the implementer of a FASP system needs to handle these loop formulas, not the developer who writes the FASP programs. This is exactly the power of FASP: providing an elegant and concise modeling language for representing continuous problems, which, thanks to the results in this chapter, can be automatically translated to lower-level languages for solving continuous problems such as MIP. Of course, to make FASP really practical it needs to be augmented with high-level constructs such as choice rules. This is similar to ASP, where

---

[4]Though in general the Gödel negation $\mathscr{N}_M$ cannot be implemented in MIP, in the ATM example we can implement the *gloc* rules using integer variables.

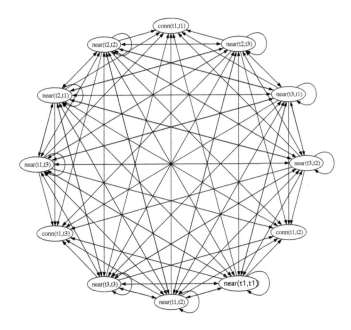

Fig. 6.4: Dependency graph of P_{ATM}

solvers support numerous high-level language extensions that are translated to regular rules before solving the program.

6.5   Discussion

The reader might wonder why we limit our approach to CFASP$^\perp$ programs with t-norms in their body, because at first sight it seems the presented approach is easily extendable to arbitrary functions. It turns out that this is not the case, however. Consider CFASP$^\perp$ with the Łukasiewicz t-norm in rule bodies. As mentioned before, the completion of such a program, and its loop formulas, are formulas in Łukasiewicz logic and are implementable using MIP. Now let us consider CFASP$^\perp$ where both the Łukasiewicz t-norm and the Łukasiewicz t-conorm may occur in rule bodies. At first, one would suspect that the loop formulas of such a program would again be formulas in Łukasiewicz logic. This turns out to be wrong however. To see this, consider the following rules:

$$b \leftarrow \mathcal{N}_W(a)$$
$$b \leftarrow \mathcal{S}_W(b,b)$$

One can readily verify that in the answer sets of a program containing these rules, literal b will be equal to $\mathcal{N}_M(a)$ (provided that b does not occur in the head of any other rule). However, the negation $\mathcal{N}_M$ cannot be implemented in MIP, as the solution space of a MIP problem is always a topologically closed set (viz. the union of a finite number of polyhedra), whereas the solution space of a constraint $b \approx \mathcal{N}_M(a)$ cannot be represented as a closed set due to the strict negation in the definition of $\mathcal{N}_M$. This means that as soon as the Łukasiewicz t-conorm is allowed, in general, there will not exist a Łukasiewicz logic theory such that the models of that theory coincide with the answer sets of a given program. Hence, it is clear that the case where other operators than t-norms are used requires a different strategy.

Finding generalized loop formulas that cover e.g. both the Łukasiewicz t-norm and t-conorm is not a trivial problem. To illustrate some of the issues, let us examine two intuitive candidates. First, remark that the loop formulas introduced in Section 6.3 eliminate certain answer sets (i.e. they are too strict). Consider the following program P:

$$a \leftarrow \mathcal{S}_W(a,b)$$
$$b \leftarrow \mathcal{S}_W(a,b)$$
$$b \leftarrow k$$

where $k \in [0,1]$. This program has a loop $\{a,b\}$ with corresponding loop formula $\max(a,b) \leqslant k$. Now note that for $k > 0$ the value of a in any answer set is equal to 1. Hence, the loop formula incorrectly eliminates all answer sets in this case. One might think this can be solved by including a condition in the loop formula: $(\max(a,b) \leqslant l) \vee (b > 0)$. This formula however fails to eliminate models that are not answer sets (i.e. it is not strict enough) on the following program:

$$a \leftarrow \mathcal{T}_M(\mathcal{S}_W(a,b),0.8)$$
$$b \leftarrow \mathcal{S}_W(a,b)$$
$$b \leftarrow k$$

If $k > 0$ the unique answer set of this program is $\{a^{0.8},b^1\}$. However, $\{a^1,b^1\}$ is also a model of the completion of this program and satisfies the above loop formula.

Although again more refined loop formulas can be thought of that handle the latter program correctly, we are pessimistic about the possibility of finding loop formulas that cover all cases. It appears that such a general solution should be able to capture some underlying idea of recursion: one loop may justify the truth value of some atom a, up to a certain level, which may then trigger other rules that justify the truth value of a, up to some higher level, etc.

Note that this problem does not occur in classical ASP (or when using the maximum t-conorm), since e.g. $a \leftarrow b \vee c$ is equivalent to $a \leftarrow b$ and $a \leftarrow c$, which is indeed why disjunctions in the body of rules are not considered in classical ASP.

Finally, we would like to remark that due to the translations defined in the preceding chapter our solving method can also be used for (A)FASP programs on $([0, 1], \leqslant)$ with only t-norms and negators in rule bodies.

6.6 Summary

Motivated by the existence of ASP solvers that translate ASP to a SAT problem we investigated in this chapter whether fuzzy SAT solvers can likewise be used for solving FASP. First we defined the completion of a FASP program and demonstrated that answer sets of a program are models, but that the reverse does not hold. Since the reverse property is important to be able to use fuzzy SAT solvers for solving FASP, we investigated whether there are conditions under which it holds. We showed that for programs that do not have loops in their positive dependency graph, the models of the completion of a program coincide with the answer sets of the program. For programs with loops in their positive dependency graph we demonstrated that we can create a fuzzy logic theory whose models coincide with the answer sets of a program P by adding formulas corresponding to the loops in the positive dependency graph of P to the completion of P. In the worst-case scenario the number of loop formulas that need to be added can grow exponentially in the number of atoms in the Herbrand Base, however. To cope with this problem we generalized the ASSAT procedure that exists for ASP to FASP. This procedure solves a FASP program P by first using a fuzzy SAT solver to find a model of the completion of P. If the returned model M is an answer set, the procedure ends; otherwise the loop formula of the loops that are violated by M are added to the completion and the resulting fuzzy logic theory is solved by the fuzzy SAT solver. This is repeated until an answer set is found. We illustrated this procedure on a variant of the k-center problem where ATMs need to be placed along roads connecting towns such that each town is close to an ATM.

The results we obtained in this chapter are only valid for a subset of CFASP$^\perp$ where the monotonic functions are t-norms. We discussed the reason for this limitation and argued that a generalization of the loop formulas to arbitrary (C)FASP programs is very difficult due to the need of capturing some underlying idea of recursion. Nevertheless, the class of $CFASP^{\perp}$ programs with t-norms as monotonic functions is already quite large and due to the results in the previous chapter includes, among others, $CFASP^{f}$ and AFASP programs with t-norms as monotonic functions and, in the latter case, also an aggregator that can be written using only t-norms and negators. Hence, our results provide an important first step towards the development of fast FASP solvers that are based on fuzzy SAT solvers.

Chapter 7

Conclusions

With the ever-growing importance of computers in our modern-day society, the need for languages that allow to quickly write non-defective programs instructing these machines is pressing. While programming languages have come a long way since the days of punched cards, the large number of errors in current software shows that we have not yet attained this goal. A growing trend in computer science is to solve problems using a language-oriented approach. The idea is that instead of solving a problem in a general-purpose programming language such as Java or Haskell, we first create a *domain-specific language* that is very close to the problem domain and then model the problem in this high-level language. The advantage of this approach is that programs can be written much faster and that it becomes easier to spot differences between the implementation and the intentions of the programmer. One such domain-specific language is answer set programming (ASP). ASP is a declarative programming language with roots in logic programming that allows to model combinatorial optimization problems in a concise and elegant manner. Among others it has been used to implement planning problems, configuration optimizations and decision support systems. Furthermore it has also been used as an intermediate language for other domain-specific languages, such as those used for modeling biological networks. However, while ASP provides a rich language for modeling combinatorial problems, it is not directly suitable for modeling problems with continuous domains. Such problems occur naturally in diverse fields such as the design of gas and electricity networks, computer vision, business process management and investment portfolios. To overcome this problem, we studied the combination of ASP with fuzzy logic – a class of multi-valued logics that can handle continuity. The resulting formalism is called fuzzy answer set programming (FASP). After a short chapter that recalled some preliminary notions on ASP and fuzzy logic we described FASP in Chapter 3.

An important issue when modeling continuous optimization problems is how we should handle *overconstrained* problems, i.e. problems that have no solutions. In many cases we can opt to accept an imperfect solution, i.e. a solution that does not satisfy all the stated rules (constraints). However, this leads to the question: what imperfect solutions should we choose? Current approaches to FASP implement approximate solutions in a rather limited way, where users are required to state to what extent each rule is satisfied. However, this leads to the problem of guessing the right weights and does not allow to rank candidate solutions. In Chapter 4 we proposed a method that is more flexible, called *aggregated fuzzy answer set programming* (AFASP). The basic idea is not to state the extent to which each rule should be satisfied beforehand, but to make this dynamic and let an aggregator function determine an overall score of suitability of a solution. The AFASP approach we proposed extends a previous proposal of FASP with aggregators in two ways. First, the aggregator expression is decoupled from the lattice underlying the truth values. This results in a more flexible language. Second, the semantics are based on fixpoint semantics for FASP instead of unfounded-based semantics. This ensures that we are no longer restricted to t-norms in rule bodies and furthermore reveals more closely the underlying links between different FASP formalisms. Moreover it solves a problem with the previous proposal when generalizing from $([0, 1], \leqslant)$ to arbitrary (complete) lattices. Finally, we illustrated AFASP on two examples: continuous graph coloring and the reviewer assignment problem. By means of these examples we illustrated the practical usefulness and the advantages of the flexibility of our framework.

While the addition of aggregators and other language constructs to FASP is very useful for programmers, it makes it harder to implement and reason about FASP. Therefore, in Chapter 5, we investigated whether it was possible to create a core language for FASP that was still able to express many FASP constructs. To this end, we proposed a language, called CFASP, that only consists of non-constraint rules with monotonically increasing functions and negators in rule bodies. We showed that CFASP is capable of simulating constraints, monotonically decreasing functions, AFASP with restricted aggregators, S-implicators and a generalization of classical negation. We also showed that the simulations of constraints and classical negation bear a great resemblance with their simulations in ASP, which provides additional insight into the connections between ASP and FASP.

The analysis in this chapter is important both from a theoretical and practical point of view. From the theoretical perspective, CFASP makes reasoning over FASP simpler, while our simulation results show that the theoretical results are still strong enough to cover a whole range of FASP programs. From the practical perspective our results show that solvers only need to implement the core language. Note that the fact that many extensions of FASP can be compiled to CFASP does not mean that these extensions are useless: many of the simulations provided in this chapter are cumbersome. To make FASP an intuitive language that is easy to model in, these extensions are thus of crucial importance.

Motivated by the need for an implementation method for FASP we focused on the translation of FASP programs to particular satisfiability problems in Chapter 6. Such a translation provides us additional theoretical insights with respect to the links between FASP and fuzzy SAT on the one hand, and a practical implementation for FASP by reducing it to a fuzzy SAT problem on the other hand. We introduced the completion of a program and showed that in the case of programs without loops, the models of the completion are exactly the answer sets. Hence, the use of FASP has no real advantage over the use of fuzzy SAT when programs do not contain loops as writing such a FASP program requires the same amount of effort as writing the equivalent fuzzy SAT problem. This is similar to ASP, where a similar link between ASP programs without loops and boolean SAT exists.

For programs that do contain loops, we showed that we can reduce them to a fuzzy SAT problem by generalizing the notion of loop formulas in ASP to FASP. Since this translation is not as straightforward as for programs without loops, we can conclude that the real advantage of FASP over fuzzy SAT lies in problem domains that give rise to programs with loops. We illustrated this with a continuous version of the k-center problem. Moreover, this translation is important because it allows us to solve FASP programs using fuzzy SAT solvers. Under appropriate restrictions, for example, the satisfiability problems that are obtained can be solved using off-the-shelf mixed integer programming methods.

Although the results in this book provide the theoretical foundations for building an (A)FASP solver, some important issues still need to be tackled to build a real working system. One of the most important ones is optimizing the grounding of FASP programs. At first sight it seems that the grounding in FASP is more complex than in ASP, since atoms can be true to a certain degree, which leaves less room for removing rules. However, a promising technique is to combine reasoning over the upper and lower bounds of atoms with properties of the functions that are used. For example, if the upper bounds of a and b are 0.5, we know that the body of the rule $c \leftarrow \mathcal{T}_W(a, b)$ is never greater than 0, meaning the rule can be removed. Investigating such optimizations thus seems to be an interesting and important path for future research in the implementation of FASP, especially since the availability of robust solvers is a prerequisite for creating real-world applications.

Another interesting path for future research is investigating the complexity of FASP. While for ASP it is known that determining the existence of answer sets is in NP (or in Σ_2^P if disjunctions in the head are allowed), as of yet no such membership results are known for FASP. Clearly such bounds on the expressiveness of FASP are important both for the creation of fast solvers as for the creation of practical applications.

In conclusion, we have performed a thorough theoretical investigation of FASP that is important from both a theoretical as a practical perspective. We contributed to the theory by introducing a new language called AFASP and by demonstrating that essential properties of ASP can be generalized to both FASP and AFASP. From a practical point of view we have shown that implementers of FASP can focus on a core language and can leverage the power of efficient fuzzy SAT solvers. Our results show that the combination of ASP with fuzzy logic results in a flexible domain-specific language that allows to solve continuous optimization problems in a concise and elegant manner without it becoming unwieldy to reason about.

Bibliography

Alsinet, T., Godo, L. and Sandri, S. (2002). Two formalisms of extended possibilistic logic programming with context-dependent fuzzy unification: A comparative description, *Electronic Notes in Theoretical Computer Science* **66**, 5, pp. 1 – 21.

Arenas, M., Bertossi, L. and Chomicki, J. (1999). Consistent query answers in inconsistent databases, in *Proceedings of the 18th ACM SIGMOD-SIGACT-SIGART Symposium on Principles of Database Systems*, pp. 68–79.

Ausiello, G., Crescenzi, P., Gambosi, G., Kann, V., Marchetti-Spaccamela, A. and Protasi, M. (1999). *Complexity and Approximation* (Springer-Verlag).

Babovich, Y., Erdem, E. and Lifschitz, V. (2000). Fages' theorem and answer set programming, *CoRR* .

Baral, C. (2003). *Knowledge Representation, Reasoning and Declarative Problem Solving* (Cambridge University Press).

Baral, C., Chancellor, K., Tran, N., Tran, N., Joy, A. and Berens, M. (2004). A knowledge based approach for representing and reasoning about signaling networks, *Bioinformatics* **20**, pp. 15–22.

Baral, C. and Subrahmanian, V. (1993). Duality between alternative semantics of logic programs and nonmonotonic formalisms, *Journal of Automated Reasoning* **10**, pp. 399–420.

Bauer, F. L. and Wössner, H. (1972). The Plankalkül of Konrad Zuse: a forerunner of today's programming languages, *Communications of the ACM* **15**, pp. 678–685, doi:http://doi.acm.org/10.1145/361454.361515, URL http://doi.acm.org/10.1145/361454.361515.

Bauters, K., Schockaert, S., De Cock, M. and Vermeir, D. (2010). Possibilistic answer set programming revisited, in *Proceedings of the 26th Conference on Uncertainty in Artificial Intelligence (UAI)*.

Ben-Eliyahu, R. and Dechter, R. (1994). Propositional semantics for disjunctive logic programs, *Annals of Mathematics and Artificial Intelligence* **12**.

Birkhoff, G. (1973). *Lattice Theory, AMS Colloquium Publications*, Vol. XXV (American Mathematical Society).

Bobillo, F. and Straccia, U. (2007). A fuzzy description logic with product t-norm, in *Proceedings of the 16th IEEE International Conference on Fuzzy Systems (FUZZ-IEEE 2007)*, pp. 652–657.

Bochvar, D. (1938). Ob odnom trechznacnom iscislenii i ego primenenii k analizu paradoksov klassiceskogo rassirennogo funkcional'nogo iscislenija, *Matematiceskij Sbornik* **46**, pp. 287–308, english translation: On a three-valued logical calculus and its application to the analysis of the paradoxes of the classical extended functional calculus, History and Philosophy of Logic, 2: 87–112.

Borkowski, L. (1970). *Jan Łukasiewicz: Selected Works* (North-Holland Publishing Company).

Brewka, G. (1991). Cumulative default logic: In defense of nonmonotonic inference rules, *Artificial*

Intelligence **50**, 2, pp. 183–205.

Brewka, G. (2004). Complex preferences for answer set optimization, in *Proceedings of the Ninth International Conference on the Principles of Knowledge Representation and Reasoning (KR2004)*, pp. 213–223.

Brewka, G., Niemelä, I. and Truszczyński, M. (2003). Answer set optimization, in *Proceedings of the 18th International Joint Conference on Artificial Intelligence*, pp. 867–872.

Buccafurri, F., Leone, N. and Rullo, P. (2000). Enhancing disjunctive datalog by constraints, *IEEE Transactions on Knowledge and Data Engineering* **12**, 5, pp. 845–860, doi:http://dx.doi.org/10.1109/69.877512.

Cao, T. H. (2000). Annotated fuzzy logic programs, *Fuzzy Sets & Systems* **113**, 2, pp. 277–298.

Chang, C. (1958). Algebraic analysis of many valued logics, *Transactions of the American Mathematical Society* **88**, pp. 476–490.

Chang, C. (1959). A new proof of the completeness of the Łukasiewicz axioms, *Transactions of the American Mathematical Society* **93**, pp. 74–80.

Choquet, G. (1954). Theory of capacities, *Annales de l'Institut Fourier* **5**, pp. 131–295.

Cignoli, R., Esteva, F., Godo, L. and Torrens, A. (2000). Basic fuzzy logic is the logic of continuous t-norms and their residua, *Soft Computing - A Fusion of Foundations, Methodologies and Applications* **4**, pp. 106–112.

Clark, K. L. (1977). Negation as failure, in *Logic and Data Bases*, pp. 293–322.

Damásio, C. V., Medina, J. and Ojeda-Aciego, M. (2004). Sorted multi-adjoint logic programs: termination results and applications, in *Proceedings of the 9th European Conference on Logics in Artificial Intelligence (JELIA'04)*, pp. 260–273.

Damásio, C. V., Medina, J. and Ojeda-Aciego, M. (2007). Termination of logic programs with imperfect information: applications and query procedure, *Journal of Applied Logic* **5**, 3, pp. 435–458.

Damásio, C. V. and Pereira, L. M. (2000). Hybrid probabilistic logic programs as residuated logic programs, in *Proceedings of the 7th European Workshop on Logics in Artificial Intelligence (JELIA'00)*, ISBN 3-540-41131-3, pp. 57–72.

Damásio, C. V. and Pereira, L. M. (2001a). Antitonic logic programs, in *Proceedings of the 6th International Conference on Logic Programming and Nonmonotonic Reasoning (LPNMR'01)*, ISBN 3-540-42593-4, pp. 379–392.

Damásio, C. V. and Pereira, L. M. (2001b). Monotonic and residuated logic programs, in *Proceedings of the 6th European Conference on Symbolic and Quantitative Approaches to Reasoning with Uncertainty (ECSQARU'01)*, ISBN 3-540-42464-4, pp. 748–759.

Damásio, C. V. and Pereira, L. M. (2004). Sorted monotonic logic programs and their embeddings, in *Proceedings of Information Processing and Management of Uncertainty (IPMU04)*, pp. 807–814.

Davis, M. and Putnam, H. (1960). A computing procedure for quantification theory, *Journal of the ACM* **7**, 3, pp. 201–215, doi:http://doi.acm.org/10.1145/321033.321034.

De Baets, B. (1995). *Oplossen van vaagrelationele vergelijkingen: een ordetheoretische benadering*, Ph.D. thesis, Universiteit Gent.

De Cock, M. (2002). *Een grondige studie van linguïstische wijzigers in de vaagverzamelingenleer*, Ph.D. thesis, Universiteit Gent.

De Cooman, G. and Kerre, E. E. (1994). Order norms on bounded partially ordered sets, *The Journal of Fuzzy Mathematics* **2**, pp. 281–310.

De Finetti, B. (1936). La logique de la probabilité, in *Actes Congrés International de la Philosophy Scientifique*.

De Vos, M. and Vermeir, D. (1999). Choice logic programs and nash equilibria in strategic games, in *Proceedings of the 13th International Workshop and 8th Annual Conference of the EACSL on Computer Science Logic*, pp. 266–276.

Dekhtyar, A. and Subrahmanian, V. S. (1997). Hybrid probabilistic programs, in *Proceedings of the Fourteenth International Conference on Logic Programming (ICLP'97)*, pp. 391–405.

Detyniecki, M. (2001). Numerical aggregation operators: state of the art, in *Proceedings of the First International Summer School on Aggregation Operators and their Applications*.

Dubois, D., Fargier, H. and Prade, H. (1996). Refinements of the maximin approach to decision-making in a fuzzy environment, *Fuzzy Sets & Systems* **81**, 1, pp. 103–122.

Dubois, D., Lang, J. and Prade, H. (1991). Towards possibilistic logic programming, in *Proceedings of the Eigth International Conference on Logic Programming (ICLP'91)*, pp. 581–595.

Dubois, D., Ostasiewicz, W. and Prade, H. (1999). *Fundamentals of Fuzzy Sets: The Handbook of Fuzzy Sets Series*, chap. Fuzzy Sets: History and Basic Notions (Kluwer Academic), pp. 21–124.

Dubois, D. and Prade, H. (1986). Weighted minimum and maximum operations in fuzzy sets theory, *Information Sciences* **39**, 2, pp. 205–210.

Dubois, D. and Prade, H. (2001). Advances in the egalitarist approach to decision-making in a fuzzy environment, in Y. Yoshida (ed.), *Dynamical Aspect in Fuzzy Decision Making, Studies in Fuzziness and Soft Computing*, Vol. 73, pp. 213–240.

Dummet, M. (1959). A propositional calculus with denumerable matrix, *Journal of Symbolic Logic* **24**, pp. 97–106.

Eiter, T., Faber, W., Leone, N. and Pfeifer, G. (1999). The diagnosis frontend of the DLV system, *AI Communications* **12**, 1-2, pp. 99–111.

Eiter, T., Faber, W., Leone, N., Pfeifer, G. and Polleres, A. (2000). Planning under incomplete knowledge, in *Proceedings of the First International Conference on Computational Logic (CL2000)*, pp. 807–821.

Eiter, T., Faber, W., Leone, N., Pfeifer, G. and Polleres, A. (2002). The dlv^k planning system, in *Logic in artificial intelligence*, pp. 541–544.

Eiter, T., Gottlob, G. and Mannila, H. (1994). Expressive power and complexity of disjunctive datalog under the stable model semantics, in *Management and Processing of Complex Data Structures*, Vol. 777, pp. 83–103.

Emden, M. H. v. (1986). Quantitative deduction and its fixpoint theory, *Journal of Logic Programming* **30**, 1, pp. 37–53.

Faber, W. and Pfeifer, G. (2005). DLV homepage, http://www.dlvsystem.com.

Fages, F. (1994). Consistency of Clark's completion and existence of stable models, *Methods of Logic in Computer Science* **1**, pp. 51–60.

Fagin, R. and Wimmers, E. L. (1998). A formula for incorporating weights into scoring rules, *Theoretical Computer Science* **239**, pp. 309–338.

Fitting, M. (1991). Bilattices and the semantics of logic programming, *Journal of Logic Programming* **11**, 2, pp. 91–116.

Fodor, J. C., Yager, R. R. and Rybalov, A. (1997). Structure of uninorms, *International Journal of Uncertainty, Fuzziness and Knowledge-Based Systems* **5**, 4, pp. 411–427.

Fuhr, N. (2000). Probabilistic datalog: implementing logical information retrieval for advanced applications, *Journal of the American Society for Information Science* **51**, 2, pp. 95–110.

Gabbay, M. and Woods, J. (2007). *The many valued and nonmonotonic turn in logic* (Elsevier).

Garg, N., Kavitha, T., Kumar, A., Mehlhorn, K. and Mestre, J. (2008). Assigning papers to referees, Unpublished.

Gebser, M., Kaufmann, B. and Schaub, T. (2009). The conflict-driven answer set solver clasp: Progress report, in E. Erdem, F. Lin and T. Schaub (eds.), *Proceedings of the 10th International Conference on Logic Programming and Nonmonotonic Reasoning (LPNMR'09), LNCS*, Vol. 5753 (Springer Berlin / Heidelberg), pp. 509–514.

Gebser, M., Schaub, T. and Thiele, S. (2007). Gringo: A new grounder for answer set programming, in *Proceedings of the 9th International Conference on Logic Programming and Nonmonotonic*

Reasoning (LPNMR'07), pp. 266–271.

Gelfond, M. and Lifschitz, V. (1988). The stable model semantics for logic programming, in *Proceedings of the Fifth International Conference and Symposium on Logic Programming (ICLP/SLP'88)*, pp. 1081–1086.

Gelfond, M. and Lifschitz, V. (1991). Classical negation in logic programs and disjunctive databases, *New Generation Computing* **9**, pp. 365–385.

Giunchiglia, E., Lierler, Y. and Maratea, M. (2004). SAT-based answer set programming, in *Proceedings of the 19th national conference on Artifical intelligence (AAAI'04)* (AAAI Press / The MIT Press), ISBN 0-262-51183-5, pp. 61–66.

Gödel, K. (1932). Zum intuitionistischen aussagenkalkül, *Anzeiger Akademie der Wissenschaften Wien (Math.-naturwiss. Klasse)* **69**, pp. 65–66.

Grabisch, M. (1996). k-additive fuzzy measures, in *Proceedings of the 6th international conference on information processing and management of uncertainty in Knowledge-Based systems (IPMU96)*.

Hähnle, R. (1994). Many-valued logic and mixed integer programming, *Annals of Mathematics and Artificial Intelligence* **12**, 3-4, pp. 231–263.

Hájek, P. (1998). *Metamathematics of fuzzy logic* (Kluwer Academic Press).

Hanqing, J. (2004). *Continuous-Time Portfolio Optimization*, Ph.D. thesis, Chinese University of Hong Kong.

Hay, L. (1963). Axiomatization of the infinite-valued predicate calculus, *Journal of Symbolic Logic* **28**, pp. 77–86.

Horn, A. (1969). Logic with truth values in a linearly ordered Heyting algebra, *Journal of Symbolic Logic* **34**, pp. 395–409.

Horn, B. K. P. and Schunck, B. G. (1981). Determining optical flow, *Artificial Intelligence* **17**, pp. 185–203.

Ishizuka, M. and Kanai, N. (1985). Prolog-elf incorporating fuzzy logic, in *Proceedings of the 9th international joint conference on Artificial intelligence (IJCAI'85)*, ISBN 0-934613-02-8, 978-0-934-61302-6, pp. 701–703.

Janssen, J., Schockaert, S., Vermeir, D. and De Cock, M. (2009). Fuzzy answer set programming with literal preferences, in *Proceedings of the Joint 2009 International Fuzzy Systems Association World Congress and 2009 European Society of Fuzzy Logic and Technology Conference (IFSA/EUSFLAT2009)*, pp. 1347–1352.

Jaskowski, S. (1936). Recherches sur le systéme de la logique intuitioniste, in *Actes du Congrés Internationale de Philosophie Scientifique*, pp. 58–61, english translation: Studia Logica, 34 (1975): 117–120.

Kerre, E. E. (1993). *Introduction to the basic principles of fuzzy set theory and some of its applications* (Communication and Cognition).

Kifer, M. and Li, A. (1988). On the semantics of rule-based expert systems with uncertainty, in *Proceedings of the 2nd International Conference on Database Theory (ICDT'88)*, ISBN 0-387-50171-1, pp. 102–117.

Kifer, M. and Subrahmanian, V. S. (1992). Theory of generalized annotated logic programming and its applications, *Journal of Logic Programming* **12**, 3&4, pp. 335–367.

Kleene, S. (1938). On notation for ordinal numbers, *Journal of Symbolic Logic* **3**, pp. 150–155.

Klement, E., Mesiar, R. and Pap, E. (2002). *Triangular norms* (Kluwer Academic Publishers).

Lakshmanan, L. V. S. (1994). An epistemic foundation for logic programming with uncertainty, in *Proceedings of the 14th Conference on Foundations of Software Technology and Theoretical Computer Science (FSTTCS'94)*, ISBN 3-540-58715-2, pp. 89–100.

Lakshmanan, L. V. S. and Sadri, F. (1994a). Modeling uncertainty in deductive databases, in *Proceedings of the 5th International Conference on Database and Expert Systems Applications (DEXA'94)*, ISBN 3-540-58435-8, pp. 724–733.

Lakshmanan, L. V. S. and Sadri, F. (1994b). Probabilistic deductive databases, in *Proceedings of the 1994 International Symposium on Logic programming (ILPS'94)* (MIT Press, Cambridge, MA, USA), ISBN 0-262-52191-1, pp. 254–268.

Lakshmanan, L. V. S. and Sadri, F. (1997). Uncertain deductive databases: a hybrid approach, *Information Systems* **22**, 9, pp. 483–508.

Lakshmanan, L. V. S. and Shiri, N. (2001). A parametric approach to deductive databases with uncertainty, *IEEE Transactions on Knowledge and Data Engineering* **13**, 4, pp. 554–570.

Lakshmanan, V. S. (1997). *Towards a generalized theory of deductive databases with uncertainty*, Ph.D. thesis, Concordia University.

Leone, N., Perri, S. and Scarcello, F. (2004). Backjumping techniques for rules instantiation in the dlv system, in *Proceedings of the Tenth International Workshop on Nonmonotonic Reasoning (NMR'04)*, pp. 258–266.

Lifschitz, V. (1999). Answer set planning, in *Proceedings of the 16th International Conference On Logic Programming (ICLP'99)*, pp. 23–37.

Lifschitz, V. (2002). Answer set programming and plan generation, *Artificial Intelligence* **138**, pp. 39–54.

Lifschitz, V. and Woo, T. (1991). Answer sets in general nonmonotonic reasoning (preliminary report), in *Proceedings of the Third International Conference on Principles of Knowledge Representation and Reasoning*, pp. 603–614.

Lin, F. and Zhao, Y. (2004). ASSAT: computing answer sets of a logic program by SAT solvers, *Artificial Intelligence* **157**, 1-2, pp. 115–137, doi:http://dx.doi.org/10.1016/j.artint.2004.04.004.

Liu, L. and Truszczyński, M. (2005). Pbmodels – software to compute stable models by pseudo-boolean solvers, in C. Baral, G. Greco, N. Leone and G. Terracina (eds.), *Proceedings of the 8th international conference on Logic Programming and Nonmonotonic Reasoning (LP-NMR'05)*, LNCS, Vol. 3662 (Springer Berlin / Heidelberg), pp. 410–415.

Loyer, Y. and Straccia, U. (2002). The well-founded semantics in normal logic programs with uncertainty, in *Proceedings of the 6th International Symposium on Functional and Logic Programming (FLOPS'02)*, ISBN 3-540-44233-2, pp. 152–166.

Loyer, Y. and Straccia, U. (2003). The approximate well-founded semantics for logic programs with uncertainty, in *Proceedings of the 28th International Symposium on Mathematical Foundations of Computer Science (MFCS'03)*, pp. 541–550.

Loyer, Y. and Straccia, U. (2005). Any-world assumptions in logic programming, *Journal of Theoretical Computer Science* **342**, pp. 351–381.

Loyer, Y. and Straccia, U. (2006). Epistemic foundation of stable model semantics, *Theory and Practice of Logic Programming* **6**, pp. 355–393.

Loyer, Y. and Straccia, U. (2009). Approximate well-founded semantics, query answering and generalized normal logic programs over lattices, *Annals of Mathematics and Artificial Intelligence* **55**, pp. 389–417.

Luhandjula, M. K. (1982). Compensatory operators in fuzzy linear programming with multiple objectives, *Fuzzy Sets & Systems* **8**, 3, pp. 245–252.

Łukasiewicz, J. (1920). O logice trójwartościowej, *Ruch Filozoficzny* **5**, pp. 170–171.

Lukasiewicz, T. (1998). Probabilistic logic programming, in *Proceedings of the 13th European Conference on Artificial Intelligence (ECAI'98)*, pp. 388–392.

Lukasiewicz, T. (1999). Many-valued disjunctive logic programs with probabilistic semantics, in *Proceedings of the 5th International Conference on Logic Programming and Nonmonotonic Reasoning (LPNMR'99)*, ISBN 3-540-66749-0, pp. 277–289.

Lukasiewicz, T. (2006). Fuzzy description logic programs under the answer set semantics for the semantic web, in *Proceedings of the Second International Conference on Rules and Rule Markup Languages for the Semantic Web (RuleML'06)*, pp. 89–96.

Lukasiewicz, T. and Straccia, U. (2007a). Tightly integrated fuzzy description logic programs under the answer set semantics for the semantic web, in *Proceedings of the First International Conference on Web Reasoning and Rule Systems (RR'07)*, pp. 289–298.

Lukasiewicz, T. and Straccia, U. (2007b). Top-k retrieval in description logic programs under vagueness for the semantic web, in *Proceedings of the 1st international conference on Scalable Uncertainty Management (SUM'07)*, pp. 16–30.

Lukasiewicz, T. and Straccia, U. (2010). Tightly integrated fuzzy description logic programs under the answer semantics for the semantic web, in M. L. . A. Sheth (ed.), *Progressive Concepts for Semantic Web Evolution: Applications and Developments*, chap. 11 (IGI Global), pp. 237–256.

Lukaszewicz, W. (1984). Considerations on default logic, in *Proceedings of the Non-Monotonic Reasoning Workshop (NMR'84)*, pp. 165–193.

Madrid, N. and Ojeda-Aciego, M. (2008). Towards a fuzzy answer set semantics for residuated logic programs, in *Proceedings of the 2008 IEEE/WIC/ACM International Conference on Web Intelligence and Intelligent Agent Technology (WI-IAT'08)*, pp. 260–264.

Madrid, N. and Ojeda-Aciego, M. (2009). On coherence and consistence in fuzzy answer set semantics for residuated logic programs, in *Proceedings of the 8th International Workshop on Fuzzy Logic and Applications (WILF'09)*, pp. 60–67.

Madrid, N. and Ojeda-Aciego, M. (2010a). Measuring instability in normal residuated logic programs: discarding information, *Communications in Computer and Information Science* **80**, pp. 128–137.

Madrid, N. and Ojeda-Aciego, M. (2010b). On the measure of instability in normal residuated logic programs, in *Proceedings of FUZZ-IEEE'10*.

Marek, V. and Truszczyński, M. (1999). Stable models and an alternative logic programming paradigm, in *The Logic Programming Paradigm: a 25-Year Perspective* (Springer Verlag), pp. 169–181.

Mateis, C. (1999). Extending disjunctive logic programming by t-norms, in *Proceedings of the 5th International Conference on Logic Programming and Nonmonotonic Reasoning (LPNMR'99)* (Springer-Verlag), pp. 290–304.

Mateis, C. (2000). Quantitative disjunctive logic programming: Semantics and computation, *AI Communications* **13**, 4, pp. 225–248.

McCarthy, J. (1980). Circumscription—a form of non-monotonic reasoning, *Artificial Intelligence* **13**, pp. 27–39.

McDermott, D. (1982). Nonmonotonic logic ii: Nonmonotonic modal theories, *Journal of the ACM* **29**, pp. 33–57.

McNaughton, R. (1951). A theorem about infinite-valued sentential logic, *Journal of Symbolic Logic* **16**, pp. 1–13.

Moore, R. C. (1985). Semantical considerations on nonmonotonic logic, *Artificial Intelligence* **25**, pp. 75–94.

Nerode, A., Remmel, J. B. and Subrahmanian, V. S. (1997). Annotated nonmonotonic rule systems, *Theoretical Computer Science* **171**, 1-2, pp. 111–146.

Ng, R. and Subrahmanian, V. S. (1993). A semantical framework for supporting subjective and conditional probabilities in deductive databases, *Journal of Automated Reasoning* **10**, 2, pp. 191–235.

Ng, R. and Subrahmanian, V. S. (1994). Stable semantics for probabilistic deductive databases, *Information and Computation* **110**, 1, pp. 42–83.

Nguyen, H. T., Walker, E. A. and Grabisch, M. (1995). *Fundamentals of Uncertainty Calculi with Applications to Fuzzy Inference* (Kluwer Academics Publishers).

Nicolas, P., Garcia, L. and Stéphan, I. (2005). Possibilistic stable models, in *Nonmonotonic Reasoning, Answer Set Programming and Constraints*, Dagstuhl Seminar Proceedings.

Nicolas, P., Garcia, L., Stéphan, I. and Lefèvre, C. (2006). Possibilistic uncertainty handling for answer set programming, *Annals of Mathematics and Artificial Intelligence* **47**, 1-2, pp. 139–

181.

Niemelä, I. (1999). Logic programs with stable model semantics as a constraint programming paradigm, *Annals of Mathematics and Artificial Intelligence* **25**, pp. 241–273.

Niemelä, I. (2003). WASP WP3 report: Language extensions and software engineering for ASP, http://www.tcs.hut.fi/Research/Logic/wasp/wp3/wasp-wp3-web/.

Nogueira, M., Balduccini, M., Gelfond, M., Watson, R. and Barry, M. (2001). An a-prolog decision support system for the space shuttle, in *Proceedings of the Third International Symposium on Practical Aspects of Declarative Languages (PADL'01)*, pp. 169–183.

Osiadacz, A. J. and Górecki, M. (1995). Optimization of pipe sizes for distribution gas network design, in *Proceedings of the 27th PSIG Annual Meeting*.

Pavelka, J. (1979). On fuzzy logic, *Zeitschrift für Mathematischen Logik und Grundlagen der Mathematik* **25**, part I: 45–52, Part II: 119–134, Part III: 447–464.

Pearce, D., Sarsakov, V., Schaub, T., Tompits, H. and Woltran, S. (2002). A polynomial translation of logic programs with nested expressions into disjunctive logic programs: Preliminary report, in *Proceedings of the 18th International Conference on Logic Programming (ICLP'02)*, pp. 405–420.

Pelov, N., Denecker, M. and Bruynooghe, M. (2003). Translation of aggregate programs to normal logic programs, in *Answer Set Programming: Advances in Theory and Implementation, CEUR Workshop Proceedings*, pp. 29–42.

Perri, S., Scarcello, F. and Leone, N. (2005). Abductive logic programs with penalization: semantics, complexity and implementation, *Theory and Practic of Logic Programming* **5**, 1-2, pp. 123–159.

Post, E. L. (1921). Introduction to a general theory of elementary propositions, *American Journal of Mathematics* **43**, pp. 163–185.

Przymusińska, H. and Przymusiński, T. (1994). Stationary default extensions, *Fundamenta Informaticae* **21**, 1-2, pp. 67–87.

Ragaz, M. (1983). Die Unentscheidbarkeit der einstelligen unendlichwertigen Prädikatenlogik, *Archiv mathematische Logik Grundlagenforschung* **23**, pp. 129–139.

Reiter, R. (1980). A logic for default reasoning, *Artificial Intelligence* **13**, 1-2, pp. 81–132.

Rojas, R., Göktekin, C., Friedl, G. and Krüger, M. (2000). Plankalkl: The first high-level programming language and its implementation, .

Saad, E. (2009a). Extended fuzzy logic programs with fuzzy answer set semantics, in *Proceedings of the 3rd International Conference on Scalable Uncertainty Management (SUM'09)*, pp. 223–239.

Saad, E. (2009b). Probabilistic reasoning by SAT solvers, in C. Sossai and G. Chemello (eds.), *Proceedings of the 10th European Conference on Symbolic and Quantitative Approaches to Reasoning with Uncertainty (ECSQARU'09)*, *LNCS*, Vol. 5590 (Springer Berlin / Heidelberg), ISBN 978-3-642-02905-9, pp. 663–675, doi:http://dx.doi.org/10.1007/978-3-642-02906-6_57.

Scarpellini, B. (1962). Die Nichtaxiomatisierbarkeit des unendlichwertigen Prädikatenkalküls von Łukasiewicz, .

Schiex, T., Fargier, H. and Verfaillie, G. (1995). Valued constraint satisfaction problems: hard and easy problems, in *Proceedings of the Fourteenth International Joint Conference on Artificial Intelligence (IJCAI'95)*, pp. 631–637.

Schockaert, S., Janssen, J., Vermeir, D. and De Cock, M. (2009). Finite satisfiability in infinite-valued Łukasiewicz logic, in *Proceedings of the Third International Conference on Scalable Uncertainty Management (SUM'2009)*, pp. 240–254.

Shapiro, E. Y. (1983). Logic programs with uncertainties: a tool for implementing rule-based systems, in *Proceedings of the Eighth international joint conference on Artificial intelligence (IJCAI'83)*, pp. 529–532.

Simons, P. and Niemelä, I. (2000). Smodels homepage, http://www.tcs.hut.fi/Software/ smodels/.

Soininen, T. and Niemelä, I. (1999). Developing a declarative rule language for applications in product configuration, in *Proceedings of the First International Workshop on Practical Aspects of Declarative Languages (PADL'99)*, pp. 305–319.

Soininen, T., Niemelä, I., Tiihonen, J. and Sulonen, R. (2001). Representing configuration knowledge with weight constraint rules, in *Proceedings of the AAAI Spring 2001 Symposium on Answer Set Programming: Towards Efficient and Scalable Knowledge*.

Straccia, U. (2005). Query answering in normal logic programs under uncertainty, in *In 8th European Conferences on Symbolic and Quantitative Approaches to Reasoning with Uncertainty (ECSQARU-05)*, pp. 687–700.

Straccia, U. (2006a). Annotated answer set programming, in *Proceedings of the 11th International Conference on Information Processing and Management of Uncertainty in Knowledge-Based Systems (IPMU'06)*.

Straccia, U. (2006b). Query answering under the any-world assumption for normal logic programs, in *Proceedings of the 10th International Conference on Principles of Knowledge Representation (KR-06)* (AAAI Press), pp. 329–339.

Straccia, U. (2007). A top-down query answering procedure for normal logic programs under the any-world assumption, in *Proceedings of the 9th European Conference on Symbolic and Quantitative Approaches to Reasoning with Uncertainty* (Springer-Verlag), pp. 115–127.

Straccia, U. (2008). Managing uncertainty and vagueness in description logics, logic programs and description logic programs, in *Reasoning Web: 4th International Summer School 2008*, pp. 54–103.

Straccia, U., Ojeda-Aciego, M. and Damásio, C. V. (2009). On fixed-points of multivalued functions on complete lattices and their application to generalized logic programs, *SIAM Journal on Computing* **38**, 5, pp. 1881–1911.

Subrahmanian, V. S. (1994). Amalgamating knowledge bases, *ACM Transactions on Database Systems* **19**, 2, pp. 291–331.

Sugeno, M. (1974). *Theory of fuzzy integrals and its application*, Ph.D. thesis, Tokyo Institute of Technology.

Syrjänen, T. (2001). Omega-restricted logic programs, in *Proceedings of the 6th International Conference on Logic Programming and Nonmonotonic Reasoning (LPNMR'01)*, pp. 267–279.

Syrjänen, T. (2004). Cardinality constraint programs, in *Proceedings of the 9th European Conference on Logics in Artificial Intelligence (JELIA'04)*, pp. 187–199.

Tarski, A. (1955). A lattice theoretical fixpoint theorem and its application, *Pacific Journal of Mathematics* **5**, pp. 285–309.

Turksen, I. B. (1992). Interval-valued fuzzy sets and "compensatory and", *Fuzzy Sets & Systems* **51**, 3, pp. 295–307.

Van Emden, M. H. and Kowalski, R. A. (1976). The semantics of predicate logic as a programming language, *Journal of the ACM* **23**, pp. 569–574.

Van Gelder, A., Ross, K. A. and Schlipf, J. S. (1991). The well-founded semantics for general logic programs, *Journal of the ACM* **38**, pp. 619–649.

Van Nieuwenborgh, D. (2005). *Preferences in Answer Set Programming*, Ph.D. thesis, Vrije Universiteit Brussel.

Van Nieuwenborgh, D., De Cock, M. and Vermeir, D. (2007a). Computing fuzzy answer sets using DLVHEX, in V. Dahl and I. Niemelä (eds.), *Proceedings of the 23rd International Conference on Logic Programming (ICLP'07)*, LNCS, Vol. 4670 (Springer Berlin / Heidelberg), pp. 449–450.

Van Nieuwenborgh, D., De Cock, M. and Vermeir, D. (2007b). An introduction to fuzzy answer set programming, *Annals of Mathematics and Artificial Intelligence* **50**, 3-4, pp. 363–388.

Vojtás, P. (2001). Fuzzy logic programming, *Fuzzy Sets and Systems* **124**, 3, pp. 361–370.

Wagner, G. (1998). Negation in fuzzy and possibilistic logic programs, *Uncertainty Theory in Artificial Intelligence Series* , 3, pp. 113–128.

Ward, M. P. (1994). Language-oriented programming, *Software - Concepts and Tools* **15**, 4, pp. 147–161.

Yager, R. R. (1981). A new methodology for ordinal multiple aspect decisions based on fuzzy sets, *Decision Sciences* **12**, pp. 589–600.

Yager, R. R. (1988). On ordered weighted averaging aggregation operators in multicriteria decision-making, *IEEE Transactions on Systems, Man and Cybernetics* **18**, 1, pp. 183–190.

Yager, R. R. and Kacprzyk, J. (eds.) (1997). *The ordered weighted averaging operators: theory and applications* (Kluwer Academic Publishers), ISBN 0-7923-9934-X.

Zadeh, L. A. (1965). Fuzzy sets, *Information and Control* **8**, 3, pp. 338–353.

Zuse, K. (1943). Ansätze einer Theorie des allgemeinen Rechnens unter besonderer Berücksichtigung des Aussagenkalkls und dessen Anwendung auf Relaisschaltungen, Zuse Papers 045/018.

Zuse, K. (1948–1949). Über den allgemeinen Plankalkül als Mittel zur Formulierung schematisch-kombinativer Aufgaben, *Archiv der Mathematik* **1**, pp. 441–449.

Index